ACCOUNTANT'S COMPLETE MODEL LETTER BOOK

Mitchell Hakoun, CPA
Gerald Tomlinson

PRENTICE HALL
Englewood Cliffs, New Jersey 07632

Prentice-Hall International, Inc., *London*
Prentice-Hall of Australia, Pty. Ltd., *Sydney*
Prentice-Hall Canada, Inc., *Toronto*
Prentice-Hall of India Private Ltd., *New Delhi*
Prentice-Hall of Japan, Inc., *Tokyo*
Prentice-Hall of Southeast Asia Pte. Ltd., *Singapore*
Editora Prentice-Hall do Brasil Ltda., *Rio de Janeiro*
Prentice-Hall Hispanoamericana, S.A., *Mexico*

10 9 8 7 6 5 4 3 2 1

Library of Congress Cataloging-in-Publication Data

Hakoun, Mitchell.
Accountant's complete model letter book.

Includes index.
1. Commercial correspondence. 2. Accounting.
3. Form letters. I. Tomlinson, Gerald.
II. Title.
HF5726.H3257 1987 657 87-11548

ISBN 0-13-001199-1

PRENTICE HALL
BUSINESS & PROFESSIONAL DIVISION
A division of Simon & Schuster
Englewood Cliffs, New Jersey 07632

PRINTED IN THE UNITED STATES OF AMERICA

About the Authors

MITCHELL HAKOUN, CPA, is a partner in the accounting firm of Hakoun and Frizzell, Sparta, New Jersey. Upon graduation from Rider College, he joined the audit staff of Touche Ross & Co., where he was promoted to senior accountant in charge of various audit engagements. After leaving Touche Ross & Co. in 1975 to further diversify his accounting background, Mr. Hakoun became associated with a medium-sized local firm in New Jersey where, in addition to his regular responsibilities, he and two staff members developed the firm's first report writing manual. Mr. Hakoun is currently an adjunct faculty member at Upsala College, has previously taught accounting courses at Fairleigh Dickinson University and Middlesex Community College, and has lectured to the County Bar Association and Bankers. He is a member of the New Jersey Society of CPAs and has served on the Advisory Grading Service of the American Institute of Certified Public Accountants.

GERALD TOMLINSON, a writer and editor, specializes in business and education. After graduating from Marietta College, he began his career as a teacher of English in upstate New York. For more than twenty years he has held various editorial positions in book publishing companies, including that of executive editor. His nonfiction writings include the *School Administrator's Complete Letter Book,* published by Prentice-Hall, and, as co-author, three computer-based training programs on word processing for DSI Micro. Listed in *Contemporary Authors* and *The International Authors and Writers Who's Who,* he is a member of the Association for Supervision and Curriculum Development, the National Council of Teachers of English, and the Mystery Writers of America.

This book is dedicated to those professionals who have set quality as their goal.

A Note About This Book

This book has been written, compiled, and edited to assist accounting professionals in writing letters of consistently high quality. The use of diligence and due professional care should accompany the use and/or modification of any of the model or specimen letters in the book. Specific circumstances determine the appropriate wording of a particular piece of correspondence, and it is the individual accountant's responsibility to ensure the letters sent under his or her name, or under the name of his or her firm, accurately reflect the facts, conditions, and accounting principles in the given circumstances.

In the course of their work, accounting professionals must take into consideration constantly shifting factors: accounting principles, tax laws, governmental regulations, financial and legal ramifications, and it is entirely possible that changes will result from future actions by government departments or agencies, Congress, state legislatures, or the courts. No attempt has been made, or can be made, to predict future parameters. If legal or other expert assistance is required, the services of a competent professional should be sought.

How This Letter Book Will Help You Build a More Profitable Accounting Practice

The *Accountant's Complete Model Letter Book* gives you all the letters you need for virtually every business situation—from a letter clarifying the status of a taxpayer, to a transmittal to a bank regarding a real estate mortgage, to an engagement letter for an employee benefit pension plan.

This *Letter Book* saves you time by putting all the letters you need right at your fingertips. The letters have been carefully chosen, edited, and assembled from those submitted by accounting firms across the nation. Each letter focuses on a real situation, with names and other specifics changed to preserve confidentiality. The situations included are ones that are common to accountants with a general practice.

The *Accountant's Complete Model Letter Book* gives you over 300 ready-to-use model letters that cover every possible accounting situation in today's business environment. This is not a book on letter-writing techniques. Rather, it is a collection of well-written, result-producing letters that can easily be used.

You can begin using the *Letter Book* immediately. Glance through the table of contents. You are almost sure to come across a letter that fits a specific and immediate need. Use the letter. You may find that it serves best as a general model for the kind of letter you have to write. If so, you can modify it to suit your needs.

As an accountant, you are sure to be judged by what you commit to paper. Therefore, it will pay to make thorough and continuing use of the model letters in this book, adapting all or parts of them to fit your own situation when necessary. If you do this, you can rest assured that the letters you sign and send out will show an impressive and visible degree of competence. By means of these letters you will represent yourself, and rightly so, as the kind of precise and informed accountant that clients want to engage—and in fact do engage.

From letters dealing with fees to letters explaining a client's situation to the IRS, the *Accountant's Complete Model Letter Book* provides:

- More than two-dozen tested proposal and engagement letters. These include everything from general preliminary proposals, audit proposals, and proposals for management advisory services engagements to various general engagement letters, audit engagement letters, and a number of engagement letters for special situations. (See Chapters 1 and 2.)

- Sample confirmation letters on a wide range of topics. These thirty-three confirmation letters, which free you from writing countless individual letters, can be tremendous timesavers. (See Chapters 3 and 4.)
- Precisely written and carefully edited client representation letters. The representation letter, acknowledging management's responsibility in regard to the engagement, is one that has to be just right—and these models will help ensure that it is. (See Chapter 5.)
- Dozens of standard audit reports covering the most common situations. This chapter is almost a reference volume in itself—the source you will come to rely on for a specific, needed audit report. (See Chapter 6.)
- Key paragraphs to use in your letters of recommendation to management. These varied and proven paragraphs cover a host of circumstances that you have probably seen, or may see, in the business activities of your clients. The ready-to-use wording of these paragraphs can save you hours of writing and rewriting. (See Chapters 7 and 8.)
- Proven letters concerning financial services and estate planning. There are letters on setting up a financial accounting system, helping a small business client obtain financing, and advising the client on how to improve the collection of accounts receivable. Other letters deal with personal financial planning and working with an estate planning team. (See Chapter 9.)
- Letters dealing with tax preparation and transmittal. Tax-preparation letters range from simple reminders to clients to compile their tax data to more complex tax matters. Transmittal letters provide ready-made coverage of the most common documents. (See Chapters 10 and 11.)
- Effective letters to the IRS. Whether filing late tax returns, resolving a continuing problem, asking the Internal Revenue Service how to proceed with a tough problem, clarifying the status of your client, or postponing an audit to obtain documents, you will find it here in a group of letters that have successfully served their purpose. (See Chapter 12.)
- Fee-collection letters that get results, including explanations of billing policies and invoices, an increase in fees, confirmation of fee agreements, reminder letters on overdue accounts, requests to arrange payment plans, and more. (See Chapter 13.)
- Letters concerning employment and employees. Responses to application letters, requests for interviews, acceptance and rejection letters, letters dealing with jury duty, reserve meetings, salary increases, and various personal matters. (See Chapter 14.)
- Tested public-relations letters for becoming better known in the community, creating the right image, and building a solid practice. Twenty letters from respected accountants and accounting firms that show the capabilities and exhibit the competence of their writers. (See Chapter 15.)

- Time-saving general transmittal letters to accompany a host of different documents—draft and completed audits, pension fund reports, reports to stockholders, recommendations to management, and documents to banks. (See Chapter 16.)
- Concise yet complete guide to word processing, report writing, and letter style and format for accountants. (See Chapters 17, 18, and 19.)

Whenever you need a letter, look first in this book. Choose the letter you need, adapt it to fit your needs, or use the exact phrasing when it is appropriate. The *Accountant's Complete Model Letter Book* is designed as your one-source reference for all accounting correspondence.

Contributors

A number of accounting firms, accounting associations, and individual accountants throughout the country have generously submitted samples of their correspondence for inclusion in this collection. In some cases the letters have been edited for consistency or excerpted for conciseness. In all cases the names, titles, and addresses, as well as the exact facts, figures, and circumstances, have been changed to ensure confidentiality.

The original letters were typed in a variety of styles—full block, semiblock, and so on. In this book, they appear in a standard block format with one line space between paragraphs. That is only one of many acceptable formats, and its use here should not be construed as a special recommendation. Any traditional format is equally good. Various letter formats are illustrated on pages 411–414.

The authors are deeply grateful to the following contributors for their invaluable, indeed indispensable, assistance in assembling the model letters in this book.

American Institute of Certified Public Accountants
New York, New York

Banks, Finley, White & Co.
Certified Public Accountants
Memphis, Tennessee

Brooks & Albin
Certified Public Accountants
Portland, Maine

Judith H. Byrum
Certified Public Accountant
Shawnee Mission, Kansas

Cannon & Company
Certified Public Accountants
Memphis, Tennessee

Mary L. Craig
Certified Public Accountant
Helena, Montana

Graubart & Company
Certified Public Accountants
Anaheim, California

Harrison & Company
Certified Public Accountants
Tuscaloosa, Alabama

International Affiliation of Independent Accounting Firms
Miami, Florida

Israeloff, Trattner & Co.
Certified Public Accountants
Valley Stream, New York

Laventhol & Horwath
Certified Public Accountants
Philadelphia, Pennsylvania

Linden, Klain, Israel & Ross
Certified Public Accountants
Southfield, Michigan

Motes, Schroeder & Company
Certified Public Accountants
Sacramento, California

Retirement Concepts, Inc.
Bloomfield, New Jersey

Society of Insurance Accountants
Crozet, Virginia

Somerville & Company
Certified Public Accountants
Huntington, West Virginia

Thomas A. Stark & Associates
Certified Public Accountants
DeKalb, Illinois

Sterling, Nappen & Chavkin
Certified Public Accountants
Livingston, New Jersey

Workman Rhine & Co.
Certified Public Accountants
Boca Raton, Florida

Alan S. Zipp
Certified Public Accountant
Rockville, Maryland

Acknowledgments

Most of the letters in this book appear in print for the first time. Many of them deal with everyday accounting topics and contain familiar terminology. A few of the letters and a number of the audit reports are reprinted with the permission of the following copyright holders.

Pages

48–49 *Memorandum of Information to Be Furnished by Client.* Reprinted by permission of *The Practical Accountant* and Victor Harrison. Copyright © 1980 by Warren, Gorham & Lamont, Inc., 1633 Broadway, New York, NY 10019.

87 *Standard Bank Confirmation Inquiry.* Copyright © 1966 by American Institute of Certified Public Accountants, 1211 Avenue of the Americas, New York, NY 10036.

135–157 Reprinted with permission from *AICPA Audit and Accounting Manual.* Copyright © 1979 by the American Institute of Certified Public Accountants, Inc.

390 *Selecting a Vendor: Advantages and Disadvantages of Vendor Options.* From "Fact Sheet 17, Selecting a Vendor," in *Executive Education: Realistic Applications of Personal Computers to Business.* Copyright © 1985 by Peat, Marwick, Mitchell & Co.

403 From George E. Hunt, "Errors in Reports: What to Do," *The Journal of Accountancy,* May 1976, pp. 97–98. Copyright © 1976 by the American Institute of Certified Public Accountants, Inc. Opinions expressed in *The Journal of Accountancy* are those of editors and contributors. Publication in *The Journal of Accountancy* does not constitute endorsement by the AICPA.

Contents

How This Letter Book Will Help You .... *vii*

PART I
PROPOSALS AND ENGAGEMENTS *1*

1. Proposal Letters That Get Results *3*

- General Preliminary Proposal *5*
- Introductory Proposal Based on Conference *7*
- Style for Résumé Included with Proposal *11*
- Proposal Letter for Audit *12*
- Proposal for Audit of Nonprofit Organization *14*
- Proposal for Management Advisory Systems (MAS) Engagement *18*
- New Client Acceptance Data Sheet *21*

2. The All-Important Engagement Letter 22

- General Engagement Letter—Small Business Client *24*
- General Engagement Letter—Special Circumstances *27*
- Engagement Letter for Representing Client Before the IRS *30*
- Engagement Letter for IRS Examination *32*
- Review Engagement Letter *34*
- Compilation Engagement Letter *36*
- Engagement Leading to an Opinion *38*
- Audit Engagement Letter *40*
- Audit Engagement Letter to Longtime Client *42*
- Engagement for Audit Not Including Tax Preparation *44*

- Engagement for Audit of Personal Financial Statements *46*
- Memorandum of Information to Be Furnished by Client *48*
- Special Engagement Letter, Expert Witness *50*
- Engagement Letter for Employee-Benefit Pension Plan *52*
- Specification Sheet for Benefit Pension Plan *54*
- General Information Form for Benefit Pension Plan *56*
- Change in Circumstances from Original Engagement Letter *58*

PART II
AUDIT CORRESPONDENCE:
CONFIRMATIONS, REPRESENTATIONS *61*

3. Confirmation Letters That Bring Responses *63*

- Confirmation of Accounts Receivable *65*
- The Positive Approach to Confirmation *67*
- Printed Letter of Confirmation *69*
- Negative Confirmation Request *70*
- The Sticker or Stamp Method of Confirmation *71*
- Amount Being Held in Special Fund *72*
- Confirmation of Petty Cash and Advances *73*
- Schedule of Notes Receivable *74*
- Notes Payable to Vendors *75*
- Marketable Securities Held by Others *77*
- Insurance Policies Held by Others *79*
- Confirmation of Client's Inventory in Public Warehouse *80*
- Inventory on Consignment *81*
- Deposit Premium Confirmation *82*

4. Ready-to-Use Requests for Confirmation *83*

- Request for Bank Cutoff Statements *85*
- Standard Bank Confirmation Inquiry *86*
- Cash and Securities in Custodian or Trust Accounts *88*
- Confirmation of Accounts Payable *89*
- Request for List of Payables and Consignment Items *90*
- General Request for Statement of Indebtedness *91*
- Request for Schedule of Notes Payable *92*
- Information on Long-term Debt *93*
- Request for Confirmation of Mortgage Indebtedness *94*

■ **Letter to Capital Stock Registrar** *95*
■ **Request for Information on Bond Issue** *96*
■ **Cash Value of Life Insurance** *97*
■ **Request for Details on Contracts or Grants** *98*
■ **Letter to Client's Attorney** *99*
■ **Letter to Collection Agency** *100*
■ **Auditor's Direct Request for Statement of Client's Account** *101*
■ **Inventory Request to Warehouse** *102*
■ **Engaging an Out-of-Town Auditor to Observe Inventory** *103*
■ **Serving as Local Auditor for Another Accounting Firm** *104*

5. Effective Client Representation Letters ***105***

■ **Inventory Certificate Letter** *107*
■ **General Client Representation Letter** *108*
■ **Modification of Letter to Fit Circumstances** *111*
■ **Concise Client Representation Letter** *113*
■ **Alternate Client Representation Letter** *115*
■ **Explanation of Key Technical Terms** *117*

6. A Portfolio of Standard Audit Reports ***118***

■ **Unqualified Opinion—Standard Report** *121*
■ **Unqualified Opinion on Two Years' Financial Statements** *122*
■ **Unqualified Opinion Accepting Other Auditors' Report** *122*
■ **Unqualified Opinion Reversing Prior Year's Qualified Opinion** *123*
■ **Paragraph Indicating Review of Prior Year's Statements** *124*
■ **Disclaimer of Opinion on Prior Year's Unaudited Statements** *124*
■ **Qualified Opinion—Departure from Generally Accepted Accounting Principles** *124*
■ **Qualified Opinion—Inconsistent Application of Generally Accepted Accounting Principles** *125*
■ **Qualified Opinion—Limitation on Scope of Audit** *126*
■ **Qualified Opinion—Inadequate Disclosure** *126*
■ **Qualified Opinion—Uncertainty about Lawsuit** *127*
■ **Qualified Opinion—Uncertainty about "Going Concern"** *128*
■ **Adverse Opinion** *128*
■ **Disclaimer of Opinion—Unobserved Inventory** *130*
■ **Disclaimer of Opinion—Inadequate Records** *131*
■ **Disclaimer of Opinion—Limited Examination** *131*

- Disclaimer of Opinion—Lack of Independence *132*
- Personal Financial Statements—Standard Report *132*
- Personal Financial Statements—Adverse Opinion *133*
- Personal Financial Statements—Disclaimer of Opinion *133*
- Twelve Review Reports *135*
- Sixteen Compilation Reports *144*
- Seven Special Reports *153*

PART III
LETTERS OF RECOMMENDATION TO MANAGEMENT 159

7. Client-Centered Letters of Recommendation 161

- Basic Introductory Paragraph *163*
- Expanded Introduction *164*
- General Management Letter *165*
- Brief Business Advisory Letter *167*
- Organization and Facilities *169*
- Personnel and Payroll *172*
- Budgeting and Forecasting *174*
- Cash Receipts and Disbursements *176*

8. Key Paragraphs in Management Letters 179

- Purchasing and Payments *181*
- Inventory and Warehousing *182*
- Sales and Collections *184*
- Computers and Data Processing *185*
- Assets and Liabilities *187*

9. Financial Services and Estate Planning 189

- Engagement to Set Up Financial Accounting System *191*
- Fund Raising Engagement for Small Business Client *193*
- Feasibility Study for Office Building *195*
- Projected Financial Statements for Proposed Venture *197*
- Interim Progress Report on Pricing of Products *199*
- Covering Note for Business Advisory Letter *201*
- Paragraphs on How to Maximize Cash Position *202*
- Paragraphs on Improving Collection of Accounts Receivable *204*
- Engagement Letter for Business Planning Session *205*
- Approach Letter Regarding Personal Financial Planning *206*

- Notice of Talk on Personal Financial Planning *208*
- Engagement Letter for Estate Planning *209*
- Letter Concerning Client's Personal Goals *211*
- Checklist for Real Estate Holdings *213*
- Letter Dealing with Continuation of Family Business *215*
- Checklist for Estate Administration and Probate *217*

PART IV
TAX-RELATED CORRESPONDENCE *219*

10. Better Tax Return Preparation Letters **221**

- Letter Advising Client to Compile Tax Data *223*
- Reminder on Filing Tax Forms *224*
- Items Needed for Payroll Tax Returns *225*
- Instructions for Filing IRS Declaration of Estimated Tax *226*
- Letter to Client's Prior Tax Accountant *228*
- Client's Letter of Authorization *229*
- Request for Tax Data from Client's Internal Accountant *230*
- Letter Asking for Details on Deductible Expenses *231*
- Informing Client of Changes in Tax Law *232*
- Letter to IRS for Qualification of Retirement Plan *233*
- Note to IRS on Final Partnership Return *234*
- Explanatory Note to State Requesting Refund Due *235*
- Notice of Termination of Business *236*

11. Tax Transmittal Letters **237**

- All-Purpose Tax Transmittal Letter *239*
- General Purpose Transmittal Letter for Form 1040 *240*
- Individual Letter to Filer of Form 1040, Tax Owed *241*
- Individual Letter to Filer of Form 1040, Refund Due *242*
- Combined Federal and State Transmittal, "Boxed" Format *243*
- Combined Federal and State Transmittal, Open Format *246*
- Happy Face/Sad Face Federal and State Transmittal *248*
- U.S. Estimated Tax Payments with Checklist *250*
- U.S. Fiduciary Income Tax Transmittal *251*
- Alternate Form for U.S. Fiduciary Income Tax Return *252*
- Form for Sending Client Application for Tax ID Number *253*
- Transmittal for U.S. Partnership Tax Return *254*

■ Alternate Form for U.S. Partnership Tax Return *255*
■ Transmittal for U.S. Corporation Tax Return *256*
■ Alternate Form for U.S. Corporation Tax Return *257*
■ Transmittal for U.S. Short-form Corporation Tax Return *259*
■ U.S. Corporation Estimated Tax Payments *260*
■ State Corporation Tax Return *261*
■ State Corporation Estimated Tax Payments *262*
■ Transmittal Letter for Form 1139 (Corporate Refund) *263*
■ Transmittal Letter for Form 5500-C (Pension Plan) *264*

12. Letters Concerning Tax Returns and IRS Tax Audits *265*

■ Reason for Late Filing of Tax Returns *267*
■ Request for Credit for IRS Payment Already Made *268*
■ Request for Correction of Taxpayer's Account *269*
■ Request for Status of Taxpayer's Account *270*
■ Resolving a Continuing Problem with the IRS *271*
■ Request for Abatement of Penalties Assessed on Underpayment *272*
■ Explanation and Request for Abatement of Penalties *273*
■ Correcting Errors Made by Previous Accountant *275*
■ Asking the IRS How to Proceed with Problem Resolution *277*
■ Apology for Late Reply to Notices *278*
■ Letter Clarifying Status of Taxpayer *279*
■ Eliminating State Taxpayer Registration Number *280*
■ Humorous Letter Explaining a State Tax Mistake *281*
■ Relaying IRS Agent's Request for More Data *283*
■ Postponement of Audit to Obtain Documents *284*
■ Letter Asking Client for Information for Tax Exam *285*
■ Letter Summarizing Results of Tax Examination *287*
■ Notification of Acceptance of Form 1040 as Filed *289*
■ Recommendation That Client Accept Deficiency *290*
■ Letter Advising Client to Sign Waiver *291*

PART V
OFFICE OPERATIONS LETTERS *293*

13. Invoices, Fees, and Fee Collection *295*

■ Explanation of Billing Policies—Individual Income Tax *297*
■ Explanation of Billing Policies—Small Business *299*

- Invoice Listing Services *302*
- Accompanying Letter Explaining Invoice *303*
- Detailed Request for Fee Increase *304*
- Brief Letter Announcing Fee Increase *305*
- Letter Explaining Increase in Amount Billed *306*
- Confirmation of Oral Fee Agreement *307*
- Answering a Complaint Concerning Fees *308*
- Friendly Reminder Letter *309*
- Reminder Letter on Overdue Amount *310*
- Letter Referring to Unpaid Invoices *311*
- Request for Payment of Overdue Fees *312*
- Payment Request Tied to Performance *313*
- Request to Arrange Payment Plan *314*
- Promissory Note *315*
- Urgent Request for Payment of Past Due Fees *316*
- Letter to Attorney Confirming Fee Collection Agreement *317*
- Thank-You Note for Payment of Overdue Bill *318*

14. Employee Relations Letters *319*

- Response to Inquiry About Employment *321*
- Letter Inviting Applicant for an Interview *322*
- Letter Stating That No Position Is Open *323*
- Letter Noting That Résumé Will Be Kept in Active File *324*
- Request for Second Interview with Desirable Candidate *325*
- Letter Offering Position with Firm *326*
- Confirmation of Offer of Position *327*
- Letter to Candidate Who Has Declined Offer *328*
- Rejection Letter *329*
- Letter Requesting Postponement of Jury Duty *330*
- Request for Employee to Be Excused from Reserve Meeting *331*
- Letter Advising of Salary Increase *332*
- Congratulations on Outstanding Work *333*
- Best Wishes on Employee's Marriage *334*
- Congratulations on Birth of Child *335*
- Get-Well Note to Hospitalized Employee *336*

15. Image Building Through Public Relations *337*

- Brochure Explaining Firm's Capabilities *339*

- Letter Accompanying Newsletter *341*
- Request to Reprint Article in Newsletter *342*
- Advice to Staff on Public Relations *343*
- Press Release to Local Newspapers *344*
- Letter Inviting Press to Speaking Engagement *345*
- Follow-up Letter on Media Coverage *346*
- Letter to Editor Presenting Accountant's Viewpoint *347*
- Letter Accompanying Article *349*
- Welcome Letter to New Client *350*
- Thanks for Recommending Client *351*
- Letter Accepting Speaking Engagement *352*
- Letter Declining Speaking Engagement *353*
- Best Wishes on Opening New Business *354*
- Congratulations on Appointment to Office *355*
- Congratulations on Joining Organization *356*
- Praise for Achievement in Community *357*
- Congratulations on Promotion *358*
- Congratulations on New Position *359*
- Best Wishes on Retirement *360*

16. Time-Saving General Transmittal Letters ***361***

- Letter of Transmittal for Adjusting Entries *363*
- Letter of Transmittal for Fiscal Closing *364*
- Transmittal of Draft Audit for Comments *365*
- Transmittal of Audited Financial Statements *366*
- Transmittal of Unaudited Financial Statements *367*
- Letter Accompanying Annual Report to Stockholders *368*
- Transmittal of Printed Annual Report *369*
- Transmittal of Working Papers Used for Annual Report *370*
- Letter Transmitting Notice About Employee Benefit Plan *371*
- Letter Transmitting Pension Fund Report *372*
- Letter Transmitting Pension Plan Amendment *373*
- Transmitting Letter of Recommendations to Management *374*
- Letter to Bank Supporting Proposed Plant-Expansion Mortgage *375*
- Transmittal to Bank of Financial Statements re Mortgage *376*
- Transmitting Copies of Prior Correspondence *377*

■ Letter Accompanying Accounting Report to Partners *378*
■ Transmittal of Special Report to Stockholders *379*

PART VI
WRITING MORE EFFECTIVE LETTERS AND REPORTS *381*

17. Word Processing in the Accounting Office *383*

■ The Power of Word Processing *385*
■ Nine Specific Applications *386*
■ A Hard Look at Software *387*
■ Storage Media in Transition *388*
■ Choosing Among Printers *389*
■ The Right Vendor *389*
■ Ten Tips on Word Processing *391*

18. A Practical Guide to Report Writing *394*

■ Toward Better Audit Reports *396*
■ Who Receives the Audit Report? *397*
■ Guidelines for Dating the Report *398*
■ The Management Advisory Services Report *398*
■ Parts of a Management Advisory Services Report *399*
■ Ten Tips for Report Writers *401*

19. Handbook of Letter Format *404*

■ Date *406*
■ Inside Address *406*
■ Salutation *407*
■ Body of Letter *407*
■ Closing *408*
■ Signature *408*
■ Optional Elements *409*
■ Identification Line *410*
■ Full-Block Format *411*
■ Block Format *412*
■ Semiblock Format *413*
■ Short Letter Format *414*

Bibliography *415*

Index *417*

PART I

PROPOSALS AND ENGAGEMENTS

CHAPTER 1

Proposal Letters That Get Results

- General Preliminary Proposal
- Introductory Proposal Based on Conference
- Style for Résumé Included with Proposal
- Proposal Letter for Audit
- Proposal for Audit of Nonprofit Organization
- Proposal for Management Advisory Services (MAS) Engagement
- New Client Acceptance Data Sheet

There are two basic kinds of proposal letters. The first is a general letter that spells out what you can do and expect to do for a prospective client. Since it is introductory in nature, it does not end (as an engagement letter does) with a line calling for the prospective client's approval and signature. This kind of proposal letter follows an inquiry that may ask for one of two things: a general picture of your accounting capabilities (or your firm's) or more commonly, a statement of what services you expect to provide and what fees you will charge in a particular kind of engagement. Like all proposals, each of these is made in response to an approach from a prospective client.

The second kind of proposal letter is more specific. It assumes that an engagement will follow, and accordingly it ends with an approval line for the prospective client's signature. If the proposal is accepted and signed as submitted—and if it is as complete as it needs to be for the engagement—then a separate engagement letter becomes unnecessary. The signed proposal *is* the engagement letter.

A good proposal letter is clear, precise, and confidence-inspiring. It contains as little technical language as possible, yet still makes the necessary accounting points. The proposal is clearly responsive to the client's request, showing that you understand what is needed and have the expertise to perform it.

GENERAL PRELIMINARY PROPOSAL

The following letter is in response to a nonspecific request for information on the services that a particular accounting firm can perform. For an example of the kinds of résumés that are included with the proposal, see page 11.

Mr. Ernest Preston, President
Nutrition, Inc.
Industry Circle
Whitman City, New York 14800

Dear Mr. Preston:

As you requested during our recent conversation, I am pleased to outline the kinds of services we can provide your company.

Knowles & Farnham is an accounting firm founded in 1975 as a partnership under the laws of the state of New York. Our professional staff consists of three partners, one manager, one supervisor, four seniors, and three staff accountants.

Our corporate clients are numerous and varied. Over the years, as you are aware, we have become especially identified with the health food industry. We are presently engaged by the following publicly owned companies:

Apex Tofutti, Inc.
Calories Strictly Ltd.
Nutrihealth Company
Verdant Valley Farms, Inc.

Since you expressed a desire to get a general picture of the types of engagements we perform, let me list some of them. This is by no means an exhaustive list, but it does show our range of activities.

Auditing and Accounting Services

1. Monthly, quarterly, and annual audits
2. Compilation of financial statements
3. Review of financial statements
4. Examination of financial statements for the purpose of rendering an opinion

Tax Services

1. Preparation of income tax returns:
   a. Corporation, partnership, individual
   b. Federal, state, city
2. Income tax examinations
3. Preparation of other tax returns—payroll, sales, and so on
4. Estates and trusts
5. Tax opinions

Management Advisory Services

1. Analysis of accounting system
2. Analysis of proposed investments
3. Analysis of proposed construction
4. Analysis of feasibility and applications

Other Engagements

1. Reports to regulatory agencies
2. Assistance to counsel in legal matters

All of us at Knowles & Farnham are dedicated to providing prompt and efficient service of the highest standards. Our staff is skilled in all phases of accounting. We have particular expertise in your business—the health food industry.

We are pleased to present this description of our firm for your consideration. If you would like additional information, we will gladly furnish it. We would welcome the opportunity to meet with you, your officers, or directors at a mutually convenient time.

Sincerely yours,
KNOWLES & FARNHAM

____

Partner

INTRODUCTORY PROPOSAL BASED ON CONFERENCE

A conference in which the client's needs were discussed in detail prompted this letter. It therefore deals with specific procedures of the bank examination that is being proposed. At the same time, since this is the first engagement the accounting firm Fairlee & Company has had with First United Bank, it is also an introductory letter, spelling out the background and expertise of the firm.

Mr. Philip Hart
First United Bank
P.O. Box 5555
Rumsey, West Virginia 25300

Dear Mr. Hart:

It was a pleasure for me to talk with you and discuss the types of accounting services your bank desires. I would personally like to thank you for the opportunity of submitting this proposal.

Introduction

Fairlee & Company came into existence in 1933, and by the early 1940s a partnership was organized under the laws of the state of West Virginia for the practice of public accounting.

The firm consists of a professional staff of three partners, one manager, one supervisor, and six staff members. We feel that the segregation of our staff into various specialized departments—tax, auditing, and management advisory services—has enabled our firm to provide our clients with the proper diversification of services in the most professional and efficient manner possible.

Fairlee & Company is a member of the Private Companies Practice Section of the American Institute of Certified Public Accountants. All our partners and CPAs are members of the American Institute and the West Virginia Society of CPAs, and most have made significant contributions to the profession as officers and committee members in various organizations.

Our firm's basic philosophy is that service to each client is based on a substantive knowledge of and specialization in the services to be provided. Because of the unique aspects of banking and auditing, we feel that previous experience and knowledge in this area are of vital importance in providing the best and most efficient service to First United Bank.

The founding partner of Fairlee & Company was one of the incorporators of the Exchange National Bank in Huntington. Since that time Fairlee & Company has been extensively involved in servicing commercial banks in the Tri-State area.

Most of the partners of the firm are past presidents of the West Virginia Society of Certified Public Accountants and on occasion have chaired the Cooperation with Financial Institutions Committee of the West Virginia Society of CPAs.

We have offered seminars to enlighten bankers on the aspects of the accounting profession that relate to their industry. Our partners and staff have attended seminars on such banking topics as auditing, one-bank holding companies, and the new West Virginia banking law. On two occasions we have assisted in the training of two other West Virginia CPA firms to become proficient in the auditing of banks. Our firm has also developed manuals for assisting banks in their accounting and tax functions.

Following is a partial list of the banks we now serve. Feel free to contact any of them if you desire a reference concerning the quality of service we provide.

Bank of Greater Rumsey
Fourth National Bank of Westville
Mountaineer State Bank
National Trade Bank
Pioneer State Bank and Trust

Proposal for Director's Examination

We propose to perform an examination following the procedures outlined below. The principal limitations of such an examination are (1) It does not test detail transactions on a daily basis, and (2) It does not evaluate certain accounts requiring extensive judgmental discretion.

Because the procedures are not intended to be sufficient to constitute an examination made in accordance with generally accepted auditing standards, we will not express an opinion on the financial statements.

Our examination will include the review of internal controls, however. This review will not necessarily discover fraud or other irregularities should they exist, but we will promptly report any items we encounter that appear unusual. At the conclusion of the engagement, we will convey any comments or recommendations we may have accumulated on internal controls and accounting procedures of the bank that we feel are worthy of your consideration.

During the performance of the engagement, we will endeavor to use your personnel to the extent practicable to assist us in schedule preparation, confirmation procedures, document retrieval, and filing. The specific details of such assistance, and the timing thereof, will be planned so as to cause as little disruption in your normal operations as possible. Having your people assist can hold the cost involved to a minimum.

Our examination will include the following procedures. We will

1. Count cash of tellers and cash in vault on a surprise basis.
2. Confirm and reconcile correspondent bank account.
3. Review and perform follow-up procedures on cash items.
4. Confirm and review investments.
5. Reconcile loan accounts at cash-count date. Confirm a portion of loans outstanding.
6. Review procedures for accounting for reserve for loan losses.
7. Review fixed assets and depreciation expense.
8. Reconcile deposit accounts at cash-count date. Confirm a portion of deposits outstanding.
9. Analyze stockholders' equity accounts. Account for stock certificates authorized.
10. Utilize internal control questionnaire to review existing system of internal control.
11. Account for numerical sequencing of official checks, CDs, and so forth.
12. Tape official checks outstanding at cash-count date.
13. Analyze significant profit-and-loss accounts.

If other procedures are warranted, in our opinion, and under the circumstances, we will discuss them with you beforehand.

Attached are résumés of our bank client service team.

Our services are normally billed at our standard rates plus direct expenses. We estimate that our fee for all the services outlined above will be approximately $14,000. In addition, if you wish, we will prepare your federal income tax return. We believe that a reasonable estimate for this additional service is $2,600.

We would be pleased to discuss the terms of this letter with you at any time, and would sincerely appreciate the opportunity of serving you.

Again, let me say thanks for the opportunity of submitting this proposal.

If the above meets with your approval, please sign this letter in the space provided and return it to us. A copy is enclosed for your files.

Very truly yours,
FAIRLEE & COMPANY

____
Partner

Approved:
FIRST UNITED BANK

______________________________ ____________
Signature/Title Date

STYLE FOR RÉSUMÉ INCLUDED WITH PROPOSAL

When submitting a proposal, it is often wise to include a résumé, or profile, of each key staff member who may be involved in the engagement. The résumé should include educational background and career experience, as well as any special distinctions or honors he or she has earned, such as offices in national or state CPA organizations, involvement in civic or community affairs, speaking engagements, published books or articles, and the like.

DUDLEY R. BOUCHARD

CERTIFICATION	Certified Public Accountant licensed by the state of New Jersey. Member: New Jersey Society of CPAs.
EXPERIENCE	Bouchard & Grey: Partner In addition to establishing the firm in 1975 and developing it to its present size, Mr. Bouchard has served on the faculties of Darney-Glenn University and Pierce College, teaching Principles of Accounting and Management of an Accounting Practice. He has been a member of the Advisory Grading Staff of the American Institute of Certified Public Accountants and has written three articles for *Accounting Today* on the use of microcomputers by accounting firms.
	Loomis, Schwartz, & Kehoe, CPAs: Senior Accountant Experience included planning, coordinating, and performing certified audits; preparing financial statements and SEC filings; preparing federal and state tax returns from individual through multicorporate consolidations.
	Gavin Prinz and Company, CPAs: Senior Accountant Diversified client exposure: manufacturing, real estate, banking, retail, personal audit, corporate and personal taxes.
EDUCATION	B.S. in Accounting, Rutledge College M.B.A., with honors, University of the North
COMMUNITY SERVICE	Mr. Bouchard has served three terms on the Halsey County Board of Supervisors. Last year he was chairman of the Halsey County United Fund drive.

PROPOSAL LETTER FOR AUDIT

This proposal letter, like all such letters, is in response to an inquiry from a prospective client. It outlines briefly the work you will perform and includes a statement of your standard fees. It usually gives an estimate of the total fee, sometimes as an approximation, sometimes as a limit not to be exceeded.

Mr. Avery Jones, President
High Impact Plastics, Inc.
1189 Highway 47
Fosterville, Pennsylvania 19100

Dear Mr. Jones:

At the request of Mr. Jared Overton, Controller of your company, we are pleased to submit this proposal.

1. We will examine the balance sheet of High Impact Plastics, Inc., as of December 31, 19x8, and the related statements of income and surplus for the year then ended. Our examination will be made in accordance with generally accepted auditing standards, and will include tests of the accounting records and such other audit procedures as we consider necessary in the circumstances. We will not, however, make any tests or follow any other auditing procedures with respect to the opening inventories as of January 1, 19x9. Because of this limitation on the scope of our examination, we will not be in a position to express an opinion on the statements of income and surplus. Except in this respect, however, our examination will be for the purpose of expressing an opinion on the financial statements.
2. We will prepare your company's federal and state income tax returns and also the franchise tax returns for the year ended December 31, 19x8.

For performing the services described above, we will charge you our usual hourly rates, which are $100 for partners, $75 for supervisors, $60 for senior accountants and $32 for assistant accountants, plus out-of-pocket expenses. It is understood that our total fee will not exceed $12,500. Should we find it possible to complete the work for a lesser amount, you will be billed for the lesser amount.

If this proposal meets with your approval, please sign this letter in the space provided below and return it to us. A duplicate copy of the proposal is enclosed.

Very truly yours,
DANNAY & LEE

____
Partner

Approved:
HIGH IMPACT PLASTICS, INC.

______________________________ ____________
Signature/Title Date

PROPOSAL FOR AUDIT OF NONPROFIT ORGANIZATION

A proposal letter, like any other letter, has to be responsive to the requests of the client. In the following proposal letter for an audit, the prospective client has asked for information on a number of specific points, some of which are only indirectly related to the audit. The letter deals with these points in order. Notice that brief notes about some of the firm's members are included as part of the letter, rather than as an appended group of résumés.

Ms. Evelyn O'Connor
Great Lakes Maritime Association
2347 Dunes Highway
Quaife, Michigan 48100

Dear Ms. O'Connor:

Thank you for inviting us to submit a proposal for the audit of Great Lakes Maritime Association for the five-year period beginning with the year ended March 31, 19x6. We are pleased to submit to you the following information that will provide the audit committee with pertinent facts about Stein, Kleberg & Jones.

Stein, Kleberg & Jones was founded in 1962 by J. Arnold Stein, and has since grown to become one of the leading firms in the metropolitan Detroit area. The firm represents clients in a broad range of business activities in southeastern Michigan. By playing an integral yet independent role in our clients' management teams, we have achieved expertise in a number of industries.

The firm was founded on the principle of commitment to providing personal service and producing the highest quality work. To advance our efforts in this regard, the firm belongs to the Private Companies Practice Section of the Division for CPA Firms of the American Institute of Certified Public Accountants. As a member of this Section, we periodically undergo peer reviews of our audit practice and system of quality control. Accompanying this letter is a copy of our most recent peer review, which resulted in an unqualified opinion.

You requested in your letter that we respond to three key questions, the first of which pertains to our experience with similar nonprofit organizations.

Here is a partial list of such clients, which will give the committee some idea of our background in this area.

Contractors Alliance of Southern Michigan
Midwest Homeowners Warranty Corporation
Greater Detroit Association of Civil Engineers
Pope Pius XII High School
Michigan Council for Quality Education

Your second question concerns the areas other than audit in which our firm has expertise. Accompanying this proposal is an outline of the services we perform for clients. Stein, Kleberg & Jones has particular expertise in the following areas:

Management Advisory Services

Experienced consultants in our management advisory services (MAS) department have the depth of knowledge necessary to serve clients in a wide range of areas, such as profit planning and controls, problem solving, organization and administration, accounting systems and support, tax support, litigation support, and personal financial planning. Harry Spence, one of our firm's MAS partners has been involved in the area for more than fifteen years. Mr. Spence currently sits on the AICPA MAS Standards Committee, which is the body charged with the responsibility of developing and issuing MAS standards for the profession. Another MAS partner, Gary Jones, has focused on the field for more than thirty years.

Management Information Systems

As one of the integrated services Stein, Kleberg & Jones provides, our MAS staff helps clients plan, install, and maintain the kinds of management information and control systems required for effective, efficient and profitable operation. Our electronic data processing (EDP) consultants have the knowledge and experience necessary to assist clients with feasibility studies, system design, hardware and software evaluation, training and support, and microcomputer applications. In addition to Gary Jones, our EDP partner who has more than twenty years of consulting experience in the computer field, our EDP consultants include individuals with backgrounds in programming and in microcomputer training and support.

Tax Services

One of our main objectives in tax services is constructive and creative tax planning. Tax planning problems of the closely held corporations' shareholders, and of corporate executives generally, are areas in which our firm is especially knowledgeable. That same expertise is applied to all our business clients, including nonprofit organizations, by having a tax specialist assigned to every major corporate client as part of the planning team. This facilitates the planning process by having a tax person become as familiar as possible with key client personnel and with ongoing business affairs. Our tax library is comprehensive, and we use one of our microcomputers to access Prentice-Hall's tax data bases, which allows our tax specialists to keep abreast of the most recent tax developments.

Employee-Benefit Plans

Many of our corporate clients have employee-benefit plans. In most cases, Stein, Kleberg & Jones was involved in the planning process leading to implementation. We constantly monitor changes in the tax laws affecting this area, and our library contains extensive reference material on the subject. We have a consulting relationship with some of the leading attorneys in this field.

Your third question deals with the backgrounds of our proposed engagement personnel. Our philosophy of personalized service means, among other things, that the audit of your organization will be under the personal supervision of Mr. Francis Price, who is in charge of the firm's auditing and accounting areas. Mr. Price holds a Bachelor's degree from Woodward College and a Master of Business Administration degree from Xenia University.

Mr. Price has more than ten years of auditing experience, dealing with a wide variety of businesses, including nonprofit organizations. He is a member of the American Institute of Certified Public Accountants and the Michigan Association of Certified Public Accountants, and currently sits on the MACPA's State Tax Committee.

Assisting Mr. Price on the audit, as the accountant in charge, will be Mr. Mario DeSilva. Mr. DeSilva is an audit manager in the firm and supervises a number of our key engagements. In his thirty-two years of practice, Mr. DeSilva has developed a strong background in many industries. His experience with nonprofit organizations spans more than twenty-five years. Mr. DeSilva holds Bachelor's and Master's degrees in Business Administration from Danforth University.

In summary, Stein, Kleberg & Jones recognizes that its most important product is prompt and efficient service of the highest quality. All our efforts are directed toward achieving that aim. We believe we can serve the Michigan Maritime Association to its complete satisfaction. The highest level of skills and resources available to our firm will be brought to bear in servicing your organization's needs.

We appreciate the opportunity to present our firm for your consideration and will be pleased to furnish additional information or meet with your audit committee.

Sincerely,
STEIN, KLEBERG & JONES

____

Armin J. Kleberg
Partner

PROPOSAL FOR MANAGEMENT ADVISORY SERVICES (MAS) ENGAGEMENT

When a proposal letter is based upon a substantial amount of prior investigation (whether the client is a new or existing one), the nature of the engagement is quite clear. Under these circumstances, there is no need for the letter to introduce the firm and its personnel. Rather, the letter begins with the project at hand, spelling out the objectives of the engagement, the extent of the work, the exact role of the accountant or accounting firm, the organization of the project, the estimated fees, and the method of billing. Since the letter anticipates an engagement, it requests a signature indicating approval.

Mr. Ernest Martin, President
Zeus Manufacturing Company, Inc.
23 South Perry Street
White River, Colorado 80700

Dear Mr. Martin:

As a result of our several meetings with you, your controller Mr. Ward, and your vice president for purchasing, Mr. Ruiz, it was agreed that our firm undertake to study the accounting system and office procedures of Zeus Manufacturing Company, Inc. This letter, based on our preliminary findings, sets forth the objectives of our proposed study and explains how we intend to proceed.

A principal goal will be to upgrade the punctuality and accuracy of inventory records for use by the sales staff, the purchasing department, and the accounting department. We will also attempt to improve sales-costing and inventory-pricing procedures. Our overall aim is to streamline accounting and other office procedures so as to ensure prompt, correct closings of the books, thereby providing management with clear, current information.

We will consider additional automation as a possible means to bring the degree of efficiency to your operation that modern electronic equipment and accompanying procedures permit. Throughout the study, we will keep in mind (and will keep you informed of) the control features of any system we recommend.

Here is how we plan to proceed. We will

- Examine the current methods used for purchasing materials, processing vendors' invoices, and handling accounts payable.
- Review the present procedures for order processing, billing, accounts receivable, and cash receipts.
- Study the existing methods of inventory analysis and control, transportation arrangements, and warehousing methods and controls.
- Assess the information needs and operating requirements of key managers, partly through in-depth discussions with them, partly through independent observation.
- Submit a written report presenting our conclusions and recommendations, including specific equipment requirements.
- Meet with you and your staff to discuss the report.

After you have received and evaluated the report, you will undoubtedly wish to go over it. We view that meeting as an integral part of the engagement.

Our fees will be based on the time spent by members of our firm at their regular rates plus any out-of-pocket costs. We will work closely with your accounting personnel and will make every effort to keep costs to a minimum. Our anticipated fee for this study is between $2,500 and $3,200, with statements to be rendered twice a month for fees incurred during that period. We would appreciate payment of these as they are received. Upon your approval of this proposal, we will require a $1,500 retainer.

Our report may very possibly recommend the purchase of new equipment, the installation of which is not included in this engagement. Installation could, if you wish, become the subject of a separate engagement. We have the capability of helping to install office systems, selecting or designing appropriate forms, and training personnel in the use of new equipment.

We can begin the engagement within one month. Upon acceptance of this proposal, we will contact you to set the exact date.

If the above meets with your approval, please sign the enclosed letter and return it to us with your check for $1,500. A copy of the letter is enclosed for your files.

Thank you for your confidence in our firm. We look forward to the engagement and, we hope, to a continuing and mutually beneficial relationship.

Very truly yours,
WESTON, LAYNE, BATES & CO.

____
Partner

Approved:
ZEUS MANUFACTURING COMPANY, INC.

______________________________ ____________
Signature/Title Date

NEW CLIENT ACCEPTANCE DATA SHEET

Client Name ______________________________

Address ______________________________

Fiscal Year ____________________ Phone (   ) ____________
Area Code

Nature of Business ______________________________

Name of Principal Owners, Officers, etc. ______________________________

____

Form of organization Corp.______ Part.______ Indiv.______ Other______

Estimated annual fees ______________

How did we obtain client? ______________________________

Related clients, parent or affiliates ______________________________

Any special technical or industry expertise needed, or other significant matters?

____

Engagement Letter Sent ______________ Date______________

Fed. I.D. No. ____________ State W/H No. ____________ Sales Tax No. ____________

Corp. Charter No. ____________ Unempl. Tax No. ____________

DUE DATE CONTROL

Type	Req. ✓	Period Ending	Due Date
Payroll		March 31 June 30 September 30 December 31	April 30 July 31 October 31 January 31
Sales Tax			
Property Taxes			
1065			
1120			
1120S			
MO			
KS			
Other States			
MO Franchise			
KS Annual Report			
MO Registration Rep.			
Kansas City			

Financial Statements

Audit			
Review			
Compilation			

Client list______

Card file______

Tax file______

W/P file______

Billing file______

Approval ______________________________ Date ______________________________

CHAPTER 2

The All-Important Engagement Letter

- General Engagement Letter—Small Business Client
- General Engagement Letter—Special Circumstances
- Engagement Letter for Representing Client Before the IRS
- Engagement Letter for IRS Examination
- Review Engagement Letter
- Compilation Engagement Letter
- Engagement Leading to an Opinion
- Audit Engagement Letter
- Audit Engagement Letter to Longtime Client
- Engagement for Audit Not Including Tax Preparation
- Engagement for Audit of Personal Financial Statements
- Memorandum of Information to Be Furnished by Client
- Special Engagement Letter, Expert Witness
- Engagement Letter for Employee-Benefit Pension Plan
- Specification Sheet for Benefit Pension Plan
- General Information Form for Benefit Pension Plan
- Change in Circumstances from Original Engagement Letter

An engagement letter can be long or short depending on the nature and extent of the work being undertaken. Whatever its length, this letter is well worth the time it takes to prepare. An engagement letter is the best tool you have for clarifying the accounting tasks you are to perform and, at the same time, preventing future misunderstandings about what was agreed upon.

In preparing an engagement letter, consider including the following items. Not all of them will be appropriate for every engagement letter, but they should be included when needed.

- *Indication of how the engagement originated:* "As we discussed at our meeting on March 22, 19x8 . . . ."
- *Nature of the engagement:* "We will review the annual balance sheet . . . ."
- *Name of client and year-end date(s):* ". . . of Deep River Diving Gear, Inc., for the year ended June 30, 19x8."
- *Statements to be examined, compiled, or reviewed:* "[annual balance sheet and] related statements of income, retained earnings, and changes in financial position. . . ."
- *Kind of opinion to be rendered:* ". . . to render an opinion on the fairness of your financial statements."
- *Disclaimer concerning irregularities:* "These services are not designed to disclose any defalcation or other irregularities that may exist."
- *How fee will be determined:* "Our charges for the engagement will be at our standard rates and are not expected to exceed $4,000 plus out-of-pocket expenses.
- *Responsibility of client's staff:* ". . . fee is based on the understanding that your personnel will prepare the audit schedules and locate the documents we need."
- *Request for signature:* "If these arrangements meet with your approval, please sign. . . ."
- *Approval (or acceptance) line and date:*

  Approved:

  DEEP RIVER DIVING GEAR, INC.

  ______________________________ ____________

  Signature/Title Date

GENERAL ENGAGEMENT LETTER—SMALL BUSINESS CLIENT

This letter follows a meeting and an agreement between an independent accountant and the president of a small incorporated business. It specifies the range of services that the accountant will provide on behalf of the client, and describes specifically what will and will not be covered under the terms of the engagement.

Ms. Dorothy Kurtz, President
Kurtz Dental Services, Inc.
443 Market Street
Sinclair, Maryland 21600

Dear Ms. Kurtz:

As we discussed, I would be happy to serve your accounting, tax, and management advisory services needs.

In accordance with standards established by the American Institute of Certified Public Accountants, an engagement letter is necessary to set forth our understanding of the terms and objectives of our relationship, and the nature and limitations of the services to be provided.

I will provide the following services:

1. I will compile, from the information you provide, the annual balance sheet and related statements of income, retained earnings, and changes in financial position of Kurtz Dental Services, Inc., for the year ended December 31, 19x7. I will not audit or review such financial statements. The transmittal letter for these statements will conform to standards established by the AICPA. If for any reason I am unable to complete the compilation of your financial statements, I will not issue a report on such statements as a result of this engagement.
2. Beginning with the month of January 19x7, I will prepare, from the information you provide, a monthly balance sheet and statement of income on the cash basis of accounting. You agree to provide me with the following documents on a monthly basis at my office: bank statements, cancelled checks, check stubs or register, payroll records, documents concerning asset acquisitions and dispositions, liabilities and notes payable, and other relevant documents. All check stubs MUST BE CODED by you as to the proper account number for recording in the ledgers.

3. I will record all income and expenses, on a monthly basis, from the above documents you provide, in a computerized general ledger system. Each month I will provide you with a copy of the general ledger account listing, which shows each check, deposit, and adjustment affecting each account during the month. You agree to review this general ledger report each month and notify me of any changes necessary in the classification or distribution of expense. Unless you notify me of a change, I will assume that all transactions have been properly coded and have been posted to the correct accounts. These ledgers will record, on a monthly basis, all cash receipts (identified by you as to source) and all cash disbursements (identified by you as to expense category). The ledgers will also include adjusting journal entries made by me in accordance with generally accepted accounting principles. These ledgers will be used in the preparation of the annual financial statements and income tax returns.
4. Each month I will reconcile your checking account with your bank statement and identify errors in the checkbook. I will make correcting entries directly in the checkbook and identify the specific source of each adjustment. I will inform you of these adjustments and request that you correct your checkbook balance at your earliest convenience.
5. Each month I will review the payroll records which you have prepared and record the appropriate amounts in the ledgers. I will discuss with you any errors identified and indicate to you the appropriate action required on your part to correct the payroll records.
6. On a quarterly basis, I will prepare the federal payroll tax return and the state unemployment tax return. You will prepare and file the monthly state withholding reports for all months except December, at which time I will reconcile the entire year's state withholding and prepare the December report. You agree to provide me with the forms needed, which are sent to you by the federal and state tax offices.
7. On an annual basis, I will reconcile all payroll tax returns with the payroll withholding records and prepare the year-end payroll tax returns, including federal and state unemployment tax returns, Forms W-2, W-3, 1099, and 1096, as required.
8. On a periodic basis, as needed, and at least four times each year, I will meet with you to discuss your accounting records and the management implications of your financial statements. These meetings are important to your financial well-being and should be held as often as considered necessary.

This engagement cannot be relied upon to disclose errors, irregularities, or illegal acts, including fraud or defalcations, that may exist. However, I will inform you of any such matters that come to my attention.

The fee for the above services will be $400 per month, payable at the time the documents are delivered for processing. The fee will remain at this level for a period of one year beginning with the January 19x7 processing. At the end of the year, I will evaluate the time actually spent on this work in relation to this fixed-fee arrangement. The fee does not include the preparation of any income tax returns, property tax returns, information reports required by any organization, or other services of a similar nature. No services outside the scope of the accounting services identified above are included in this fee.

If you would like me to perform additional services, including tax return preparation, tax consulting, management advisory services, and the like, I would be pleased to do so. This type of work will be billed separately at my standard billing rates. I will always be willing to estimate the fee for any special service in advance of the service and will give you a fixed-fee quote if at all possible.

I look forward to working with you and will be happy to discuss this letter and our arrangements with you at any time.

If the foregoing is agreeable to you, please sign this letter in the space provided and return it to me in the enclosed envelope. The second copy is for your files.

Sincerely yours,

James Ackerman
Certified Public Accountant

Acknowledge and agree

____

Dorothy Kurtz, President
Kurtz Dental Services, Inc.

GENERAL ENGAGEMENT LETTER—SPECIAL CIRCUMSTANCES

In this letter a careful distinction is drawn between the two parts of the engagement. The first part deals with the ongoing affairs of the new company, while the second deals with a short, earlier period following recapitalization. Because of the disparate nature of the two tasks, the services and fees for each one are explained separately.

Mr. John Hayes, President
Softwarehouse, Inc.
27 Route 82
Fitchburg, New Jersey 07700

Dear Mr. Hayes:

This will confirm the understanding arrived at by you, Mr. Emil Burton, Chairman of the Board; Mrs. Rhoda Fox, Secretary-Treasurer; and our accounting firm represented by Messrs. Henry Roe and Morris Weinfeld at the January 5, 19x6 meeting at your offices. Our understanding concerns the fiscal years ending (1) March 31, 19x7 and (2) March 31, 19x6.

(1) For the fiscal year ending March 31, 19x7, we will examine the company's balance sheet as of March 31, 19x7, and the related statements of income, retained earnings, shareholders' equity, and changes in financial position for the year then ended. Our examination will be in accordance with generally accepted auditing standards, and will include such tests of the accounting records and such other audit procedures as we consider necessary to render an opinion on the fairness of your financial statements.

These services will not be designed to disclose any defalcations or other irregularities that may exist, and should not be relied on to do so. However, we will notify you of anything that comes to our attention which appears to be unusual or abnormal.

We will prepare unaudited compilation of financial statements as of the end of the first three quarters of the fiscal year. This will be solely an accounting service, and we will disclaim an opinion on these unaudited statements.

We will prepare the company's federal, state of New Jersey, and state of California returns for the fiscal year ending March 31, 19x7.

We will also prepare all quarterly and annual federal and state (New Jersey and California) payroll tax returns and related required filings.

Our fee for the above will be $8,400 plus out-of-pocket expenses. We will render four quarterly invoices, which will be due and payable upon receipt. If any extraordinary matters come to our attention during the engagement, we will immediately consult with you.

(2) For the year ending March 31, 19x6—which encompasses the "short period" of "new" Softwarehouse, Inc., from recapitalization December 1, 19x5 to March 31, 19x6—we will compile an unaudited balance sheet as of November 30, 19x5 and as of March 31, 19x6, and related audited statements of income, retained earnings, and changes in financial position for the eight and twelve months then ended. This will be solely an accounting function. No auditing procedures will be performed, and we will disclaim an opinion on these unaudited financial statements.

We will perform such bookkeeping services as may be required to compile the unaudited statements, such as assisting in adjusting and closing the general books. These services are not designed to disclose any defalcations or other irregularities that may exist, and should not be relied on to do so. However, we will notify you of anything that comes to our attention which appears to be unusual or abnormal.

We will also prepare the federal and state income and franchise tax returns for the fiscal year ending March 31, 19x6.

In addition, we will be available for consultation regarding such matters as the recapitalization with respect to federal and state tax laws, payroll setup and related payroll tax requirements, and any other areas that require our expertise.

Because of the complexities in the development of a business such as Softwarehouse, Inc. in such a short period of time, it is impossible for us to establish a fixed fee for our services for the year ending March 31, 19x6. Our fee, therefore, will be billed at our standard rates together with any out-of-pocket costs on a monthly basis as the work progresses.

It is expressly understood that the services detailed above do not refer to Studio 5-1/4 Software Company or any other business acquired or to be acquired relating to the recapitalization or formation of "new" Softwarehouse, Inc.

We are pleased to be able to offer this proposal and look forward to a long and mutually beneficial association.

Please indicate your approval of these arrangements by signing this letter and returning it to us. The enclosed copy is for your files.

Very truly yours,
BALLOU & SCHMIDT

____
Partner

Approved:
SOFTWAREHOUSE, INC.

______________________________ ____________
Signature/Title Date

ENGAGEMENT LETTER FOR REPRESENTING CLIENT BEFORE THE IRS

Not all engagement letters are long, but all of them—even the shortest—should include these elements:

- A statement indicating the limitations of the accountant's responsibility for discovering fraud and other irregularities.
- The terms of billings and payment.
- A description of any special services that are to be performed.

The following tax engagement shown on page 31 is short, but it contains those elements.

Paul and Christine Kovacs
435 El Segundo Boulevard
Alvarez, California 92300

Dear Mr. and Mrs. Kovacs:

This letter summarizes our discussion of May 23, 19x3, concerning the terms of our engagement. It describes the nature and extent of the tax services we will provide.

We will represent you before the Internal Revenue Service and exert our best efforts to obtain a satisfactory settlement of any issues that may arise in the examination of your 19x2 joint income tax return.

We will not audit or otherwise attempt to verify the information you have submitted, although we may ask for clarification or further details on some matters.

Our fee, charged at our standard billing rates for tax work plus out-of-pocket expenses, will be based upon the amount of time required for our services. We request payment of all invoices upon presentation.

If this letter accurately sets forth your understanding of the engagement, please sign below in the space provided and return it to us, retaining the copy for your files.

We are pleased to have you as clients and trust that the association will prove to be mutually beneficial.

Very truly yours,
POLLARA & ASSOCIATES

____
Partner

Approved:

__________________________ ____________
Paul Kovacs Date

__________________________ ____________
Christine Kovacs Date

ENGAGEMENT LETTER FOR IRS EXAMINATION

This letter is similar to the preceding one, but it is more specific in regard to billing and also in setting forth the specific responsibilities of the client.

Mr. Walter Crane
2323 Highpoint Road
Spring Hill, New Jersey 07800

Dear Mr. Crane:

This confirms our discussion of the services we will provide in connection with the Internal Revenue Service audit of your 19x2 and 19x3 federal income tax returns, as well as the manner of determining our fee and the time of its payment.

We will represent you before the Internal Revenue Service and exert our best efforts to obtain a satisfactory settlement of any issues that may arise in the examination.

Our fee will be at our standard rate of $75 per hour plus any out of-pocket-expenses we may incur.

You agree to pay a $250 retainer which will be applied against our final billing under this engagement. Invoices to you for fees and out-of-pocket expenses will be due and payable on presentation.

You agree to:

- Cooperate in furnishing and in helping us to obtain information.
- Furnish us with such documents and affidavits as we may from time to time request.

If the above correctly sets forth your understanding, please sign the copy of this letter in the space provided, and return it to us in the enclosed envelope.

We appreciate your retaining us, and we assure you that we will make every effort to resolve this tax examination satisfactorily.

Very truly yours,
VOORHEES & BATSTO

____
Partner

Approved:

______________________________ ____________
Walter Crane Date

REVIEW ENGAGEMENT LETTER

It is a good practice to have an engagement letter for every year—or at most every two years—of a continuing accountant-client relationship. The review engagement letter that follows is fairly short because its main purpose is to summarize existing practices. Notice the informality of the salutation. Notice also (from the final paragraph) that two copies of the letter are being sent—one to be returned to the accounting firm and one for the client's files. Even in the age of reprographics, that is an excellent idea for all engagement letters.

Mr. Everett Borders
LVR Corporation
P.O. Box 7865
Vance Mills, West Virginia 26400

Dear Ev:

May I personally, and on behalf of our firm, thank you and those in your organization for the opportunity to serve as your accountant.

For the year ended November 30, 19x5, and for next year, we would like to confirm our understanding of the terms and objectives of this engagement and review the accounting services our firm will provide.

We will perform the following services:

1. We will review the balance sheet of LVR Corporation as of November 30, 19x5, and the related statements of operations, retained earnings, and changes in financial position for the year then ended, in accordance with standards established by the American Institute of Certified Public Accountants. This service does NOT constitute an audit of such financial statements, the object of which is to express an opinion regarding the financial statements taken as a whole, and, accordingly, we will not express an opinion. Our report will be in the standard format for a review statement, as set forth by the American Institute of Certified Public Accountants, which is familiar to you.
2. Throughout the twelve-month period ended November 30, 19x6, we will compile interim balance sheets and statements of income through the use of our computer. Such statements will substantially omit all disclosures, including a statement of changes in financial position. These

financial statements will be for management purposes only, and our report will so indicate.

3. We will prepare federal and state income tax returns of LVR Corporation for the year ended November 30, 19x5. We will be available at your request to perform other tax and accounting services, especially income and estate tax planning and other business-related matters.

Our engagement cannot be relied upon to disclose errors or other irregularities that may exist. However, we will inform you of any such matters that come to our attention.

Our fees for this engagement and any additional services will be computed at our standard rate plus direct expenses.

We will be pleased to discuss this letter with you at any time.

If the foregoing is in accordance with your understanding, please sign one of the enclosed two copies of this letter and return it to us.

Very truly yours,
FAIRLEE & COMPANY

____
Partner

Approved:
LVR CORPORATION

______________________________ ____________
Signature/Title Date

COMPILATION ENGAGEMENT LETTER

A compilation engagement letter is similar in many respects to a review engagement letter. Both should contain a paragraph that clearly states the limitations of the engagement. A client may assume that any irregularities will come to light during a review or compilation. They may not, of course, and you should make that clear. The following paragraph is recommended for both a review and a compilation letter:

> Our engagement cannot be relied upon to disclose errors, irregularities or illegal acts, including fraud or defalcations, that may exist. However, we will inform you of any such matters that come to our attention.

The key word is *engagement*. In a review or compilation letter, you should not state or suggest that you are making an *examination*. Both the previous letter and the one that follows include a version of the paragraph above.

Ms. Carolyn Newby, President
Leprechaun Boutique, Inc.
Hidden Valley Road
Wayne, Vermont 05600

Dear Ms. Newby:

I would like to thank you for the opportunity to serve as your accountant.

The purpose of this letter is to set forth the terms and objectives of our engagement, including any limitations on the services to be performed.

As we have discussed, I will provide the following services:

1. I will compile, from information you supply, the annual balance sheet and related statements of income, retained earnings, and changes in financial position of Leprechaun Boutique, Inc., for the year ended June 30, 19x7. This service is not an audit or a review of the financial statements submitted. A compilation is limited to presenting in the form of a report, including financial statements, information that is the representation of management.
2. I will prepare the annual federal and state income tax returns of Leprechaun Boutique, Inc., for the year ended June 30, 19x7.

The engagement outlined in this letter cannot be relied upon to disclose irregularities or illegal acts, including fraud or defalcations, that may exist. However, I will inform you of any errors, aberrations, or other questionable items or activities that come to my attention.

My fee for this engagement will be computed at my standard hourly rate plus out-of-pocket expenses. A bill will be rendered upon completion of the work and will be due and payable upon receipt.

Should you find that you require additional tax-related services—preparation of federal payroll tax returns, state sales tax or unemployment tax returns, local property tax returns, or tax planning or consulting—I will gladly provide them. These would be billed at my standard hourly rate plus out-of-pocket expenses.

If you have any questions about this letter or about compilation procedures in general, do not hesitate to get in touch with me. To indicate your agreement to the arrangements above, please sign this letter and return it to me. The duplicate copy is for your files.

Sincerely yours,

Marcus Smith
Certified Public Accountant

Approved:

__________________________ ____________

Carolyn Newby, President — Date
Leprechaun Boutique, Inc.

ENGAGEMENT LEADING TO AN OPINION

To achieve the best possible understanding of a client's needs and expectations, as well as to spell out the client's responsibilities, a pre-engagement conference is highly desirable. The information gained in this conference will largely determine what needs to be said in the engagement letter. In addition, a conference allows you to explain the background and services of your firm and to discover pertinent information about the client's circumstances. Was there a predecessor accountant? What is his or her current status? The following letter was preceded by such a conference.

Mr. Willard Vroman, President
Vroman Industries, Inc.
400 South Main Street
Oak Grove, Alabama 36200

Dear Mr. Vroman:

This letter is to confirm our understanding that we will examine the balance sheet of Vroman Industries, Inc., as of December 31, 19x8, and the related statements of income, retained earnings, and changes in financial position for the year then ended.

We will perform this examination in accordance with generally accepted accounting standards and will include such tests of the accounting records and other procedures as we consider necessary in the circumstances.

Our objective in this examination is to express an unqualified opinion on the financial statements listed above, although it is possible that facts or circumstances encountered may require us to qualify or disclaim an opinion.

This examination is subject to the inherent risk that it will not detect material errors, irregularities, illegal acts, or fraud or defalcations should they exist. However, we will inform you of any matters of this kind should they come to our attention during the examination.

As part of this engagement, we will prepare the federal and state income tax returns for Vroman Industries, Inc., for the year ended December 31, 19x8.

Our charges for the engagement will be at our standard rates and will not exceed $9,500 plus out-of-pocket expenses. Bills will be submitted monthly and are due upon presentation. If unforeseen circumstances arise, requiring additional services that exceed the maximum fee, we will consult with you before undertaking such work or increasing the fee.

We wish to emphasize that our fee is based on the understanding that your personnel will prepare the audit schedules and locate the documents we need.

If this letter accurately reflects your understanding of the engagement, please sign below in the space provided and return the letter to us. A copy is enclosed for your files.

Sincerely,
BRADSHAW, STIMPSON, BERG & O'SHEA

____
Partner

Approved:
VROMAN INDUSTRIES, INC.

____________________________ ______________
Signature/Title Date

AUDIT ENGAGEMENT LETTER

Clients can easily have misconceptions about an audit. Some clients may think that once an audit has been completed, the resulting financial statements are the auditor's representations, not the client company's. That is not the case, as the annual report of any large public company reveals. Some clients suppose that an audit will inevitably disclose frauds or embezzlements. It may not. Poor internal controls within a company, illegal collusion, or some other subterfuge may escape the most careful audit. Consequently, an audit engagement letter should emphasize the limitations on the accountant's responsibility for detecting irregularities.

Mr. Thomas Chauvin, Controller
Evangeline Produce Company, Inc.
Beauregard Building
Polk, Louisiana 70400

Dear Mr. Chauvin:

This letter will confirm the understanding between you and Mr. Gene Harder, a partner in this firm, concerning the examination of your company's financial statements for the year ended December 31, 19x8.

Our examination will be made in accordance with generally accepted auditing standards and will include tests of the accounting records and other audit procedures that we consider necessary to enable us to render an opinion on the fairness of your financial statements.

Since we do not contemplate making a detailed examination of specific company transactions, we may not uncover material errors, irregularities, illegal acts, frauds, or defalcations should they exist. If such irregularities come to our attention, we will discuss them with you to determine what action should be taken.

Our work will include a review and critique of your system of internal controls, which, as Mr. Harder recommended, will be the subject of a separate report.

We will prepare federal and state income tax returns of Evangeline Produce Company, Inc., for the year ended December 31, 19x8, and will represent your company through the informal conference level if either or both of the returns are selected for audit by the taxing authorities.

At the conclusion of the audit, we will submit a report that contains our opinion, comments on your financial position and operating results, and certain supplementary schedules.

Our charges for these services will be based on our standard rates. It is understood that our fee is not to exceed $10,000 plus out-of-pocket expenses that we incur. If, at any time during the engagement, extraordinary matters come to our attention which appear to require an extension of services, we reserve the right to increase our fee, but only after consultation with you.

If these arrangements meet with your approval, please sign the original copy of this letter in the space provided and return it to us. The copy is for your files.

Sincerely,
K. M. KILCOYNE & COMPANY

____
Partner

Approved:
EVANGELINE PRODUCE COMPANY, INC.

______________________________ ____________
Signature/Title Date

AUDIT ENGAGEMENT LETTER TO LONGTIME CLIENT

Even though a particular accountant-client relationship may cover many years, it is wise to update the audit engagement each year. Sometimes the letter can be virtually identical from year to year, but at other times you may have to make changes that reflect changed circumstances, as in the second paragraph of the following letter.

Board of Directors
Malabar Corporation
21789 West Shore Highway
Douglas, Arkansas 72500

Gentlemen:

We would like to express our sincere appreciation for the opportunity of serving you over the years. Our continuing goal is to provide you with the type and quality of service that will be most beneficial to you. Following is an outline of the services we propose for the year ending June 30, 19x5.

The objective of our examination will be to express an opinion on the June 30, 19x5, balance sheet. Since we did not confirm accounts receivable or observe inventory for the preceding year, we will not express an opinion on the statements of income, retained earnings, or changes in financial position for the year ended June 30, 19x5.

Our audit procedures will include the review, evaluation, and testing of internal control. However, our examination cannot be relied upon to disclose errors or other irregularities. We will, of course, inform you of any such matters that come to our attention. At the end of the engagement, we will report to you any comments or recommendations we have accumulated on Malabar Corporation's internal control and accounting procedures that we think are worthy of your consideration.

During the performance of the engagement, we will endeavor to use Malabar's personnel to the fullest practical extent to assist in schedule preparation, document retrieval, and filing. The specific requirements of such assistance, along with its timing, will be organized so as to cause as little disruption in the company's normal operations as possible.

We will prepare federal and state income tax returns of Malabar Corporation for the year ended June 30, 19x5. We will also be available at your request to perform other tax- and accounting-related services.

Our fees for the services outlined above will be computed at our standard rates plus out-of-pocket expenses. We estimate that the fee for the audit and the preparation of tax returns will be approximately $12,000.

If you have any questions regarding this engagement, or if you desire further elaboration, we would be pleased to meet with you and discuss your concerns at a mutually convenient time.

To indicate your approval of the engagement as outlined above, please sign and return one of the two enclosed copies of this letter. The other is for your files. Thank you.

Sincerely,
FROMME & LEIFIELD

____
Partner

Approved:
MALABAR CORPORATION

______________________________ ________________
Signature/Title Date

ENGAGEMENT FOR AUDIT NOT INCLUDING TAX PREPARATION

Like all good audit engagement letters, the one below includes five important elements: (1) a statement that an understanding has been reached, (2) an explanation of what is and is not to be covered by the audit, (3) a disclaimer concerning fraud or embezzlement, (4) a paragraph concerning fees, and (5) a request for signed approval.

Mr. Edwin Zoar, President
The Glassworks
Upper Lake Road
Elm City, New York 14900

Dear Mr. Zoar:

This letter is to confirm our understanding of the examination that our firm will make of your company's financial statements for the year ended December 31, 19x7.

Our examination will be made in accordance with generally accepted auditing standards. It will include such tests of the accounting records and other such auditing procedures as we consider necessary in the circumstances to express an opinion on the financial statements.

Please note that this examination leading to the expression of an opinion on financial statements is not designed to disclose defalcations and irregularities, and cannot be relied upon to do so. If any such irregularities come to our attention during the examination, however, we will bring them to your attention and discuss with you what action should be taken.

As we agreed at our meeting, this engagement will not include the preparation of The Glassworks' federal or state tax returns. Nevertheless, should you wish to consult with us on tax matters, we are prepared to act in that capacity, although extensive consultation on tax matters would require a separate agreement.

The fee for this engagement will be based on our regular rates. We estimate that the fee will be somewhere between $4,000 and $5,000. If circumstances should require us to exceed this estimate, we will point it out to you and discuss the matter before proceeding.

As you know, our estimate is based on the understanding that your personnel will assist us by preparing the audit schedules and locating documents that we require.

Please indicate your approval of these arrangements by signing and dating one copy of this letter and returning it to us. The other copy is for your files.

Very truly yours,
DANNAY & LEE

____
Partner

Approved:
THE GLASSWORKS

______________________________ ____________
Signature/Title Date

ENGAGEMENT FOR AUDIT OF PERSONAL FINANCIAL STATEMENTS

This letter is similar to the preceding one, but it concerns an individual or individuals rather than a company.

Ms. Charlene Morrissey
9599 Eucalyptus Drive
Auraria, California 95700

Dear Ms. Morrissey:

We would like to confirm our understanding of the audit engagement that we discussed on October 7, 19x8.

Our examination will include the following:

We will examine your personal financial statement as of December 31, 19x8 and the accompanying statement of changes in net worth for the year then ended. We will conduct this examination according to generally accepted auditing standards and, in doing so, will undertake whatever tests or other auditing procedures we consider necessary in the circumstances.

Our objective is to be able to express an opinion as to whether the financial statements are fairly presented in conformity with generally accepted accounting principles. As of now, we expect our report on the financial statements to read as follows:

> [The paragraph or paragraphs included here will be in standard audit report format. See Chapter 6.]

In addition, we will prepare your federal and state income tax returns of December 31, 19x8.

If you wish, we can perform any other tax and accounting services that you may need. Such services would become the subject of a separate agreement.

Our fee for the examination outlined above will be charged at our standard rates plus out-of-pocket expenses. We expect the fee to be approximately $2,800. If circumstances require it to exceed that amount by more than $600, we will consult with you on how to proceed.

If this letter accurately states your understanding of the engagement, please sign it below in the space provided and return it to us, keeping the copy for your files.

Very truly yours,
POLLARA & ASSOCIATES

____
Partner

Approved:

______________________________ ____________
Charlene Morrissey Date

MEMORANDUM OF INFORMATION TO BE FURNISHED BY CLIENT

An engagement can be greatly facilitated if all necessary information is at hand. To that end, the client needs a clear, succinct statement of what will be required. The following memorandum covers most of the items you may want to include.

Mr. Darwin Williams, Controller
Greenleaf Co., Inc.
1334 Semmes Street
Talullah, Alabama 35600

Dear Mr. Williams:

In accordance with our pre-engagement conference, we request that you provide the following information for the year ended December 31, 19x0:

- Financial statements or a trial balance of the general ledger
- A reconciliation of each bank account
- Bank confirmation forms, furnished by us and completed by you, ready for mailing to the banks. (We will mail these confirmations.)
- An aged listing of accounts receivable as of December 31, 19x0
- Accounts receivable confirmation requests, furnished by us and completed by you, ready for mailing to customers. (We will mail these confirmations.)
- A list of bad debts charged off during the year
- A schedule of notes receivable, showing in columnar form:

Maker	Due date	Original amount
Date of note	Interest rate	Balance at 12/31/x0

- A completed copy of the physical inventory sheets
- An analysis of marketable securities, showing in columnar form:

For Bonds:	*For Stocks:*
Title of issue	Title of issue
Bond number	Certificate number
Date of acquisition	Date of acquisition
Face value	Number of shares
Book value	Book value

- A schedule of insurance coverage, showing in columnar form:

Policy number	Property covered	Period covered
Insurance company	Amount of coverage	Premium paid

- A schedule of property and equipment additions (please have invoices available) and retirements during the year, showing:

Description	Cost of asset acquired
Date of transaction	Sales price of asset sold

- A depreciation schedule
- A schedule of life insurance coverage, showing in columnar form:

Name of employee	Issue date of policy	Cash surrender value
Insurance company	Face amount	Annual premium
Policy number		

- A list of accounts payable as of December 31, 19x0
- A schedule of notes payable, showing in columnar form:

Payee	Original balance	Rate of interest
Issue date	Balance at end of year	Collateral
Maturity date	Periodic payment	

- A schedule of repairs
- A schedule of officers' salaries and expenses
- A schedule of professional expenses, including, but not limited to, legal fees
- A schedule of contributions
- A schedule of tax expense

Please have available for our use:

- Copies of minutes of board of directors' meetings
- Copies of all leases
- Copies of employment or sales contracts
- Copy of corporate charter
- Copy of bylaws
- Copy of profit-sharing agreement

Please call or write if there is any question regarding the requested information.

Sincerely,
ALEX & BAKER

____

SPECIAL ENGAGEMENT LETTER, EXPERT WITNESS

If you are called upon to perform services that are outside the scope of your regular activities, you will need a special engagement letter. Since the letter must fit the circumstances precisely, and since the range of possible activities is so broad, no uniform, standard letter will fit all occasions. The following letter shows the general form of such a special engagement letter.

Norman Brennan, Esq.
Wechter, Foxx, Rowe & Peterson
Attorneys at Law
1211 East Stevenson Avenue
Darrow, Illinois 61700

Dear Mr. Brennan:

Let me summarize the results of our meeting on September 15 concerning the case of *Carnaby* v. *Save-A-Dime Stores, Inc.*, in which your client, Mr. Bruce Carnaby, a toy wholesaler, alleges that he was defrauded by the retail chain and suffered substantial monetary loss as a result.

In accordance with our understanding, I will perform the following services:

1. I will study the relevant financial documents now in your possession, both those of Mr. Carnaby and those of Save-A-Dime Stores, Inc., which, as I understand, were obtained through disclosure proceedings.
2. After reviewing these documents, I will submit to Wechter, Foxx, Rowe & Peterson a report of my findings, including a statement of my opinion as to whether Mr. Carnaby has, in fact, through financial misrepresentations made to him in writing by executives of Save-A-Dime Stores, Inc., suffered the specific losses he claims.
3. If my conclusion is that Mr. Carnaby has suffered such losses through apparent misrepresentation, I will be available to appear in court to testify on his behalf.

My fee for the foregoing services will be $100 per hour. Invoices will be rendered twice monthly and will be due and payable upon presentation. I estimate that my fee for the first two services described above will not exceed $1,000. If unforeseen circumstances were to materially increase that fee, I would so advise you, and we could then determine how to proceed. Should I appear in court, you can predict better than I the time that will be required, and consequently can estimate with some accuracy the fee for that service.

If this letter correctly expresses our understanding, I would appreciate your signing it in the space provided and returning it to me. The second copy is for your files.

Sincerely yours,

Darryl Clancy
Certified Public Accountant

Approved:
WECHTER, FOXX, ROWE & PETERSON

____

Partner

ENGAGEMENT LETTER FOR EMPLOYEE-BENEFIT PENSION PLAN

Employee-benefit plans comprise a broad and complex range of activities. If the individual accountant or small accounting firm has an in-house expert in the field, the expert will probably use a number of letters that are beyond the scope of this book. The model engagement letter below comes from a company that specializes in handling employee-benefit pension plans. If an accounting firm, rather than an outside specialist, were dealing directly with the retirement plan, the firm's engagement letter would be similar to this one.

PERSONAL AND CONFIDENTIAL

Mr. Edward Brice, President
Tri-City Salvage Company
2158 Highway 593
Lake Lenape, New Jersey 07700

SUBJECT: EMPLOYEE-BENEFIT RETIREMENT PLAN

Dear Mr. Brice:

Let me welcome you as a client and take this opportunity to assure you that we will provide you, in a timely manner, with all the services necessary to ensure the qualification of your combined defined benefit pension plan.

Our services will consist of preparing a plan and trust document for review by your attorney, preparing forms for submission of the plan and trust to the Internal Revenue Service (IRS) for approval, and subsequent negotiating with the IRS, if necessary.

On an annual basis, we will provide the services required to maintain your plan properly, including consultation, collection and review of employee and trust fund data, actuarial calculation of contributions, determination of benefits, preparation of employee benefit statements, and preparation of annual government Form series 5500 and attachments as applicable and appropriate.

I do not anticipate that you will have any difficulty in getting in touch with me personally. However, my partner, Candace Mercer, will be thoroughly familiar with your plan and fully prepared to answer any questions you might have in my absence.

As we discussed, our fee for implementing the plan will be $1,000, payable one half upon delivery of the enclosed documents and the balance upon submission of the plan to the IRS. Our annual fee for the administration of the retirement plan will be $700 plus $20 per participant, which will be payable upon presentation of our annual report and statements of benefits.

Enclosed are the following documents:

- One (1) copy of the plan document, based on the attached outline of specifications
- Three (3) additional copies of the signature page
- Four (4) copies of the corporate resolution adopting the plan

Please sign all four copies of the signature page and resolution, affix the corporate seal to the resolution, and return three copies of each to us.

So that we can complete Form 5300, including appropriate attachments for requesting a favorable letter from the Internal Revenue Service, please complete and return the enclosed general information form.

If you have any questions, do not hesitate to call.

Sincerely,
RETIREMENT SERVICES, INC.

____
President

SPECIFICATION SHEET FOR BENEFIT PENSION PLAN

This sheet accompanies the preceding letter. It spells out the principal features of the benefit pension plan.

TRI-CITY SALVAGE COMPANY
Specifications for Retirement Plan

1. Effective Date	October 1, 19x5
2. Anniversary Date	October 1
3. Eligibility Requirements	
a. Part-time Exclusion	Customary employment for fewer than 1,000 hours per year
b. Classification	All employees
c. Minimum Age	21
d. Maximum Age	None
e. Service	1 year
4. Enrollment	All employees on date of adoption. Thereafter, enrollment on anniversary date nearest completion of eligibility requirements.
5. Normal Retirement Date	Age 60 or tenth anniversary of date participation commenced, if later
6. Normal Retirement Benefit	30% of average annual compensation
7. Compensation	Total pay for plan year
8. Average Annual Compensation	The average of the participant's compensation over the highest three consecutive plan years of participation
9. Early Retirement	None
10. Deferred Retirement	Permitted, with employer consent required after age 70
11. Deferred Retirement Benefit	Actuarial equivalent of Normal Retirement Benefit
12. Service	Service credited for Normal Retirement Benefit for all plan years with at least 1,000 hours of service

13. Vesting Schedule	Vesting of accrued benefit as follows: 20% after 2 years of service, increasing 20% per year to 100% after 6 years
14. Definition of Disability	Inability to perform customary services
15. Disability Benefit	Actuarial value of accrued benefit
16. Death Benefit	Greater of life insurance in effect, up to 100 times the projected monthly benefit, or actuarial value of accrued benefit
17. Distribution of Benefits	Lump sum, installments, or annuity
18. Break in Service	Plan year of fewer than 501 hours of service
19. Voluntary Employee Contributions	Permitted on a deductible and nondeductible basis
20. Rollover Contributions	Permitted
21. Loans	Permitted, to the extent allowed by law
22. Administrator	Michael Brooks
23. Trustee	Michael Brooks

GENERAL INFORMATION FORM FOR BENEFIT PENSION PLAN

This form, noted in the letter on pages 52–53, lists the information needed for completion and submission of Form 5300 to the Internal Revenue Service.

Information Required for Proper Administration of Retirement Plan

1. Company's legal name__________
2. Company's legal address__________
3. Fiscal year end__________ Date of incorporation__________
4. Federal ID No.__________ Tel. No.(   )__________

   Type of organization: ( ) Regular corp. ( ) P.C. or P.A.
   ( ) Subchapter S ( ) Sole proprietor
   ( ) Tax exempt ( ) Partnership

   If you are part of a consolidated tax filing, what is the fiscal year end of the parent corporation?
   ____

   Are all companies that are parties to this consolidated filing participating in this plan?
   ____

5. Full name and title of person in company to be contacted for:
   Decisions__________
   General information__________
   Government forms__________
6. Business code__________ and industry in which most of the participants are employed:
   ( ) Manufacturing
   ( ) Transportation
   ( ) Finance, Insurance, Real Estate
   ( ) Agriculture, Forestry, Fisheries
   ( ) Construction
   ( ) Mining
   ( ) Communications and Utilities
   ( ) Services
   ( ) Wholesale and Retail Trade
   ( ) Other
7. If you have any employees covered under any plan established or maintained pursuant to one or more collective bargaining agreements, please supply photocopies of any collective bargaining agreements that relate to this plan, and complete the following:
   Name of labor organization__________
   Federal Employer ID No. (labor organization)__________
   Local No.__________ Unit No.__________
8. Agent for service of legal process__________
9. Company's accountant and attorney:
   Accountant__________
   Firm name__________
   Address__________
   __________ Tel. No.(   )__________
   Attorney__________
   Firm name__________
   Address__________
   __________ Tel. No.(   )__________
10. Stockholder participants. Provide name of each participant who directly or indirectly owns more than 1% of the company's voting or total stock.

Participant's Name	Percent of Stock Owned

11. Plan administrator (if other than company)
    ____

    Administrative committee members. Provide name, address, title, or other relationship to employer for each member. Indicate to whom mail is to be directed, and specify if member is a director or stockholder.
    ____
    ____
    ____

    Number of signatures required__________
12. Trustee(s).
    Individual. Provide name, address, title, or other relationship to employer for each trustee. Indicate to whom mail is to be directed, and specify if member is a director or stockholder.
    ____
    ____
    ____

    Corporate. Provide name of bank and address of trust department.
    ____

    Direct mail to__________ Tel. No.(   )__________

CHANGE IN CIRCUMSTANCES FROM ORIGINAL ENGAGEMENT LETTER

Whenever an estimated fee is given in an engagement letter, or, even more important, when a maximum fee is specified, the engagement letter should make clear that a change in circumstances may affect the estimate. Each engagement letter in this book includes an escape provision of that kind. The letter on page 59 refers to such a provision and goes on to explain the new circumstances that led to the revised estimate.

Ms. Heidi Lundquist, President
Orly Fashions, Inc.
Avedon Drive
Port Dobie, Texas 77500

Dear Ms. Lundquist:

In our engagement letter of February 17, 19x7, we indicated that unforeseen or changed circumstances might affect our original fee estimate of $3,000. It now seems likely that they will, and I want to bring this matter promptly to your attention.

Both unforeseen and changed circumstances have occurred during the course of the engagement. We did not anticipate, quite frankly, the problems we would encounter with your accounting procedures, which, as you now realize, included certain shortcuts and irregular practices. Nor did we make allowance for the then-imminent expansion of Orly Fashions, Inc., whose two new stores—in Hughes City and Nimitzville—added significantly to our task.

These matters are being dealt with on a continuing basis, the consequence being that we are spending nearly twice as many hours as our estimate included. Therefore, we believe that the original figure must be revised upward, and our best prediction, based on what we now know, is that the total fee will be approximately $5,500.

Since you have expressed a desire for us to continue with the engagement, we hope you will find this new estimate acceptable. If so, please sign this letter in the space provided and return it to us. A duplicate copy is enclosed for your files.

Sincerely,
CARTWRIGHT, PELL & AMICO

____
Partner

Approved:
ORLY FASHIONS, INC.

______________________________ ______________
Signature/Title Date

PART II

AUDIT CORRESPONDENCE: CONFIRMATIONS, REPRESENTATIONS

CHAPTER 3

Confirmation Letters That Bring Responses

- Confirmation of Accounts Receivable
- The Positive Approach to Confirmation
- Printed Letter of Confirmation
- Negative Confirmation Request
- The Sticker or Stamp Method of Confirmation
- Amount Being Held in Special Fund
- Confirmation of Petty Cash and Advances
- Schedule of Notes Receivable
- Notes Payable to Vendors
- Marketable Securities Held by Others
- Insurance Policies Held by Others
- Confirmation of Client's Inventory in Public Warehouse
- Inventory on Consignment
- Deposit Premium Confirmation

Instructions for completing confirmation letters must be clearly communicated to the client. This can often be facilitated by using copies of the model letters contained in this and the next chapter. As with all the letters in this book, some modifications may be necessary.

Confirmations should be signed by the client (except in those instances where no signature is requested), then returned to you for proofreading, comparison to audit controls, and mailing. You, the auditor, should control the mailing and receipt of responses so that the confirmation process is independent of the client.

Mailing envelopes should have your return address rather than the client's so that undeliverable letters are returned to you. Along with the confirmation request you should enclose a postage-paid envelope addressed to you. This will encourage responses.

Because of the number of confirmation letters included in this book, the models have been separated into two chapters for convenience. In the letters in this chapter the client is given specific figures or other information and is asked to confirm it. In Chapter 4 the client is asked for information and must supply it. Both kinds of letters, however, are confirmations.

In the first two chapters of this book, the letters include inside addresses, salutations, closings, signatures, and other necessary structural parts (except for dates). Beginning with Chapter 3, most letters include only basic content—the body of the letter—with other parts indicated graphically. You will find a detailed explanation of these graphic indicators in Chapter 19, "Handbook of Letter Format."

CONFIRMATION OF ACCOUNTS RECEIVABLE

There are two ways to confirm accounts receivable. One of them is positive—stating the amount on record and asking for a signature confirming it. The letter that follows is a positive confirmation request.

CLIENT'S LETTERHEAD

[Date]

INSIDE ADDRESS

[Salutation]:

Our auditors, [name and address of auditors], are making an examination of our financial statements. They request that you confirm the correctness of the following information relating to your indebtedness to this company as of December 31, 19x6.

Due from you: [amount receivable]

Please complete the lower portion of this letter and return it directly to [name and address of auditors]. A stamped, addressed envelope is enclosed for your reply.

Please do not send remittances to the auditors.

[Closing],

CLIENT'S AUTHORIZED SIGNATURE

NAME AND ADDRESS OF AUDITORS

[Salutation]:

The above indebtedness of $________ as of December 31, 19x6, is correct, except as noted below:

Exceptions: ____

____

SIGNATURE AND TITLE OF ADDRESSEE

THE POSITIVE APPROACH TO CONFIRMATION

Here is a second example (shown on page 68) of a confirmation letter for accounts receivable. Both time and money can be saved if confirmation requests such as this one accompany monthly billings. Whether sent separately or in the same mailing with statements, the confirmation letter should make clear that it is not a demand for payment.

CLIENT'S LETTERHEAD

[Date]

INSIDE ADDRESS

[Salutation]:

Our auditors, [name and address of auditors], are conducting their regular examination of our financial statements. In connection with this audit, would you please confirm directly to them the amount of your indebtedness to us, which according to our records as of [date] is [$amount].

If the amount shown agrees with your records for that date, please sign this letter in the space provided below and return it directly to our auditors in the enclosed stamped, addressed envelope.

If the amount shown does not agree with your records, please indicate the amount that your records show. Use the back of the letter to supply any information that may help to reconcile the difference. Then return the letter directly to our auditors in the enclosed, stamped envelope.

This is not a request for payment. Please do not send remittances to our auditors.

[Closing],

CLIENT'S AUTHORIZED SIGNATURE

The amount stated above is correct as of [date], with the following exceptions, if any: ____________

SIGNATURE AND TITLE OF ADDRESSEE

PRINTED LETTER OF CONFIRMATION

A supply of the following all-purpose printed form for accounts receivable confirmation can be kept in the supply room for ready use. Note that this printed form, unlike other confirmation letters, uses the letterhead of the accounting firm. It is signed by the client, however, after "Very truly yours."

YOUR LETTERHEAD

Date of Statement

____

____

____

FOR VERIFICATION ONLY

Our auditors, whose name is shown above, are making their regular examination of our financial statements as of the close of business on the date shown.

Please confirm the accuracy of the enclosed statement showing the balance you owed us on the date indicated. Disregard any payments or transactions made since the date shown.

If the enclosed statement is correct, please sign this letter in the space provided below. If the statement is incorrect, kindly furnish details concerning the differences.

The signed letter should be returned directly to our auditors in the enclosed stamped, addressed envelope. We will appreciate your prompt reply to this request. Thank you.

Very truly yours,

____

The statement accompanying this letter, which shows a balance of $________ owed by us, is correct.

Customer ______________________________

By ______________________________

Remarks____

____

Note: The enclosed statement is for your files. It does not have to be sent to the auditors.

NEGATIVE CONFIRMATION REQUEST

The easiest and most common way of confirming receivables is to request a reply only if an error is found. As the auditor, you must control this process to be sure that the confirmations have in fact been sent. Confirmations of this kind—negative, in that they require no action if the indicated amount is correct—can often be included with one of the client company's periodic statements, thus eliminating the need for a separate mailing.

> Please examine the accompanying statement carefully.
>
> Our auditors are making an examination of our financial statements. If our statement does not agree with your records, please report any difference to our auditors:
>
> [name and address of auditors]
>
> You need not respond if the stated amount is accurate. However, should you find any discrepancy, a stamped, addressed envelope is enclosed for your convenience. If no differences are reported to our auditors, the accompanying statement will be considered correct.

THE STICKER OR STAMP METHOD OF CONFIRMATION

This is the least time-consuming way of confirming accounts receivable. Simply have a sticker or stamp prepared containing the following wording or a variation of it. This request goes directly on the client's statements to customers.

> PLEASE EXAMINE THIS STATEMENT CAREFULLY
>
> If the amounts shown on this statement are *incorrect,* use the enclosed stamped, addressed envelope to write directly to our auditors,
>
> [name and address of auditors]
>
> who are now making their regular examination of our financial statements. If you do not write to them, they will consider the statement to be correct.
>
> NOTE:
> - If you find any error on the statement, we would appreciate a prompt reply.
> - This is NOT a request for payment. Do NOT send remittances to the auditors.

AMOUNT BEING HELD IN SPECIAL FUND

This is a form letter to members of an organization. It appears under the letterhead of the organization and is signed by one of its officers or representatives.

CLIENT'S LETTERHEAD

[Salutation]:

In connection with an audit of our financial statements as of September 30, 19x5, please confirm to us the correctness of our records by signing below and returning this letter directly to our independent auditor, [name and address of auditor]. A stamped, addressed envelope is enclosed for your convenience.

Our records at September 30, 19x5, indicate that [name of organization] is holding $________ in its Special Assessment Fund. This figure includes interest, if any.

[Closing],

____

CLIENT'S AUTHORIZED SIGNATURE

____

________ The information above is correct.

________ The information above is not correct, as explained below:

____

____

Signature____________________________
(Please sign in either case)

CONFIRMATION OF PETTY CASH AND ADVANCES

Anyone in the client company who maintains a petty cash fund or has received and not yet repaid advances should be asked to confirm the amounts involved.

CLIENT'S LETTERHEAD

________________________ [Date]

INSIDE ADDRESS

____

[Salutation]:

Our auditors, [name and address of auditors], are conducting their annual examination of our financial statements. Please confirm directly to them the balance of the petty cash fund (or amount of advances) in your possession as of December 31, 19x5. Our records show this amount to be $________.

In the space below, please indicate whether the amount above agrees with your records. If not, please send our auditors any information you have that will help them reconcile the difference.

This letter, signed and dated, is to be returned directly to the auditors in the enclosed stamped, addressed envelope.

[Closing],

____

CLIENT'S AUTHORIZED SIGNATURE

____

________ The information above is correct.

________ The information above does not agree with my records, as explained below:

____

____

Date: ____________________ Signed: ____________________

SCHEDULE OF NOTES RECEIVABLE

CLIENT'S LETTERHEAD

[Date]

INSIDE ADDRESS

[Salutation]:

Our auditors, [name and address of auditors], are making an examination of our financial statements. Please confirm directly to them the accuracy of the following list of amounts receivable from you on notes as of December 31, 19x7:

Date of Note	*Due Date*	*Interest Rate*	*Interest Paid to*	*Unpaid Balance*	*Collateral*

Your prompt attention to this request will be appreciated. An envelope is enclosed for your reply.

[Closing],

CLIENT'S AUTHORIZED SIGNATURE

CONFIRMATION
The above list is complete and accurate as of the date indicated, except as described below.

Date: ______________________ By: ______________________

NOTES PAYABLE TO VENDORS

Although the last paragraph of this letter indicates that a file copy is enclosed, there is no actual need for such a copy, and some accountants do not include it.

CLIENT'S LETTERHEAD

[Date]

INSIDE ADDRESS

[Salutation]:

According to the records of this company as of December 31, 19x8, we were indebted to you on the following unsecured note:

Date	*Payable To*	*Rate*	*Maturity*	*Amount*	*Secured By*
				$________	

For the purpose of audit, will you please confirm the correctness of the information above by signing in the space provided below. Also, please furnish our auditors with a statement of any other indebtedness outstanding against this company at the date mentioned.

In the event that you hold any assignments or collateral as security to the note or open account, please give a complete description of it in your reply.

Kindly return one copy of this letter to [name and address of auditors], using the enclosed envelope. The other copy is intended for your files.

[Closing],

CLIENT'S AUTHORIZED SIGNATURE

____

NAME AND ADDRESS OF AUDITORS

____

[Salutation]:

As of December 31, 19x8, the above company was indebted to us in the amount of $_______ represented by the note _______ described above and the open account amounting to $_______. Collateral security, amounting to $_______, held by us, consisted of

____

____

____

Date: ____________________ Signed: ____________________

MARKETABLE SECURITIES HELD BY OTHERS

This request should be sent so that it reaches the custodian sufficiently in advance of the examination date.

CLIENT'S LETTERHEAD

[Date]

INSIDE ADDRESS

[Salutation]:

Our auditors, [name and address of auditors], are making an examination of our financial statements. They request that you confirm the correctness of the following information, as shown by our records, relating to securities belonging to this company that were in your possession at December 31, 19x8.

Description	*Maturity Date of Next Interest Coupon*	*Number of Shares*	*Principal Amount*

Please indicate the maturity date of the next bond interest coupon, if any. When the lower portion of this letter has been completed, please return it directly to [name and address of auditors], retaining the duplicate copy for your files. A stamped, addressed envelope is enclosed for your reply.

[Closing],

CLIENT'S AUTHORIZED SIGNATURE

____

NAME AND ADDRESS OF AUDITORS

____

[Salutation]:

The securities listed above were held by this company at December 31, 19x8, for the account of [name of client], except as noted below:

Exceptions: ______________________________

____

____

____

Date: ______________________ Signed: ______________________

INSURANCE POLICIES HELD BY OTHERS

This request should be sent so that it reaches the custodian sufficiently in advance of the examination date.

CLIENT'S LETTERHEAD

[Date]

INSIDE ADDRESS

[Salutation]:

Our records indicate that at December 31, 19x2, you had in your possession the following fire insurance policies covering our building located at [address of building].

Policy Number	*Insuring Company*	*Term*	*Expiration Date*	*Amount of Insurance*	*Co-Ins.*

For the purpose of audit, please confirm the correctness of the information above by signing in the space provided below.

Kindly return one copy of this letter directly to our auditors, [name and address of auditors], using the enclosed envelope. The other copy is for your files.

[Closing],

CLIENT'S AUTHORIZED SIGNATURE

NAME AND ADDRESS OF AUDITORS

[Salutation]:

We were holding the policies named above at December 31, 19x2.

Date: ______________ Signed: ______________

CONFIRMATION OF CLIENT'S INVENTORY IN PUBLIC WAREHOUSE

This letter confirms that the client's list of merchandise in a particular warehouse accurately reflects the merchandise that is actually there. Although warehouse personnel are asked to check against an existing list, they must also supply additional lists and statements.

CLIENT'S LETTERHEAD

[Date]

____

NAME AND ADDRESS OF WAREHOUSE

____

[Salutation]:

Our auditors, [name and address of auditors], are conducting their regular examination of our financial statements. Please confirm directly to them the following information about the merchandise that you held in your custody for our account as of [date].

1. Please check the accuracy of the enclosed list showing the quantities of merchandise that our records indicate are in your warehouse. If this list differs from the quantities you actually hold, please explain the differences in your reply to our auditors.
2. Please state how you determined the quantities being confirmed—physical count, weight or measure, or your own existing records.
3. If applicable, please note any or all of the following:
   a. Warehouse receipts issued and, if known, whether these receipts have been assigned or pledged.
   b. Known liens against the merchandise.
   c. Amount of any unpaid charges as of [date].

Your reply should go directly to our auditors, [name and address of auditors]. A stamped, addressed envelope is enclosed for your convenience.

[Closing],

____

CLIENT'S AUTHORIZED SIGNATURE

____

INVENTORY ON CONSIGNMENT

This request should be sent so that it reaches the custodian sufficiently in advance of the examination date.

CLIENT'S LETTERHEAD

______________________ [Date]

INSIDE ADDRESS

____

[Salutation]:

In connection with an examination of our financial statements, please confirm to our auditors, [name and address of auditors], our merchandise held by you on consignment as of December 31, 19x5, as described below.

Quality *Description*

Your prompt attention to this request will be appreciated. An envelope is enclosed for your reply.

[Closing],

____

CLIENT'S AUTHORIZED SIGNATURE

____

CONFIRMATION
The list represents all merchandise of [name of client company] held by us on consignment as of December 31, 19x5, except as explained below.

____

____

____

Date: ______________________ By: ______________________

DEPOSIT PREMIUM CONFIRMATION

CLIENT'S LETTERHEAD

[Date]

INSIDE ADDRESS

[Salutation]:

In connection with an audit of our financial statements as of September 30, 19x5, please confirm the correctness of our records regarding workmen's compensation insurance policy WC-05-20275. Our records indicate that at September 30, 19x5, we had on deposit with you $________ for this policy.

To confirm the accuracy of the information above, kindly sign this letter in the space provided below and return one copy of it directly to our independent auditors, [name and address of auditors]. A stamped, addressed envelope is enclosed for your convenience. The second copy of the letter is for your files.

[Closing],

CLIENT'S AUTHORIZED SIGNATURE

NAME AND ADDRESS OF AUDITOR

[Salutation]:

As of September 30, 19x5, we held the amount shown above, $________, as a deposit premium on the indicated insurance policy.

TYPED NAME OF INSURANCE COMPANY

By________________________

Title________________________

Date________________________

CHAPTER 4

Ready-to-Use Requests for Confirmation

- Request for Bank Cutoff Statements
- Standard Bank Confirmation Inquiry
- Cash and Securities in Custodian or Trust Accounts
- Confirmation of Accounts Payable
- Request for List of Payables and Consignment Items
- General Request for Statement of Indebtedness
- Request for Schedule of Notes Payable
- Information on Long-term Debt
- Request for Confirmation of Mortgage Indebtedness
- Letter to Capital Stock Registrar
- Request for Information on Bond Issue
- Cash Value of Life Insurance
- Request for Details on Contracts or Grants
- Letter to Client's Attorney
- Letter to Collection Agency
- Auditor's Direct Request for Statement of Client's Account
- Inventory Request to Warehouse
- Engaging an Out-of-Town Auditor to Observe Inventory
- Serving as Local Auditor for Another Accounting Firm

This chapter is essentially a continuation of the preceding one. The requests are more general in that they usually ask the addressees to supply information rather than simply to check information that you have provided them. This difference is not substantive, however, and the letters in Chapters 3 and 4 are used for the same basic purposes.

All letters in this book are referenced and cross-referenced in the index at the back. If you do not see a letter in the table of contents or the chapter-opener pages, by all means check the index for its location.

REQUEST FOR BANK CUTOFF STATEMENTS

This form letter goes out under the letterhead of the company being audited, but the bank statements and cancelled checks must be sent to you. The request for bank cutoff statements should be mailed at least ten days prior to the audit date and should include a list of the account names and bank account numbers for each of the client's accounts.

CLIENT'S LETTERHEAD

[Date]

____

INSIDE ADDRESS

____

[Salutation]:

Our auditors, [name and address of auditors], are making an examination of our financial statements and request that you mail directly to them the bank statements and canceled checks for our account number ________ as of the close of business on ________.

[Closing],

____

CLIENT'S AUTHORIZED SIGNATURE

____

STANDARD BANK CONFIRMATION INQUIRY

The accounting profession and the banking profession have jointly approved a standard form to confirm accounts with banks. Ideally, the forms should be mailed sufficiently in advance of the confirmation date so as to arrive at the bank just before the confirmation date or slightly thereafter. A copy of this form is shown on page 87.

STANDARD BANK CONFIRMATION INQUIRY*

RETURN TO: [ ]

[ ]

REPORT FROM BANK [ ]

[ ]

Date:

Your completion of the following report will be sincerely appreciated. IF THE ANSWER TO ANY ITEM IS "NONE," PLEASE SO STATE. Use the enclosed envelope to return the original directly to our accountant (see name to left).

Yours truly,

(ACCOUNT NAME PER BANK RECORDS)

By ______________________

Authorized Signature

☐ Bank customer should check here if confirmation of bank balances only (Item ①) is desired.

NOTE—If the space provided is inadequate, please enter totals hereon and attach a statement giving full details called for by the columnar headings below.

① At the close of business on 19 our records showed the following balance(s) to the credit of the above named customer. In the event that we could readily ascertain whether there were any balances to the credit of the customer not designated in this request, the appropriate information is given below.

AMOUNT	ACCOUNT NAME	ACCOUNT NO.	SUBJECT TO WITHDRAWAL BY CHECK? ✓	INTEREST BEARING? GIVE RATE	REMARKS:
$					

② The customer was directly liable to us in respect of loans, acceptances, etc., at the close of business on that date in the total amount of $, as follows:

AMOUNT	DATE		INTEREST		DESCRIPTION OF LIABILITY, COLLATERAL SECURITY INTERESTS, LIENS, ENDORSERS, ETC.
	OF LOAN/DISCOUNT	DUE	RATE	PAID TO	
$					

③ The customer was contingently liable as endorser of notes discounted and/or as guarantor at the close of business on that date in the total amount of $, as below:

AMOUNT	NAME OF MAKER	DATE		REMARKS
		OF NOTE	DUE	
$				

④ Other direct or contingent liabilities, open letters of credit, and relative collateral, were:

⑤ Security agreements under the Uniform Commercial Code or any other agreements providing for restrictions, not noted above, were as follows (if officially recorded, indicate date and office in which filed):

*Approved 1966 by American Institute of Certified Public Accountants and Bank Administration Institute (formerly NABAC). Additional forms available from: AICPA—ORDER P.O. BOX 1003, NYC, NY 10108-1003

Date:

Yours truly, (Bank)

By ______________________

Authorized Signature - Bank

ORIGINAL
To be mailed to accountant

2411-B

CASH AND SECURITIES IN CUSTODIAN OR TRUST ACCOUNTS

This letter of request should be sent far enough in advance of the listing date to give the custodian or trustee sufficient time to respond properly. Although this letter can be combined with a request for cutoff bank statements, the AICPA advises sending separate letters since, as a rule, the commercial banking and trust departments of a bank are separate operations.

CLIENT'S LETTERHEAD

[Date]

INSIDE ADDRESS

[Salutation]:

Our auditors, [name and address of auditors], are now examining our financial statements. In this connection, we ask that you send directly to them a list of our securities owned at December 31, 19x7, as well as the amount of cash (principal and income) that you hold at that date for each of the following accounts.

	Name of Account	*Custodian's or Trustee's Account Number*
1.	______________	______________
2.	______________	______________
3.	______________	______________

If you are aware that any of these securities are pledged or otherwise encumbered, please indicate that to the auditors in your reply.

Your reply should go directly to [name and address of auditors]. A stamped, self-addressed envelope is enclosed for your convenience.

[Closing],

____

CLIENT'S AUTHORIZED SIGNATURE

CONFIRMATION OF ACCOUNTS PAYABLE

CLIENT'S LETTERHEAD

______________________ [Date]

INSIDE ADDRESS

____

[Salutation]:

Our auditors, [name and address of auditors], are performing their regular examination of our financial statements. In connection with their examination, please confirm directly to them whether or not there is a balance due as of [date]. If there is a balance due, please indicate the amount in the space provided below and mail your reply to [name and address of auditors]. A stamped, addressed envelope is enclosed for your convenience.

[Closing],

____

CLIENT'S AUTHORIZED SIGNATURE

____

- -

According to our records, a balance of $________ was due from [name of client] at [date].

TYPED NAME OF ADDRESSEE

By______________________

Title______________________

Date______________________

REQUEST FOR LIST OF PAYABLES AND CONSIGNMENT ITEMS

CLIENT'S LETTERHEAD

[Date]

INSIDE ADDRESS

[Salutation]:

Our auditors, [name and address of auditors], are making an examination of our financial statements. For this purpose, we ask that you please furnish them with the following information as of December 31, 19x7.

1. Itemized statements of our accounts payable to you, showing all unpaid items.
2. A complete list of any notes and acceptances payable to you (including any that have been discounted), showing the original date, dates due, original amount, unpaid balance, collateral, and endorsers.
3. An itemized list of your merchandise consigned to us.

Your prompt attention to this request will be appreciated. A stamped, addressed envelope is enclosed for your reply.

[Closing],

CLIENT'S AUTHORIZED SIGNATURE

GENERAL REQUEST FOR STATEMENT OF INDEBTEDNESS

As with the receivable confirmation, this boilerplate payable confirmation can be preprinted, if you wish, leaving the variable information blank. You can then keep a supply of them on hand for ready use.

CLIENT'S LETTERHEAD

____________________ [Date]

INSIDE ADDRESS

____

[Salutation]:

Our auditors, [name and address of auditors], are currently performing an examination of our financial statements. Please furnish them with an open item statement of our indebtedness to you, listing the unpaid items as of the close of business on December 31, 19x9.

[Closing],

____

CLIENT'S AUTHORIZED SIGNATURE

____

REQUEST FOR SCHEDULE OF NOTES PAYABLE

CLIENT'S LETTERHEAD

[Date]

INSIDE ADDRESS

[Salutation]:

Our auditors, [name and address of auditors], are making an examination of our financial statements. They request that you complete the following schedule with regard to notes payable to you as of the above date.

Date of Note	*Due Date*	*Interest Rate Paid To*	*Unpaid Balance*	*Collateral*

Please indicate the note and amount of any default or deficiency. Your prompt attention to this request will be appreciated. An envelope is enclosed for your reply.

[Closing],

CLIENT'S AUTHORIZED SIGNATURE

INFORMATION ON LONG-TERM DEBT

Many of the items requested will vary with the circumstances of the debt involved.

CLIENT'S LETTERHEAD

[Date]

INSIDE ADDRESS

[Salutation]:

Our auditors, [name and address of auditors], are currently performing an examination of our financial statements. We ask that you please furnish them with the following information concerning our mortgage note payable as of [date].

Date of note
Maturity date
Interest rate
Interest payment dates
Date to which interest has been paid
Principal amount unpaid at [date]
Amount of installments due in the next twelve months
Description of collateral, if any

Your reply, sent directly to our auditors, will be appreciated. An addressed envelope is enclosed for your convenience.

[Closing],

CLIENT'S AUTHORIZED SIGNATURE

REQUEST FOR CONFIRMATION OF MORTGAGE INDEBTEDNESS

The main difference between this letter and the preceding one is in the information requested. Items will vary from one letter to another in accordance with the terms of the mortgage.

CLIENT'S LETTERHEAD

[Date]

INSIDE ADDRESS

[Salutation]:

In connection with their regular examination of our financial statements, our auditors, [name and address of auditors], ask that you confirm directly to them the following information about our mortgage indebtedness to you as of [date].

Nature of mortgage
Description of property mortgaged
Balance of unpaid principal
Terms for payment of principal
Interest rate
Date to which interest has been paid
Amounts deposited with you in escrow for insurance and taxes
Amounts paid from [date] to [date] for insurance and taxes
Nature and amounts of defaults, if any

Please reply directly to our auditors in the enclosed addressed envelope.

[Closing],

CLIENT'S AUTHORIZED SIGNATURE

LETTER TO CAPITAL STOCK REGISTRAR

This same letter should also be sent to the transfer agent.

CLIENT'S LETTERHEAD

____________________ [Date]

INSIDE ADDRESS

____

[Salutation]:

Our auditors, [name and address of auditors], are making an examination of our financial statements. They request that you furnish the following information as of [date].

1. Titles and descriptions of all classes of stock authorized to be issued
2. Total authorized shares of each class of stock
3. Number of shares of each class issued and outstanding

Your prompt attention to this request will be appreciated. A stamped, addressed envelope is enclosed for your reply.

[Closing],

____

CLIENT'S AUTHORIZED SIGNATURE

REQUEST FOR INFORMATION ON BOND ISSUE

CLIENT'S LETTERHEAD

[Date]

INSIDE ADDRESS

[Salutation]:

For the purpose of audit, please furnish our auditors, [name and address of auditors], with the following information relative to our First Mortgage 5% Sinking Fund Bonds as of [date].

Date of issue
Amount of original issue
Amount retired
Maturity dates
Interest rate
Date to which interest has been paid
Have all requirements of the Sinking Fund been met?

Thank you for your prompt attention to this matter. Please send your reply directly to our auditors in the enclosed, stamped envelope.

[Closing],

CLIENT'S AUTHORIZED SIGNATURE

CASH VALUE OF LIFE INSURANCE

The American Institute of Certified Public Accountants (AICPA) has a standard form that you may want to use.

CLIENT'S LETTERHEAD

[Date]

INSIDE ADDRESS

[Salutation]:

REFERENCE: POLICY NO. [# of policy]

Our auditors, [name and address of auditors], are conducting their annual examination of our financial statements. Please furnish them with the following information as of [date] pertaining to the above insurance policy carried on the life of [name of company officer].

Kind of insurance
Amount of insurance
Date to which premiums have been paid
Cash value
Amount of indebtedness
If any indebtedness exists, rate of interest it bears and amount accrued
Present beneficiary
Is the policy assigned or pledged?
Has the insured the right to change the beneficiary without the consent of the present beneficiary?

Your reply, sent directly to our auditors in the enclosed envelope, will be appreciated.

[Closing],

CLIENT'S AUTHORIZED SIGNATURE

REQUEST FOR DETAILS ON CONTRACTS OR GRANTS

CLIENT'S LETTERHEAD

[Date]

INSIDE ADDRESS

[Salutation]:

Our auditors, [name and address of auditors], are currently performing an examination of our financial statements as of [date]. We request that you supply them with the following information. Your reply should be mailed directly to them in the enclosed stamped, addressed envelope.

Date of grant/contract award ____________________

Period of grant/contract ____________________

Amount awarded ____________________

Payments through (date) ____________________

Refunds, if any ____________________

Balance due to us (date) ____________________

[Closing],

____

CLIENT'S AUTHORIZED SIGNATURE

LETTER TO CLIENT'S ATTORNEY

This letter is designed to obtain additional outside assurance regarding legal considerations that involve your client. It should be modified where necessary to match the specific circumstances of the engagement. A legal inquiry should be directed to outside general counsel and to each significant special counsel. Timing of the request should be such that the lawyer's response is dated as close to the accountant's report date as is practicable.

CLIENT'S LETTERHEAD

______________________ [Date]

INSIDE ADDRESS

____

[Salutation]:

In connection with our regular audit, will you please furnish directly to our auditors, [name and address of auditors], the following information.

1. Balance this company owes you for services or expenses to [date]
2. Summary of the status of any lawsuits or pending litigation to which this company is a party
3. Information concerning any controversies of which you have knowledge that may be likely to develop into lawsuits or give rise to claims against this company

[Closing],

____

CLIENT'S AUTHORIZED SIGNATURE

____

LETTER TO COLLECTION AGENCY

If your client has turned accounts receivable over to a collection agency, you may want to verify the status of these accounts by means of a letter such as the following one.

CLIENT'S LETTERHEAD

[Date]

INSIDE ADDRESS

[Salutation]:

In connection with the annual examination of our financial statements, will you kindly send to our auditors, [name and address of auditors], a list of our accounts turned over to you for collection. For each account, please show the present balance and the date and amount of the last remittance sent to us.

Your reply should go directly to our auditors, and a stamped, addressed envelope is enclosed for that purpose. Thank you.

[Closing],

CLIENT'S AUTHORIZED SIGNATURE

AUDITOR'S DIRECT REQUEST FOR STATEMENT OF CLIENT'S ACCOUNT

Occasionally you may find it necessary to write directly to one of the companies with which your client does business. It may be that you have received no response to an earlier client letter, or there may have been an initial oversight on your part. Whatever the cause, the following brief letter can be used.

YOUR LETTERHEAD

[Date]

INSIDE ADDRESS

[Salutation]:

We are completing our audit of the books and records of our client, [name and address of client].

We would appreciate your sending to us in the enclosed, addressed envelope a statement of our client's account with you as of [date].

It is important that we deliver our final report as soon as possible. Consequently, we will appreciate your prompt attention to this matter.

[Closing],

YOUR SIGNATURE

INVENTORY REQUEST TO WAREHOUSE

If the client does not furnish a list of merchandise in a particular warehouse, the warehouse must be asked to supply it.

CLIENT'S LETTERHEAD

[Date]

NAME AND ADDRESS OF WAREHOUSE

[Salutation]:

Our auditors, [name and address of auditors], are conducting their regular examination of our financial statements. Please confirm directly to them the following information about the merchandise that you held in your custody for our account as of [date].

1. Please determine the quantities on hand, showing for each lot:
   a. Lot number
   b. Date received
   c. Number of units, kind of package, description of goods
2. Please state how you determined the quantities being confirmed—physical count, weight or measure, or your own existing records
3. If applicable, please note any or all of the following:
   a. Warehouse receipts issued and, if known, whether these receipts have been assigned or pledged
   b. Known liens against the merchandise
   c. Amount of any unpaid charges as of [date]

Your reply should go directly to our auditors, [name and address of auditors]. A stamped, addressed envelope is enclosed for your convenience.

[Closing],

CLIENT'S AUTHORIZED SIGNATURE

ENGAGING AN OUT-OF-TOWN AUDITOR TO OBSERVE INVENTORY

Clients' inventories are often located in out-of-town plants, branches, warehouses, and so on. In some cases, it may be more efficient to engage out-of-town auditors to verify an inventory count than it is to do the job yourself. This letter deals with this kind of engagement.

YOUR LETTERHEAD

[Date]

INSIDE ADDRESS

[Salutation]:

As we discussed on the telephone yesterday, we hereby engage your firm to assist us in the inventory of [name of company]. I have asked the company's home office in Elm City to notify their Fitchburg warehouse that you will observe the inventory for us.

We understand that the inventory, which consists mainly of plywood panels, has a value of approximately $227,000. We expect you to observe the inventory procedure and to furnish us with a memorandum of your observations. We would also like you to list a representative number of items verified by you as they appear on the inventory sheets.

If you should experience any difficulty with your observations, please call me immediately.

[Closing],

YOUR SIGNATURE

SERVING AS LOCAL AUDITOR FOR ANOTHER ACCOUNTING FIRM

It is often more efficient for a far-distant accounting firm to engage a local auditor to verify inventories in nearby plants, branches, and warehouses than it is to send their own personnel to do it. The following letter is a report of such an out-of-town auditor who has verified an inventory for another accounting firm.

YOUR LETTERHEAD

[Date]

INSIDE ADDRESS

[Salutation]:

At your request we have verified the inventory of [name and address of local company] as of the close of business on [date].

In accordance with your inventory instructions, the work we performed consisted of verifying quantities only. Where we found discrepancies, we corrected both original and duplicate copies of the inventory listings.

We noted on the inventory sheets all sales made after the close of business on December 31, 19x6, up to the time of our verification on January 3, 19x7. This was done by inspection of the sales tickets. We also verified layaway merchandise as of January 3, 19x7.

Enclosed with this letter are:

93 original inventory sheets
2 original layaway-recap sheets
1 schedule of shipments, transfers, and price changes

We are pleased to have been able to perform this work for you.

[Closing],

YOUR SIGNATURE

CHAPTER 5

Effective Client Representation Letters

- Inventory Certificate Letter
- General Client Representation Letter
- Modification of Letter to Fit Circumstances
- Concise Client Representation Letter
- Alternate Client Representation Letter
- Explanation of Key Technical Terms

The written representations to be obtained from the client should be based on the circumstances of the particular engagement and the presentation of the financial statements. The representation letter is a formal acknowledgment of management's responsibilities in regard to the engagement. The assurances made by management do not relieve you, the accountant, of sound auditing judgment or of fair accounting disclosure relative to the report issued.

Where circumstances exist that warrant unusual auditing procedures or present out-of-the-ordinary reporting requirements, additional representation paragraphs should be used. These paragraphs should describe the nature of such deviations from standard practice and acknowledge their effects.

INVENTORY CERTIFICATE LETTER

CLIENT'S LETTERHEAD

[Date]

INSIDE ADDRESS

[Salutation]:

In connection with your review of the financial statements of this company as of [date], we, the undersigned, who are familiar with the goods carried in inventory and with the methods used in taking inventory, confirm, to the best of our knowledge and belief, the following representations concerning the inventory of [name of client company] taken on [date].

1. A summary of the values of the merchandise on hand at [inventory date above] is as follows:

   [list of main categories with final adjusted values]

2. On [date] the goods listed above were physically located on the premises of [name and address of company] and at the warehouse of [name of company and address of warehouse].
3. Quantities were determined by actual count (or weight or measurement), except [indicate any other methods used].
4. All items are valued at the lower of cost or net realizable value. In computing the inventory value, all unsalable, damaged, and deteriorated stocks have been eliminated or appropriately written down.
5. The entire inventory as listed above represents unencumbered property of the company. It includes no items that were not paid for, nor does it include any items for which liability was not reflected on our books at [date above]. No part of the inventory has been pledged as collateral.
6. No goods held on consignment for others have been included.
7. In our opinion, the amount stated is a fair and proper valuation of the inventory.

[Closing],

SIGNATURE OF APPROPRIATE EXECUTIVE OFFICER

SIGNATURE OF PERSON WHO DIRECTLY CONTROLLED INVENTORY COUNT

GENERAL CLIENT REPRESENTATION LETTER

In one sense, this is an all-purpose letter. It includes most of the items that you will ordinarily have to put into such a letter. Indeed, it covers more than it may be necessary to include. The variable and specific circumstances of the engagement will dictate the actual wording, inclusions, and omissions. In that sense, the letter must be looked upon as an inclusive model—one to be edited and adapted—rather than as a form letter.

CLIENT'S LETTERHEAD

[Date]

____

INSIDE ADDRESS

____

[Salutation]:

This letter concerns the examination you have been conducting of the financial statements of [name of client company] as of [date] for the period [January 1, 19x7, to December 31, 19x7]. The purpose of your examination is to express an opinion as to whether the financial statements present fairly the financial position of [name of client company] in accordance with generally accepted accounting principles. In this regard, you have requested that we confirm, to the best of our knowledge and belief, the following representations that we have made to you in connection with the examination.

Documents Made Available

1. We have furnished to you all financial records and data.
2. We have supplied to you complete and authentic minutes of all meetings of stockholders and directors. If minutes of recent meetings are unavailable, we have furnished summaries of the actions taken.

Absence of Irregularities

3. To the best of our knowledge, there have been no irregularities involving management or employees that could materially affect the financial statements.

4. We have received no communications from regulatory agencies concerning our financial reporting practices that could materially affect the financial statements.

Items Recorded or Disclosed

5. Our financial statements include related party transactions and related amounts receivable or payable, if any, including sales, purchases, loans, transfers, leasing arrangements, consigned inventory, and guarantees.
6. We have disclosed any existing agreements or options to repurchase capital stock.

Plans and Intentions

7. We have adopted no plans nor do we have any present intentions that could materially affect the carrying value or classification of assets or liabilities in the financial statements.

Violations, Liabilities, Contingencies

8. We are unaware of any violations of law or regulations that should be, but are not, disclosed in the financial statements.
9. To the best of our knowledge, there are no other material liabilities or gain or loss contingencies that should be accrued or disclosed.
10. Our lawyer has advised us of no unasserted claims or assessments that are likely to be asserted and should therefore be disclosed.

Material Transactions

11. There are no material transactions that have not been properly recorded in the accounting records on which the financial statements are based.

Inventories

12. If applicable, we have reduced excess or obsolete inventories to their estimated net realizable value.

Title to Owned Assets

13. The company has satisfactory title to all owned assets, and there are no liens or encumbrances on such assets, nor has any asset been pledged.

Provisions for Material Loss

14. Provision has been made for any material loss that may be sustained in the fulfillment of, or from the inability to fulfill, any sales commitment.
15. Provision has been made for any material loss that may be sustained as a result of purchase commitments for inventory quantities in excess of normal requirements or at prices higher than the prevailing market prices.

Contractual Agreements

16. We have complied with all aspects of contractual agreements in instances where our noncompliance could materially affect the financial statements.

Subsequent Events

17. No events have occurred subsequent to the balance sheet date that would require adjustment to, or disclosure in, the financial statements.

[Closing],

____

SIGNATURE OF CHIEF EXECUTIVE OFFICER

____

____

SIGNATURE OF CHIEF FINANCIAL OFFICER

____

MODIFICATION OF LETTER TO FIT CIRCUMSTANCES

It is important to note that a client representation letter should take the specific circumstances of the engagement into account. The preceding general letter may contain points that are not applicable, and, if so, they should be eliminated. Not only may irrelevant points confuse the client, but they may also add unnecessary length to the letter. Moreover, they may be objectionable. The following letter has been shortened considerably, yet it contains everything that the accounting firm deemed necessary.

CLIENT'S LETTERHEAD

____________________ [Date]

INSIDE ADDRESS

____

[Salutation]:

In connection with your audit of the financial statements of [name of company] as of [date] and for the [period] then ended, you have requested that we confirm, to the best of our knowledge and belief, the representations made in this letter. The purpose of your examination is to express an opinion as to whether the financial statements present fairly the financial position of [name of company] in conformity with generally accepted accounting principles. We confirm the following:

1. We are responsible for the fair presentation in the financial statements of the financial position of [name of company] in conformity with generally accepted accounting principles.
2. We have made available to you all financial records and data as well as minutes of the meetings of stockholders and the board of directors.
3. There have been no irregularities involving management or employees.
4. We have disclosed to you all plans or intentions that may materially affect the carrying value or classification of assets and liabilities.
5. The following have been properly recorded or disclosed in the finanical statements: Related party transactions, if applicable, as defined in State-

ment on Auditing Standards No. 6, and related amounts receivable or payable, including sales, purchases, loans, transfers, leasing arrangements and guaranties.

6. There are no violations of laws or regulations that should be considered for disclosure in the financial statements or as a basis for recording a loss contingency.
7. We have disclosed to you all material liabilities and gain or loss contingencies as required to be accrued or disclosed by Statement of Financial Accounting Standards No. 5.
8. There are no unasserted claims that our lawyers have advised us are probable of assertion and must be disclosed in accordance with Statement of Financial Accounting Standards No. 5.
9. There are no material transactions or related assets or liabilities that have not been properly recorded in the financial records.
10. [Name of company] has satisfactory title to all assets shown in the financial statements. Assets that have been pledged are reflected in the financial statements. Liens on property have been adequately disclosed.
11. We have complied with all aspects of contractual agreements that are unrelated to, but may materially affect, the financial statements.
12. Other than those already noted, no events have occurred subsequent to the balance sheet date that would require adjustment to, or disclosure in, the financial statements.

[Closing],

____

SIGNATURE OF CHIEF EXECUTIVE OFFICER

____

CONCISE CLIENT REPRESENTATION LETTER

Here is another modification, and shortening, of the general representation letter. The format is slightly different, and the wording has been changed in certain places to fit the circumstances.

CLIENT'S LETTERHEAD

[Date]

INSIDE ADDRESS

[Salutation]:

In connection with your review of the financial statements of [name of company] as of [date] and for the year then ended, for the purpose of expressing limited assurance that there are no material modifications that should be made to the statements in order for them to be in conformity with generally accepted accounting principles, we confirm, to the best of our knowledge and belief, the following representations made to you during your review.

1. The financial statements referred to above present the financial position, results of operations, and changes in financial position of [name of company] in conformity with generally accepted accounting principles. In that connection, we specifically confirm that:
   a. The company's accounting principles, and the practices and methods followed in applying them, are as disclosed in the financial statements.
   b. There have been no changes during the year ended [date as above] in the company's accounting principles and practices.
   c. We have no plans or intentions that may materially affect the carrying value or classification of assets and liabilities.
   d. There are no material transactions that have not been properly reflected in the financial statements.
   e. There are no material losses (such as from obsolete inventory or

purchase or sales commitments) that have not been properly accrued or disclosed in the financial statements.

f. There are no violations or possible violations of laws or regulations whose effects should be considered for disclosure in the financial statements or as a basis for recording a loss contingency, and there are no other material liabilities or gain or loss contingencies that are required to be accrued or disclosed.

g. The company has satisfactory title to all owned assets, and there are no liens or encumbrances on such assets, nor has any asset been pledged which has not been disclosed.

h. There are no related party transactions or related amounts receivable or payable that have not been properly disclosed in the financial statements.

i. We have complied with all aspects of contractual agreements that would have a material effect on the financial statements in the event of noncompliance.

j. No events have occurred subsequent to the balance sheet date that would require adjustment to, or disclosure in, the financial statements.

2. We have advised you of all actions taken at meetings of stockholders and boards of directors that may affect the financial statements.

We have responded fully to all inquiries that you have made to us during your review.

[Closing],

____

SIGNATURE OF CHIEF EXECUTIVE OFFICER

____

ALTERNATE CLIENT REPRESENTATION LETTER

Strictly speaking, this is a limited, or partial, representation letter. Concentrating on liabilities, it lacks some of the key points of previous letters in this chapter, but is included to show the extent of modification—and the amount of alternate wording—that may be appropriate in some circumstances.

CLIENT'S LETTERHEAD

[Date]

INSIDE ADDRESS

[Salutation]:

In connection with your examination of the financial statements of [name of company] as of [date] and for the year then ended, we confirm that to the best of our knowledge and belief:

1. All known liabilities of the company at [date as above] have been provided for and are recorded in the financial statements.
2. All known assets of the company at [date as above] were recorded in the financial statements as of that date.
3. Adequate provision has been made to cover possible losses that may be sustained in the collection of accounts receivable recorded in the financial statements at [date as above].
4. No purchase commitments have been made in excess of normal requirements or at prices in excess of the prevailing market prices, nor are there any agreements to repurchase items previously sold. [except as follows:]
5. Through the date of this letter, the company was not contingently liable as endorsers or guarantors of obligations of others.
6. The company has not entered into any contract of an unusual nature or material amount not disclosed in the financial statements, nor are there any lawsuits or judgments pending against the company. [except as follows:]

7. At [date as above] there were no defaults in payment of principal or interest on notes, bonds, or debentures payable, nor defaults or breaches of underlying agreements.
8. Except as reflected in the balance sheet, there were no agreements under which any of the liabilities of the company have been subordinated to any other of its liabilities, nor were any receivables owned by the company subordinated to any other liabilities of the debtor companies.
9. No events have occurred subsequent to the balance sheet date that would require adjustment to, or disclosure in, the financial statements.

[Closing],

____

SIGNATURE OF CHIEF EXECUTIVE OFFICER

____

____

SIGNATURE OF CHIEF FINANCIAL OFFICER

____

EXPLANATION OF KEY TECHNICAL TERMS

Since a representation letter is ostensibly written by the client (although, in fact, more commonly by the accountant), the client must understand exactly what is being said. If the letter contains technical terms, the client may need definitions. There are various ways to meet this need. One is to include standard definitions in the letter, either as notes or as parenthetical statements. Another is to refer to published definitions: ". . . transactions with related parties (as defined in Statement on Auditing Standards No. 6) . . . ." If neither of these methods has been used, a brief letter defining a questioned term may be needed.

YOUR LETTERHEAD

[Date]

INSIDE ADDRESS

[Salutation]:

This letter is in response to your question about the meaning of the term "irregularities" as used in the representation letter dated [date].

You point out that two people in your organization have questioned why the letter cannot use a more specific term, such as "fraud," for example. They feel that "irregularities" may be too broad a term.

The term "irregularities" is recommended by the American Institute of Certified Public Accountants. As defined by the AICPA, it has two specific meanings: (1) "Intentional distortions of financial statements," (2) "Misappropriations of assets."

Its meaning in the representation letter is limited to those two particular kinds of acts. There is no cause to fear that "irregularities" means minor or unintentional errors. It does not.

I hope this explanation will resolve the doubts raised about the meaning of this rather technical term.

YOUR SIGNATURE

CHAPTER 6

A Portfolio of Standard Audit Reports

- Unqualified Opinion—Standard Report
- Unqualified Opinion on Two Years' Financial Statements
- Unqualified Opinion Accepting Other Auditors' Report
- Unqualified Opinion Reversing Prior Year's Qualified Opinion
- Paragraph Indicating Review of Prior Year's Statements
- Disclaimer of Opinion on Prior Year's Unaudited Statements
- Qualified Opinion—Departure from Generally Accepted Accounting Principles
- Qualified Opinion—Inconsistent Application of Generally Accepted Accounting Principles
- Qualified Opinion—Limitation on Scope of Audit
- Qualified Opinion—Inadequate Disclosure
- Qualified Opinion—Uncertainty about Lawsuit
- Qualified Opinion—Uncertainty about "Going Concern"
- Adverse Opinion
- Disclaimer of Opinion—Unobserved Inventory
- Disclaimer of Opinion—Inadequate Records
- Disclaimer of Opinion—Limited Examination
- Disclaimer of Opinion—Lack of Independence
- Personal Financial Statements—Standard Report
- Personal Financial Statements—Adverse Opinion
- Personal Financial Statements—Disclaimer of Opinion
- Twelve Review Reports
  - —Predecessor's Compilation Report on Prior Period Not Presented—Comparative Financial Statements
  - —Prior Period Audited—Comparative Financial Statements

—Predecessor's Review Report on Prior Period Not Presented—Comparative Financial Statements

—Changed Reference to a Departure from Generally Accepted Accounting Principles—Comparative Financial Statements

—Review Report on Current Period and Reference to Compilation Report on Prior Period—Comparative Financial Statements

—Review Each Period—Comparative Financial Statements

—Review of Financial Statements of a Nonpublic Entity—Standard Report

—Departure from GAAP—Accounting Principle Not Generally Accepted

—Departure from GAAP—Change in Accounting Principle Without Reasonable Justification

—Departure from GAAP—Omission of Statement of Changes in Financial Position

—Cash Basis Statements

—Income Tax Basis Statements

- Sixteen Compilation Reports

—Compilation of Financial Statements of a Nonpublic Entity—Standard Report

—Omission of Substantially All Disclosures

—Omission of Statement of Financial Position and Substantially All Disclosures

—Departure from GAAP—Omission of Statement of Changes in Financial Position

—Departure from GAAP—Accounting Principles Not Generally Accepted

—Cash Basis Statements

—Cash Basis Statements—Omission of Substantially All Disclosures

—Income Tax Basis Statements

—Income Tax Basis Statements—Omission of Substantially All Disclosures

—Compilation Each Period—Comparative Financial Statements

—Compilation Report on Current Period and Reference to Review Report on Prior Period—Comparative Financial Statements

—Changed Reference to a Departure from Generally Accepted Accounting Principles—Comparative Financial Statements

—Predecessor's Compilation Report on Prior Period Not Presented—Comparative Financial Statements

—Predecessor's Review Report on Prior Period Not Presented—Comparative Financial Statements

—Omission of Substantially All Disclosures Including Those for Prior Period Previously Not Omitted—Comparative Financial Statements

—Prior Period Audited—Comparative Financial Statements

- **Seven Special Reports**

—Cash Basis Statements

—Income Tax Basis Statements

—Royalties

—Profit Participation

—Compliance with Contractual Provisions (Separate Report)—Negative Assurance

—Compliance with Contractual Provisions (Auditor's Report Accompanying Financial Statements)—Negative Assurance

—Compliance with Regulatory Requirements—Negative Assurance

Keep in mind that the audit reports in this chapter, like the letters in the rest of the book, are presented as models, or examples. They are representative specimens only and are not intended to be viewed as appropriate for all occasions. Nor do they comprise an all-inclusive collection.

In drafting a report for a specific engagement, you may find it necessary to depart from the wording given in one of the models, since your report must match precisely the circumstances of the engagement. No attempt has been made in the chapter to refer to authoritative pronouncements. When you are faced with a particular problem in an audit engagement, you are urged to seek authoritative advice—to find the relevant pronouncements in authoritative sources. Such advice is well beyond the scope of this chapter.

In connection with these sample audit reports, you will find Chapter 17, "A Practical Guide to Report Writing," a useful supplement.

UNQUALIFIED OPINION—STANDARD REPORT

This is the basic form of a standard report for the financial statements of a single year. The first paragraph explains the scope of the audit; the second contains the opinion.

> We have examined the balance sheet of [name of company] as of December 31, 19x8, and the related statements of income and retained earnings and changes in financial position for the year then ended. Our examination was made in accordance with generally accepted auditing standards, and accordingly included such tests of the accounting records and such other auditing procedures as we considered necessary in the circumstances.
>
> In our opinion, the financial statements indicated above present fairly the financial position of [name of company] at December 31, 19x8, and the results of its operations and the changes in its financial position for the year ended, in conformity with generally accepted accounting principles applied on a basis consistent with that of the preceding year.

UNQUALIFIED OPINION ON TWO YEARS' FINANCIAL STATEMENTS

Depending upon circumstances, a number of variations are possible in the wording of an unqualified opinion. Changes from standard wording should be made only when necessary, and then, only to the extent needed to show clearly what the variation is.

> We have examined the balance sheets of [name of company] as of December 31, 19x8 and December 31, 19x9, and the related statements of income, retained earnings, and changes in financial position for the years then ended. Our examinations were made in accordance with generally accepted auditing standards and accordingly included such tests of the accounting records and other such auditing procedures as we considered necessary in the circumstances.
>
> In our opinion, the financial statements indicated above present fairly the financial position of [name of company] at December 31, 19x8 and December 31, 19x9, and the results of its operations and the changes in its financial position for the years then ended, in conformity with generally accepted accounting principles applied on a consistent basis.

UNQUALIFIED OPINION ACCEPTING OTHER AUDITORS' REPORT

This report includes common, necessary information not supplied by the standard report. The first paragraph is slightly changed because of circumstances: The words "consolidated" and "subsidiaries" have been added. The second paragraph is entirely new. The third paragraph takes into account the changes in the first and second paragraphs.

> We have examined the consolidated balance sheet of [name of company] and subsidiaries as of December 31, 19x8, and the related consolidated statements of income and retained earnings and changes in financial position for the year then ended. Our examination was made in accordance with generally accepted auditing standards, and accordingly included such tests of the accounting records and such other auditing procedures as we considered necessary in the circumstances.
>
> We did not examine the financial statements of [name of subsidiary], a consolidated subsidiary, which statements reflect total assets and revenues constituting 11 and 14 percent, respectively, of the related consolidated totals. These statements were examined by other auditors who have furnished their report to us. Our opinion expressed below, as

it relates to the amounts included for [name of subsidiary], is based solely upon the report of the other auditors.

In our opinion, based upon our examination and the report of other auditors, the financial statements referred to in the first paragraph present fairly the financial position of [name of company] and subsidiaries at December 31, 19x8, and the results of their operations and the changes in their financial position for the year then ended, in conformity with generally accepted accounting principles applied on a basis consistent with that of the preceding year.

UNQUALIFIED OPINION REVERSING PRIOR YEAR'S QUALIFIED OPINION

In this report, which covers two years, a matter that could have affected the preceding year's report has been settled, making it possible for the auditors to remove their earlier qualification.

We have examined the balance sheets of [name of company] as of December 31, 19x5 and December 31, 19x4, and the related statements of income, retained earnings, and changes in financial position for the years then ended. Our examinations were made in accordance with generally accepted auditing standards and accordingly included such tests of the accounting records and other such auditing procedures as we considered necessary in the circumstances.

Our report dated March 1, 19x5, which expressed our opinion on the 19x4 financial statements, was qualified because of certain unresolved litigation, the outcome of which could have affected the 19x4 financial statements. As explained in Note X, this litigation was settled as of September 15, 19x5, at no material cost to [name of company]. Consequently, our present opinion of the 19x4 financial statements, as noted below, differs from our previous opinion in that it is no longer qualified.

In our opinion, the financial statements indicated above present fairly the financial position of [name of company] at December 31, 19x5 and December 31, 19x4, and the results of its operations and the changes in its financial position for the years then ended, in conformity with generally accepted accounting principles applied on a consistent basis.

PARAGRAPH INDICATING REVIEW OF PRIOR YEAR'S STATEMENTS

The first two paragraphs of this report present an unqualified opinion of the financial statements of 19x9. Their wording is identical to that in the standard report on page 121. However, a final paragraph has been added, pointing out that the financial statements of the preceding year, 19x8, were reviewed, not audited. Since the two years' financial statements are presented in comparative form, this paragraph is needed to make it clear that the accompanying 19x8 financial statements are unaudited.

> We have made a review of the 19x8 financial statements of [name of company], and our report thereon, dated June 1, 19x9, stated that we were not aware of any material modifications that should be made to those statements for them to be in conformity with generally accepted accounting principles. However, a review is substantially less in scope than an audit and does not provide a basis for the expression of an opinion on the financial statements taken as a whole.

DISCLAIMER OF OPINION ON PRIOR YEAR'S UNAUDITED STATEMENTS

This paragraph, like the previous one, deals with unaudited financial statements. But in this instance neither a review nor an audit has been performed. The first two paragraphs of the standard report (page 121) express an unqualified opinion on the 19x9 financial statements. The report ends with the one-sentence paragraph below.

> We did not audit the 19x8 financial statements of [name of company], and accordingly we do not express an opinion on them.

QUALIFIED OPINION—DEPARTURE FROM GENERALLY ACCEPTED ACCOUNTING PRINCIPLES

When an opinion must be qualified, a modifying phrase is inserted in the opinion paragraph. Other explanatory statements may be included in the report as well. Here are five basic reasons for qualifying an opinion.

1. Departure from generally accepted accounting principles
2. Departure from the consistent application of generally accepted accounting principles

3. Limitation on the scope of the audit
4. Inadequate disclosure in the financial statements
5. Uncertainty concerning the financial statements

When there has been a departure from generally accepted accounting principles, a modifying phrase in the opinion paragraph signals a qualified opinion. It begins with the word "except."

> We have examined the balance sheet of [name of company] as of December 31, 19x6, and the related statements of income and retained earnings and changes in financial position for the year then ended. Our examination was made in accordance with generally accepted auditing standards, and accordingly included such tests of the accounting records and such other auditing procedures as we considered necessary in the circumstances.
>
> On March 1, 19x6, [name of company] acquired four acres of land adjacent to its place of business at a cost of $50,400. In the financial statements this land is stated at its appraised value of $84,000. Generally accepted accounting principles require that land be stated at cost.
>
> In our opinion, except for the effects of stating the newly acquired four acres of land at its appraised value rather than at cost, the financial statements present fairly the financial position of [name of company] at December 31, 19x8, and the results of its operations and the changes in its financial position for the year then ended, in conformity with generally accepted accounting principles applied on a basis consistent with that of the preceding year.

QUALIFIED OPINION—INCONSISTENT APPLICATION OF GENERALLY ACCEPTED ACCOUNTING PRINCIPLES

Except for the modifying phrase near the end of the opinion paragraph ("except for . . ."), this would be a standard report. The company has made a change in its method of valuing inventory—a change that the auditor agrees with. However, the opinion must be qualified in view of this inconsistency from one year to the next.

> We have examined the balance sheet of [name of company] as of December 31, 19x8, and the related statements of income and retained earnings and changes in financial position for the year then ended. Our examination was made in accordance with generally accepted auditing standards, and accordingly included such tests of the accounting records and such other auditing procedures as we considered necessary in the circumstances.

In our opinion, the financial statements indicated above present fairly the financial position of [name of company] at December 31, 19x8, and the results of its operations and the changes in its financial position for the year then ended, in conformity with generally accepted accounting principles, which, except for the change, with which we concur, in the method of valuing inventory, as described in Note A to the financial statements, have been applied on a basis consistent with that of the preceding year.

QUALIFIED OPINION—LIMITATION ON SCOPE OF AUDIT

Limitations on scope will generally be mentioned in the scope paragraph and detailed in a paragraph immediately following the introductory paragraph.

> . . . auditing procedures as we considered necessary in the circumstances, *except as* described in the following paragraph.
>
> The company is a participant with other developers in long-term development contracts undertaken as joint ventures. We understand that the financial statements of the joint ventures for the year ended December 31, 19x4, have not been audited. Accordingly, we do not express an opinion concerning the equity in joint ventures stated at $500,000 in the accompanying balance sheet, the equity in income of joint ventures stated at $100,000 (before income taxes) in the accompanying income statement, or the increase in equity of joint ventures stated at $300,000 in the accompanying statement of changes in financial position.
>
> In our opinion, with the exceptions stated in the previous paragraph, the financial statements indicated above present fairly . . .

QUALIFIED OPINION—INADEQUATE DISCLOSURE

If the client company, either by mistake or by intent, fails to include something in the financial statements that should be there, a qualified opinion may be necessary.

> We have examined the consolidated balance sheet of [name of company] and of [name of wholly owned subsidiary] as of December 31, 19x8, and the related statements of income and retained earnings and changes in financial position for the year then ended. Our examination was made in accordance with generally accepted auditing standards, and accordingly included such tests of the accounting records and such

other auditing procedures as we considered necessary in the circumstances.

Certain information with respect to long-term debt as of December 31, 19x8, has been omitted from the accompanying financial statements. This debt consisted of notes payable to financial institutions of $623,000 due December 31, 19x4. These notes bear interest at 1-3/4% over the prime rate and are collateralized by the stock and all of the assets of [name of subsidiary], a wholly owned subsidiary.

In our opinion, the consolidated financial statements present fairly, except for the omission of the information contained in the preceding paragraph, the consolidated financial position of [name of company] and of [name of wholly owned subsidiary] and results of operations and changes in financial position for the year then ended in conformity with generally accepted accounting principles consistently applied.

QUALIFIED OPINION—UNCERTAINTY ABOUT LAWSUIT

If the outcome of a major lawsuit against your client company is in doubt, there is clearly some uncertainty about the company's financial position, and a qualified opinion is called for.

We have examined the balance sheet of [name of company] as of December 31, 19x8, and the related statements of income and retained earnings and changes in financial position for the year then ended. Our examination was made in accordance with generally accepted auditing standards, and accordingly included such tests of the accounting records and such other auditing procedures as we considered necessary in the circumstances.

The [name of company] is defendant in a class-action lawsuit alleging that certain of its products caused personal injuries to consumers, and demanding compensatory and punitive damages. The case is scheduled to come to trial in the month following the date of this report. The outcome of the lawsuit cannot presently be determined, and no provision for any liability that may result has been made in the financial statements.

In our opinion, subject to the effects on the financial statements of such adjustments, if any, that might have been required had the outcome of the aforementioned lawsuit been known, the financial statements indicated above present fairly the financial position of [name of company] at December 31, 19x8, and the results of its operations and the changes in its financial position for the year then ended, in conformity with generally accepted accounting principles applied on a basis consistent with that of the preceding year.

QUALIFIED OPINION—UNCERTAINTY ABOUT "GOING CONCERN"

If it appears from your audit that the shaky financial position of the client company threatens its survival, this conclusion should be included as a qualification.

> We have examined the balance sheet of [name of company] as of December 31, 19x8, and the related statements of income and retained earnings and changes in financial position for the year then ended. Our examination was made in accordance with generally accepted auditing standards, and accordingly included such tests of the accounting records and such other auditing procedures as we considered necessary in the circumstances.
>
> The financial statements show that [name of company] incurred a net loss of [$ amount] during the year ended December 31, 19x7. As of that date, the company's current liabilities exceeded its current assets by [$ amount], and its total liabilities exceeded its total assets by [$ amount]. As pointed out in Note C, these facts and others suggest that the company may be unable to continue in existence. The financial statements do not include any adjustments involving the classification and recoverability of recorded asset amounts, nor do they indicate the classification and amounts of liabilities that might be necessary should the company be unable to continue in existence.
>
> In our opinion, subject to the effects on the financial statements of such adjustments, if any, that might have been required had the aforementioned uncertainty been resolved, the financial statements indicated above present fairly the financial position of [name of company] at December 31, 19x8, and the results of its operations and the changes in its financial position for the year then ended, in conformity with generally accepted accounting principles applied on a basis consistent with that of the preceding year.

ADVERSE OPINION

An adverse opinion states flatly that the financial statements do *not* present fairly what they are supposed to present. No client wants an adverse opinion, and most will want to make the changes needed to avoid one. However, if an adverse opinion is clearly required, the auditor cannot avoid it by writing a disclaimer instead.

> We have examined the balance sheet of [name of company] as of December 31, 19x5, and the related statements of income and retained earnings and changes in financial position for the year then ended. Our examination was made in accordance with generally accepted auditing standards, and accordingly included such tests of the accounting records and such other auditing procedures as we considered necessary in the circumstances.
>
> [This paragraph contains an explanation of the specific circumstances that warrant an adverse opinion.]
>
> In our opinion, because of the effects of the matters discussed in the preceding paragraph, the financial statements indicated above do not present fairly the financial position of [name of company] at December 31, 19x5, or the results of its operations and the changes in its financial position for the year then ended.

DISCLAIMER OF OPINION—UNOBSERVED INVENTORY

In an initial engagement it may be impossible to obtain enough evidence to form an opinion. If the beginning inventory was not observed, for example, there may be no way to establish the accuracy of beginning inventory quantities. In that case, the auditor must disclaim an opinion.

> We have examined the balance sheet of [name of company] as of December 31, 19x8, and the related statements of income and retained earnings and changes in financial position for the year then ended. Our examination was made in accordance with generally accepted auditing standards, and accordingly included such tests of the accounting records and such other auditing procedures as we considered necessary in the circumstances, except as stated in the following paragraph.
>
> Since we were not engaged as auditors until after December 31, 19x7, we did not observe the physical inventory taken at that date. We have tried various other procedures to verify inventory quantities, but they have proved unavailing. Consequently, we are not satisfied as to the accuracy of the amount of inventory at December 31, 19x7. As discussed in Note D, the amount of beginning inventory enters materially into the determination of the results of operations and changes in financial position for the year ended December 31, 19x8. Therefore, we do not express an opinion on the aforementioned statements of income and retained earnings and changes in financial position for the year ended December 31, 19x8.
>
> In our opinion, the accompanying balance sheet presents fairly the financial position of [name of company] at December 31, 19x8, in conformity with generally accepted accounting principles applied on a basis consistent with that of the preceding year.

DISCLAIMER OF OPINION—INADEQUATE RECORDS

An initial engagement may uncover internal accounting problems at the client company that make it impossible to express an opinion. The report should cover all reasons for a disclaimer—if there are more than one—even though one would be sufficient for the auditor to decline to express an opinion.

> We have examined the balance sheet of [name of company] as of December 31, 19x5, and the related statements of income and retained earnings and changes in financial position for the year then ended. Except as explained in the following paragraph, our examination was made in accordance with generally accepted auditing standards, and accordingly included such tests of the accounting records and such other auditing procedures as we considered necessary in the circumstances.
>
> In the course of our examination, we discovered major inadequacies in the company's accounting records for the year ended December 31, 19x5. We could not extend our auditing procedures to enable us to express an opinion on results of operations and changes in financial position for that year or on the consistency of application of accounting principles with the previous year.
>
> In our opinion, the accompanying balance sheet presents fairly the financial position of [name of company] at December 31, 19x5, in conformity with generally accepted accounting principles.

DISCLAIMER OF OPINION—LIMITED EXAMINATION

A client who needs an auditor's report for a special, limited purpose may be willing to accept a disclaimer rather than having a full physical inventory taken. In such a case, the client should be aware of what assurances the auditor's report does and does not make. It does not, for example, offer assurances as to the absence of fraud or other irregularities.

> We have examined the balance sheet of [name of company] as of December 31, 19x9, and the related statements of income and retained earnings and changes in financial position for the year then ended. Except as explained in the following paragraph, our examination was made in accordance with generally accepted auditing standards, and accordingly included such tests of the accounting records and such other auditing procedures as we considered necessary in the circumstances.
>
> The terms of this engagement did not include our observation of physi-

cal inventory taking, nor did we use alternative procedures to determine inventories.

Since the inventories at those dates enter materially into the determination of financial position, results of operations, and changes in financial position, the scope of our work was insufficient to enable us to express, and we do not express, an opinion on the aforementioned financial statements.

DISCLAIMER OF OPINION—LACK OF INDEPENDENCE

If you audit the financial statements for an organization in which you are an officer or director, or if you are related to it in any other significant way, you are not independent and must disclaim an opinion on the financial statements. In doing so, you should not explain the reason for the lack of independence, nor should you include a description of the procedures you used. Such additions could conceivably mislead readers about the importance of your lack of independence.

We are not independent with respect to [name of company] and the accompanying balance sheet as of December 31, 19x2, and we did not audit the related statements of income, retained earnings, and changes in financial position for the year then ended. Accordingly, we do not express an opinion on them.

PERSONAL FINANCIAL STATEMENTS—STANDARD REPORT

An auditor's report on personal financial statements follows the same pattern as the report on a company, although the wording is slightly different. Here, as in previous reports, if the auditor is a single practitioner, the "we's" and "our's" become "I's" and "my."

We have examined the statement of financial position of [name(s) of person or persons] as of [date] and the related statement of changes in net worth for the year [or other period] then ended. Our examination was made in accordance with generally accepted auditing standards and, accordingly, included such tests of the accounting records and such other auditing procedures as we considered necessary in the circumstances.

In our opinion, the financial statements indicated above present fairly the financial condition of [name(s) of person or persons] at [date], and the changes in their net worth for the year [or other period] then ended, in conformity with generally accepted accounting principles applied on a consistent basis with that of the previous year [or other period].

PERSONAL FINANCIAL STATEMENTS—ADVERSE OPINION

No one wants to write an adverse opinion, but there may be no alternative. If the client refuses to, or is unable to, adhere to generally accepted accounting principles, a report like the following one is the only kind possible.

> We have examined the statement of financial position of [name(s) of person or persons] as of [date] and the related statement of changes in net worth for the year [or other period] then ended. Our examination was made in accordance with generally accepted auditing standards and, accordingly, included such tests of the accounting records and such other auditing procedures as we considered necessary in the circumstances.
>
> [This paragraph contains an explanation of the specific circumstances that warrant an adverse opinion.]
>
> In our opinion, because of the effects of the matters discussed in the preceding paragraph, the financial statements indicated above do not present fairly, in conformity with generally accepted accounting principles, the financial position of [name(s) of person or persons] at [date], or the changes in their net worth for the year [or other period] then ended.

PERSONAL FINANCIAL STATEMENTS—DISCLAIMER OF OPINION

A disclaimer is more likely to be necessary in a first engagement than in later ones. Presumably, the inadequate accounting records referred to in the following letter will be straightened out by the time of the next audit. Meanwhile, if there is no way to obtain accurate records for the present engagement, a disclaimer is required.

> We have examined the statement of financial position of [name(s) of person(s)] as of [date] and the related statement of changes in net worth for the year [or other period] then ended. Except as explained in the following paragraph, our examination was made in accordance with generally accepted auditing standards and, accordingly, included such tests of the accounting records and such other auditing procedures as we considered necessary in the circumstances.
>
> The accounting records of [name(s) of person(s)] are inadequate to disclose the existence or accuracy of certain transactions. These transactions,

when entered into his [her, their] computer, are not always supported by corresponding documents. As a result, it was impossible to extend our auditing procedures sufficiently to determine that all assets, liabilities, and changes in net worth are recorded in the aforementioned financial statements.

Since the accounting records and supporting documentation of [name(s) of person(s)] are inadequate, and since we were unable to apply proper auditing procedures to the computer-recorded transactions, as noted in the preceding paragraph, the scope of our work was insufficient to enable us to express, and we do not express, an opinion on the aforementioned financial statements.

TWELVE REVIEW REPORTS

PREDECESSOR'S COMPILATION REPORT ON PRIOR PERIOD NOT PRESENTED—COMPARATIVE FINANCIAL STATEMENTS

I (we) have reviewed the accompanying balance sheet of XYZ Company as of December 31, 19x2, and the related statements of income, retained earnings, and changes in financial position for the year then ended, in accordance with standards established by the American Institute of Certified Public Accountants. All information included in these financial statements is the representation of the management (owners) of XYZ Company.

A review consists principally of inquiries of company personnel and analytical procedures applied to financial data. It is substantially less in scope than an examination in accordance with generally accepted auditing standards, the objective of which is the expression of an opinion regarding the financial statements taken as a whole. Accordingly, I (we) do not express such an opinion.

Based on my (our) review, I am (we are) not aware of any material modifications that should be made to the accompanying 19x2 financial statements in order for them to be in conformity with generally accepted accounting principles.

The 19x1 financial statements of XYZ Company were compiled by other accountants whose report dated February 1, 19x2 stated that they did not express an opinion or any other form of assurance on those statements.

PRIOR PERIOD AUDITED—COMPARATIVE FINANCIAL STATEMENTS

I (we) have reviewed the accompanying balance sheet of XYZ Company as of December 31, 19x2, and the related statements of income, retained earnings, and changes in financial position for the year then ended, in accordance with standards established by the American Institute of Certified Public Accountants. All information included in these financial statements is the representation of the management (owners) of XYZ Company.

A review consists principally of inquiries of company personnel and analytical procedures applied to financial data. It is substantially less in scope than an examination in accordance with generally accepted auditing standards, the objective of which is the expression of an opinion regarding the financial statements taken as a whole. Accordingly, I (we) do not express such an opinion.

Based on my (our) review, I am (we are) not aware of any material modifications that should be made to the accompanying 19x2 financial statements in order for them to be in conformity with generally accepted accounting principles.

The financial statements for the year ended December 31, 19x1 were examined by me (us) (other accountants) and I (we) (they) expressed an unqualified opinion on them in my (our) (their) report dated March 1, 19x2, but I (we) (they) have not performed any auditing procedures since that date.

PREDECESSOR'S REVIEW REPORT ON PRIOR PERIOD NOT PRESENTED—COMPARATIVE FINANCIAL STATEMENTS

I (we) have reviewed the accompanying balance sheet of XYZ Company as of December 31, 19x2, and the related statements of income, retained earnings, and changes in financial position for the year then ended, in accordance with standards established by the American Institute of Certified Public Accountants. All information included in these financial statements is the representation of the management (owners) of XYZ Company.

A review consists principally of inquiries of company personnel and analytical procedures applied to financial data. It is substantially less in scope than an examination in accordance with generally accepted auditing standards, the objective of which is the expression of an opinion regarding the financial statements taken as a whole. Accordingly, I (we) do not express such an opinion.

Based on my (our) review, I am (we are) not aware of any material modifications that should be made to the accompanying 19x2 financial statements in order for them to be in conformity with generally accepted accounting principles.

The 19x1 financial statements of XYZ Company were reviewed by other accountants whose report dated March 1, 19x2 stated that they were not

---

aware of any material modifications that should be made to those statements in order for them to be in conformity with generally accepted accounting principles.

CHANGED REFERENCE TO A DEPARTURE FROM GENERALLY ACCEPTED ACCOUNTING PRINCIPLES—COMPARATIVE FINANCIAL STATEMENTS

I (we) have reviewed the accompanying balance sheet of XYZ Company as of December 31, 19x2, and 19x1, the related statements of income, retained earnings, and changes in financial position for the years then ended, in accordance with standards established by the American Institute of Certified Public Accountants. All information included in these financial statements is the representation of the management (owners) of XYZ Company.

A review consists principally of inquiries of company personnel and analytical procedures applied to financial data. It is substantially less in scope than an examination in accordance with generally accepted auditing standards, the objective of which is the expression of an opinion regarding the financial statements taken as a whole. Accordingly, I (we) do not express such an opinion.

Based on my (our) review, I am (we are) not aware of any material modifications that should be made to the accompanying financial statements in order for them to be in conformity with generally accepted accounting principles.

In my (our) previous review report dated March 1, 19x2, on the 19x1 financial statements, I (we) referred to a departure from generally accepted accounting principles because the company carried its land at appraised values. However, as disclosed in Note X, the company has restated its 19x1 financial statements to reflect its land in accordance with generally accepted accounting principles.

REVIEW REPORT ON CURRENT PERIOD AND REFERENCE TO COMPILATION REPORT ON PRIOR PERIOD—COMPARATIVE FINANCIAL STATEMENTS

I (we) have reviewed the accompanying balance sheet of XYZ Company as of December 31, 19x2, and the related statements of income, retained earnings, and changes in financial position for the year then ended, in accordance with standards established by the American Institute of Certified Public Accountants. All information included in these financial statements is the representation of the management (owners) of XYZ Company.

A review consists principally of inquiries of company personnel and analytical procedures applied to financial data. It is substantially less in scope than an examination in accordance with generally accepted auditing standards, the objective of which is the expression of an opinion regarding the financial statements taken as a whole. Accordingly, I (we) do not express such an opinion.

Based on my (our) review, I am (we are) not aware of any material modifications that should be made to the 19x2 financial statements in order for them to be in conformity with generally accepted accounting principles.

The accompanying 19x1 financial statements of XYZ Company were compiled by me (us). A compilation is limited to presenting in the form of financial statements information that is the representation of management (owners). I (we) have not audited or reviewed the 19x1 financial statements and, accordingly, do not express an opinion or any other form of assurance on them.

REVIEW EACH PERIOD— COMPARATIVE FINANCIAL STATEMENTS

I (we) have reviewed the accompanying balance sheet of XYZ Company as of December 31, 19x2 and 19x1, and the related statements of income, retained earnings, and changes in financial position for the years then ended, in accordance with standards established by the American Institute of Certified Public Accountants. All information included in these financial statements is the representation of management (owners) of XYZ Company.

A review consists principally of inquiries of company personnel and analytical procedures applied to financial data. It is substantially less in scope than an examination in accordance with generally accepted auditing standards, the objective of which is the expression of an opinion regarding the financial statements taken as a whole. Accordingly, I (we) do not express such an opinion.

Based on my (our) reviews, I am (we are) not aware of any material modifications that should be made to the accompanying financial state-

---

ments in order for them to be in conformity with generally accepted accounting principles.

REVIEW OF FINANCIAL STATEMENTS OF A NONPUBLIC ENTITY—STANDARD REPORT

I (we) have reviewed the accompanying balance sheet of XYZ Company as of December 31, 19xx, and the related statements of income, retained earnings, and changes in financial position for the years then ended, in accordance with standards established by the American Institute of Certified Public Accountants. All information included in these financial statements is the representation of the management (owners) of XYZ Company.

A review consists principally of inquiries of company personnel and analytical procedures applied to financial data. It is substantially less in scope than an examination in accordance with generally accepted auditing standards, the objective of which is the expression of an opinion; I (we) do not express such an opinion.

Based on my (our) review, I am (we are) not aware of any material modifications that should be made to the accompanying financial statements in order for them to be in conformity with generally accepted accounting principles.

DEPARTURE FROM GAAP—ACCOUNTING PRINCIPLE NOT GENERALLY ACCEPTED

I (we) have reviewed the accompanying balance sheet of XYZ Company as of December 31, 19xx, and the related statements of income, retained earnings, and changes in financial position for the years then ended, in accordance with standards established by the American Institute of Certified Public Accountants. All information included in these financial statements is the representation of the management (owners) of XYZ Company.

A review consists principally of inquiries of company personnel and analytical procedures applied to financial data. It is substantially less in scope than an examination in accordance with generally accepted auditing standards, the objective of which is the expression of an opinion regarding the financial statements taken as a whole. Accordingly, I (we) do not express such an opinion.

Based on my (our) review, with the exception of the matter described in the following paragraph, I am (we are) not aware of any material modifications that should be made to the accompanying financial statements in order for them to be in conformity with generally accepted accounting principles.

As disclosed in note X of the financial statements, generally accepted accounting principles require that inventory cost consist of material, labor, and overhead. Management has informed me (us) that the inventory of finished goods and work in process is stated in the accompanying financial statements at material and labor cost only, and that the effects of this departure from generally accepted accounting principles on financial position, results of operations, and changes in financial position have not been determined.

DEPARTURE FROM GAAP—CHANGE IN ACCOUNTING PRINCIPLE WITHOUT REASONABLE JUSTIFICATION

I (we) have reviewed the accompanying balance sheet of XYZ Company as of December 31, 19xx, and the related statements of income, retained earnings, and changes in financial position for the years then ended, in accordance with standards established by the American Institute of Certified Public Accountants. All information included in these financial statements is the representation of the management (owners) of XYZ Company.

A review consists principally of inquiries of company personnel and analytical procedures applied to financial data. It is substantially less in scope than an examination in accordance with generally accepted auditing standards, the objective of which is the expression of an opinion regarding the financial statements taken as a whole. Accordingly, I (we) do not express such an opinion.

Based on my (our) review, with the exception of the matter described in the following paragraph, I am (we are) not aware of any material modifications that should be made to the accompanying financial statements in order for them to be in conformity with generally accepted accounting principles.

As disclosed in Note X to the financial statements, the company has adopted (description of newly adopted method), whereas it previously used (description of previous method). Although the (description of newly adoped method) is in conformity with generally accepted accounting principles, the company does not appear to have reasonable justification for making a change as required by Opinion No. 20 of the Accounting Principles Board.

DEPARTURE FROM GAAP—OMISSION OF STATEMENT OF CHANGES IN FINANCIAL POSITION

I (we) have reviewed the accompanying balance sheet of XYZ Company as of December 31, 19xx, and the related statements of income, and retained earnings, for the year then ended, in accordance with standards established by the American Institute of Certified Public Accountants. All information included in these financial statements is the representation of the management (owners) of XYZ Company.

A review consists principally of inquiries of company personnel and analytical procedures applied to financial data. It is substantially less in scope than an examination in accordance with generally accepted auditing standards, the objective of which is the expression of an opinion regarding the financial statements taken as a whole. Accordingly, I (we) do not express such an opinion.

Based on my (our) review, with the exception of the matter described in the following paragraph, I am (we are) not aware of any material modifications that should be made to the accompanying financial statements in order for them to be in conformity with generally accepted accounting principles.

A statement of changes in financial position for the year ended December 31, 19xx, has not been presented. Generally accepted accounting principles require that such a statement be presented when financial statements purport to present financial position and results of operations.

CASH BASIS STATEMENTS

I (we) have reviewed the accompanying statement of assets and liabilities arising from cash transactions of XYZ Company as of December 31, 19xx,

---

and the related statement of revenue collected and expenses paid for the year ended, in accordance with standards established by the American Institute of Certified Public Accountants. All information included in these financial statements is the representation of the management (owners) of XYZ Company.

A review consists principally of inquiries of company personnel and analytical procedures applied to financial data. It is substantially less in scope than an examination in accordance with generally accepted auditing standards, the objective of which is the expression of an opinion regarding the financial statements taken as a whole. Accordingly, I (we) do not express such an opinion.

As described in Note X, the Company's policy is to prepare its financial statements on the basis of cash receipts and disbursements; consequently, certain revenue and the related assets are recognized when received rather than when earned, and certain expenses are recognized when paid rather than when the obligation is incurred. Accordingly, the accompanying financial statements are not intended to present financial position and results of operations in conformity with generally accepted accounting principles.

Based on my (our) review, I am (we are) not aware of any material modifications that should be made to the accompanying financial statements in order for them to be in conformity with the basis of accounting described in Note X.

INCOME TAX BASIS STATEMENTS

I (we) have reviewed the accompanying statement of assets, liabilities, and capital—income tax basis of XYZ Company as of December 31, 19xx and the related statements of revenue and expenses—income tax basis, and of changes in assets, liabilities, and capital—income tax basis, for the year then ended, in accordance with standards established by the American Institute of Certified Public Accountants. All information included in these financial statements is the representation of the management (owners) of XYZ Company.

A review consists principally of inquiries of company personnel and analytical procedures applied to financial data. It is substantially less in scope than an examination in accordance with generally accepted auditing standards, the objective of which is the expression of an opinion regarding the financial statements taken as a whole. Accordingly, I (we) do not express such an opinion.

As described in Note X, the Company's policy is to prepare its financial statements on the accounting basis used for income tax purposes; consequently, certain revenue and the related assets are recognized when received rather than when earned, and certain expenses are recognized when paid rather than when the obligation is incurred. Accordingly, the accompanying financial statements are not intended to present financial position and results of operations in conformity with generally accepted accounting principles.

Based on my (our) review, I am (we are) not aware of any material modifications that should be made to the accompanying financial statements in order for them to be in conformity with the basis of accounting described in Note X.

SIXTEEN COMPILATION REPORTS

COMPILATION OF FINANCIAL STATEMENTS OF A NONPUBLIC ENTITY—STANDARD REPORT

The accompanying balance sheet of XYZ Company as of December 31, 19xx, and the related statements of income, retained earnings, and changes in financial position for the year then ended have been compiled by me (us).

A compilation is limited to presenting in the form of financial statements information that is the representation of management (owners). I (we) have not audited or reviewed the accompanying financial statements and, accordingly, do not express an opinion or any other form of assurance on them.

OMISSION OF SUBSTANTIALLY ALL DISCLOSURES

The accompanying balance sheet of XYZ Company as of December 31, 19xx, and the related statements of income, retained earnings, and changes in financial position for the year then ended have been compiled by me (us).

A compilation is limited to presenting in the form of financial statements information that is the representation of management (owners). I (we) have not audited or reviewed the accompanying financial statements and, accordingly, do not express an opinion or any other form of assurance on them.

Management has elected to omit substantially all of the disclosures required by generally accepted accounting principles. If the omitted disclosures were included in the financial statements, they might influence the user's conclusions about the company's financial position, results of operations, and changes in financial position. Accordingly, these financial statements are not designed for those who are not informed about such matters.

OMISSION OF STATEMENT OF FINANCIAL POSITION AND SUBSTANTIALLY ALL DISCLOSURES

The accompanying balance sheet of XYZ Company as of December 31, 19xx, and the related statements of income and retained earnings for the year then ended have been compiled by me (us).

A compilation is limited to presenting in the form of financial statements information that is the representation of management (owners). I (we) have not audited or reviewed the accompanying financial statements and, accordingly, do not express an opinion or any other form of assurance on them.

Management has elected to omit substantially all of the disclosures and the statement of changes in financial position required by generally accepted accounting principles. If the omitted disclosures and the statement of changes in financial position were included in the financial statements, they might influence the user's conclusions about the company's financial position, results of operations, and changes in financial position. Accordingly, these financial statements are not designed for those who are not informed about such matters.

DEPARTURE FROM GAAP—OMISSION OF STATEMENT OF CHANGES IN FINANCIAL POSITION

The accompanying balance sheet of XYZ Company as of December 31, 19xx, and the related statements of income and retained earnings for the year then ended have been compiled by me (us).

A compilation is limited to presenting in the form of financial statements information that is the representation of management (owners). I (we) have not audited or reviewed the accompanying financial statements and, accordingly, do not express an opinion or any other form of assurance on them. However, I (we) did become aware of a departure from generally accepted accounting principles that is described in the following paragraph.

A statement of changes in financial position for the year ended December 31, 19xx, has not been presented. Generally accepted accounting principles require that such a statement be presented when financial statements purport to present financial position and results of operations.

DEPARTURE FROM GAAP—ACCOUNTING PRINCIPLES NOT GENERALLY ACCEPTED

The accompanying balance sheet of XYZ Company as of December 31, 19xx, and the related statements of income, retained earnings, and changes in financial position for the year then ended have been compiled by me (us).

A compilation is limited to presenting in the form of financial statements information that is the representation of management (owners). I (we) have not audited or reviewed the accompanying financial statements and, accordingly, do not express an opinion or any other form of assurance on them. However, I (we) did become aware of a departure (certain departures) from generally accepted accounting principles that is (are) described in the following paragraph.

As disclosed in Note X to the financial statements, generally accepted accounting principles require that land be stated at cost. Management has informed me (us) that the company has stated its land at appraised value and that, if generally accepted accounting principles had been followed, the land account and stockholders' equity would have been decreased by $500,000.

CASH BASIS STATEMENTS

The accompanying statement of assets and liabilities arising from cash transactions of XYZ Company as of December 31, 19xx, and the related statement of revenue collected and expenses paid for the year then ended have been compiled by me (us).

A compilation is limited to presenting in the form of financial statements information that is the representation of management (owners). I (we) have not audited or reviewed the accompanying financial statements and, accordingly, do not express an opinion or any other form of assurance on them.

The Company's policy is to prepare its financial statements on the basis of cash receipts and disbursements; consequently, certain revenue and

---

the related assets are recognized when received rather than when earned, and certain expenses are recognized when paid rather than when the obligation is incurred. Accordingly, the accompanying financial statements are not intended to present financial position and results of operations in conformity with generally accepted accounting principles.

CASH BASIS STATEMENTS—OMISSION OF SUBSTANTIALLY ALL DISCLOSURES

The accompanying statement of assets and liabilities arising from cash transactions of XYZ Company as of December 31, 19xx, and the related statement of revenue collected and expenses paid for the year then ended have been compiled by me (us).

A compilation is limited to presenting in the form of financial statements information that is the representation of management (owners). I (we) have not audited or reviewed the accompanying financial statements and, accordingly, do not express an opinion or any other form of assurance on them.

The Company's policy is to prepare its financial statements on the basis of cash receipts and disbursements; consequently, certain revenue and the related assets are recognized when received rather than when earned, and certain expenses are recognized when paid rather than when the obligation is incurred. Accordingly, the accompanying financial statements are not intended to present financial position and results of operations in conformity with generally accepted accounting principles.

Management has elected to omit substantially all of the informative disclosures ordinarily included in financial statements. If the omitted disclosures were included in the financial statements, they might influence the user's conclusions about the Company's assets, liabilities, capital, revenue, and expenses. Accordingly, these financial statements are not designed for those who are not informed about such matters.

INCOME TAX BASIS STATEMENTS

The accompanying statement of assets, liabilities, and capital—income tax basis of ABC Partnership as of December 31, 19xx, and the related

---

statements of revenue and expenses—income tax basis, and of changes in partners' capital accounts—income tax basis for the year then ended have been compiled by me (us).

A compilation is limited to presenting in the form of financial statements information that is the representation of management (owners). I (we) have not audited or reviewed the accompanying financial statements and, accordingly, do not express an opinion or any other form of assurance on them.

The partnership's policy is to prepare its financial statements on the accounting basis used for income tax purposes; consequently, certain revenue and related assets are recognized when received rather than when earned, and certain expenses are recognized when paid rather than when the obligation is incurred. Accordingly, the accompanying financial statements are not intended to present financial position and results of operations in conformity with generally accepted accounting principles.

INCOME TAX BASIS STATEMENTS—OMISSION OF SUBSTANTIALLY ALL DISCLOSURES

The accompanying statement of assets, liabilities, and capital—income tax basis of ABC Partnership as of December 31, 19xx, and the related statements of revenue and expenses—income tax basis, and of changes in partners' capital accounts—income tax basis for the year then ended have been compiled by me (us).

A compilation is limited to presenting in the form of financial statements information that is the representation of management (owners). I (we) have not audited or reviewed the accompanying financial statements and, accordingly, do not express an opinion or any other form of assurance on them.

The partnership's policy is to prepare its financial statements on the accounting basis used for income tax purposes; consequently, certain revenue and the related assets are recognized when received rather than when earned, and certain expenses are recognized when paid rather than when the obligation is incurred. Accordingly, the accompanying financial statements are not intended to present financial position and results of operations in conformity with generally accepted accounting principles.

Management has elected to omit substantially all of the information disclosures ordinarily included in financial statements. If the omitted disclosures were included in the financial statements, they might influence the user's conclusions about the partnership's assets, liabilities, capital, revenue, and expenses. Accordingly, these financial statements are not designed for those who are not informed about such matters.

COMPILATION EACH PERIOD—COMPARATIVE FINANCIAL STATEMENTS

The accompanying balance sheets of XYZ Company as of December 31, 19x2 and 19x1, and the related statements of income, retained earnings, and changes in financial position for the years then ended have been compiled by me (us).

A compilation is limited to presenting in the form of financial statements information that is the representation of management (owners). I (we) have not audited or reviewed the accompanying financial statements and, accordingly, do not express an opinion or any other form of assurance on them.

COMPILATION REPORT ON CURRENT PERIOD AND REFERENCE TO REVIEW REPORT ON PRIOR PERIOD—COMPARATIVE FINANCIAL STATEMENTS

The accompanying balance sheet of XYZ Company as of December 31, 19x2, and the related statements of income, retained earnings, and changes in financial position for the year then ended have been compiled by me (us).

A compilation is limited to presenting in the form of financial statements information that is the representation of management (owners). I (we) have not audited or reviewed the accompanying 19x2 financial statements and, accordingly, do not express an opinion or any other form of assurance on them.

The accompanying 19x1 financial statements of XYZ Company were previously reviewed by me (us), and my (our) report dated March 1, 19x2, stated that I was (we were) not aware of any material modifications that

---

should be made to those statements in order for them to be in conformity with generally accepted accounting principles. I (we) have not performed any procedures in connection with that review engagement after the date of my (our) report on the 19x1 financial statements.

CHANGED REFERENCE TO A DEPARTURE FROM GENERALLY ACCEPTED ACCOUNTING PRINCIPLES—COMPARATIVE FINANCIAL STATEMENTS

The accompanying balance sheets of XYZ Company as of December 31, 19x2 and 19x1, and the related statements of income, retained earnings, and changes in financial position for the years then ended have been compiled by me (us).

A compilation is limited to presenting in the form of financial statements information that is the representation of management (owners). I (we) have not audited or reviewed the accompanying financial statements and, accordingly, do not express an opinion or any other form of assurance on them.

In my (our) previous compilation report dated March 1, 19x2, on the 19x1 financial statements, I (we) referred to a departure from generally accepted accounting principles because the company carried its land at appraised values. However, as disclosed in Note X, the company has restated its 19x1 financial statements to reflect its land at cost in accordance with generally accepted accounting principles.

PREDECESSOR'S COMPILATION REPORT ON PRIOR PERIOD NOT PRESENTED—COMPARATIVE FINANCIAL STATEMENTS

The accompanying balance sheet of XYZ Company as of December 31, 19x2, and the related statements of income, retained earnings, and changes in financial position for the year then ended have been compiled by me (us).

A compilation is limited to presenting in the form of financial statements information that is the representation of management (owners). I (we) have not audited or reviewed the accompanying 19x2 financial statements and, accordingly, do not express an opinion or any other form of assurance on them.

The 19x1 financial statements of XYZ Company were compiled by other accountants whose report dated February 1, 19x2, stated that they did not express an opinion or any other form of assurance on those statements.

PREDECESSOR'S REVIEW REPORT ON PRIOR PERIOD NOT PRESENTED—COMPARATIVE FINANCIAL STATEMENTS

The accompanying balance sheet of XYZ Company as of December 31, 19x2, and the related statements of income, retained earnings, and changes in financial position for the year then ended have been compiled by me (us).

A compilation is limited to presenting in the form of financial statements information that is the representation of management (owners). I (we) have not audited or reviewed the accompanying 19x2 financial statements and, accordingly, do not express an opinion or any other form of assurance on them.

The 19x1 financial statements of XYZ Company were reviewed by other accountants whose report dated March 1, 19x2, stated that they were not aware of any material modifications that should be made to those statements in order for them to be in conformity with generally accepted accounting principles.

OMISSION OF SUBSTANTIALLY ALL DISCLOSURES INCLUDING THOSE FOR PRIOR PERIOD PREVIOUSLY NOT OMITTED—COMPARATIVE FINANCIAL STATEMENTS

The accompanying balance sheets of XYZ Company as of December 31, 19x2 and 19x1, and the related statements of income, retained earnings, and changes in financial position for the years then ended have been compiled by me (us).

A compilation is limited to presenting in the form of financial statements information that is the representation of management (owners). I (we)

---

have not audited or reviewed the accompanying financial statements and, accordingly, do not express an opinion or any other form of assurance on them.

Management has elected to omit substantially all of the disclosures required by generally accepted accounting principles. If the omitted disclosures were included in the financial statements, they might influence the user's conclusions about the company's financial position, results of operations, and changes in financial position. Accordingly, these financial statements are not designed for those who are not informed about such matters.

The accompanying 19x1 financial statements were compiled by me (us) from financial statements that did not omit substantially all of the disclosures required by generally accepted accounting principles and that I (we) previously compiled (reviewed) as indicated in my (our) report dated March 1, 19x2.

PRIOR PERIOD AUDITED—COMPARATIVE FINANCIAL STATEMENTS

The accompanying balance sheet of XYZ Company as of December 31, 19x2, and the related statements of income, retained earnings, and changes in financial position for the year then ended have been compiled by me (us).

A compilation is limited to presenting in the form of financial statements information that is the representation of management (owners). I (we) have not audited or reviewed the accompanying 19x2 financial statements and, accordingly, do not express an opinion or any other form of assurance on them.

The financial statements for the year ended December 31, 19x1, were examined by me (us) (other accountants) and I (we) (they) expressed an unqualified opinion on them in my (our) (their) report dated March 1, 19x2, but I (we) (they) have not performed any auditing procedures since that date.

SEVEN SPECIAL REPORTS

CASH BASIS STATEMENTS

We have examined the statement of assets and liabilities arising from cash transactions of XYZ Company as of December 31, 19xx, and the related statement of revenue collected and expenses paid for the year then ended. Our examination was made in accordance with generally accepted auditing standards and, accordingly, included such tests of the accounting records and such other auditing procedures as we considered necessary in the circumstances.

As described in Note X, the Company's policy is to prepare its financial statements on the basis of cash receipts and disbursements; consequently, certain revenue and the related assets are recognized when received rather than when earned, and certain expenses are recognized when paid rather than when the obligation is incurred. Accordingly, the accompanying financial statements are not intended to present financial position and results of operations in conformity with generally accepted accounting principles.

In our opinion, the financial statements referred to above present fairly the assets and liabilities arising from cash transactions of XYZ Company as of December 31, 19xx, and the revenue collected and expenses paid during the year then ended, on the basis of accounting described in Note X, which basis has been applied in a manner consistent with that of the preceding year.

INCOME TAX BASIS STATEMENTS

We have examined the statement of assets, liabilities, and capital—income tax basis of ABC Partnership as of December 31, 19xx, and the related statements of revenue and expenses—income tax basis, and of changes in partners' capital accounts—income tax basis for the year then ended. Our examination was made in accordance with generally accepted auditing standards and, accordingly, included such tests of the accounting records and such other auditing procedures as we considered necessary in the circumstances.

As described in Note X, the partnership's policy is to prepare its financial statements on the accounting basis used for income tax purposes; consequently, certain revenue and the related assets are recognized when received rather than when earned, and certain expenses are recognized when paid rather than when the obligation is incurred. Accordingly, the accompanying financial statements are not intended to present financial position and results of operations in conformity with generally accepted accounting principles.

In our opinion, the financial statements referred to above present fairly the assets, liabilities, and capital of ABC Partnership as of December 31, 19xx, and its revenue and expenses and changes in its partners' capital accounts for the year then ended, on the basis of accounting described in Note X, which basis has been applied in a manner consistent with that of the preceding year.

ROYALTIES

Board of Directors
XYZ Company

We have examined the schedule of royalties applicable to engine production of the Q Division of XYZ Company for the year ended December 31, 19xx, under the terms of a license agreement dated May 14, 19xx, between ABC Company and XYZ Corporation. Our examination was made in accordance with generally accepted auditing standards and, accordingly, included such tests of the accounting records and such other auditing procedures as we considered necessary in the circumstances.

We have been informed that, under XYZ Corporation's interpretation of the agreement referred to above, royalties were based on the number of engines produced after giving effect to a reduction for production retirements that were scrapped, but without a reduction for field returns that were scrapped, even though the field returns were replaced with new engines without charge to customers. This treatment is consistent with that followed in prior years.

In our opinion, the schedule of royalties referred to above presents fairly the number of engines produced by the Q Division of XYZ Corporation during the year ended December 31, 19xx, and the amount of royalties

---

applicable thereto under the license agreements referred to above, on the basis indicated in the preceding paragraph.

PROFIT PARTICIPATION

Mr. John Smith

We have examined XYZ Company's schedule of John Smith's profit participation for the year ended December 31, 19x1. Our examination was made in accordance with generally accepted auditing standards and, accordingly, included such tests of the accounting records and such other auditing procedures as we considered necessary in the circumstances. We have examined the financial statements of XYZ Company for the year ended December 31, 19x1, and have issued our report thereon dated March 10, 19x2.

We have been informed that the documents that govern the determination of John Smith's profit participation are (a) the employment agreement between John Smith and XYZ Company dated February 1, 19x0, (b) the production and distribution agreement between XYZ Company and Television Network Incorporated dated March 1, 19x0, and (c) the studio facilities agreement between XYZ Company and QRX Studios dated April 1, 19x0, as amended November 1, 19x0.

In our opinion, the schedule of profit participation referred to above presents fairly John Smith's participation in the profits of XYZ Company for the year ended December 31, 19x1, in accordance with the provisions of the agreements referred to in the preceding paragraph.

COMPLIANCE WITH CONTRACTUAL PROVISIONS (SEPARATE REPORT)—NEGATIVE ASSURANCE

We have examined the balance sheet of XYZ Company as of December 31, 19x1, and the related statements of income, retained earnings, and changes in financial position for the year then ended, and have issued our report thereon dated February 16, 19x2. Our examination was made in accordance with generally accepted auditing standards and, accordingly, included such tests of the accounting records and such other auditing procedures as we considered necessary in the circumstances.

In connection with our examination, nothing came to our attention that caused us to believe that the Company was not in compliance with any of the terms, covenants, provisions, or conditions of sections XX to XX, inclusive, of the indenture dated July 21, 19x0, with ABC Bank. However, it should be noted that our examination was not directed primarily toward obtaining knowledge of such noncompliance.

COMPLIANCE WITH CONTRACTUAL PROVISIONS (AUDITOR'S REPORT ACCOMPANYING FINANCIAL STATEMENTS)—NEGATIVE ASSURANCE

We have examined the balance sheet of XYZ Company as of December 31, 19x1, and the related statements of income, retained earnings, and changes in financial position for the year then ended. Our examination was made in accordance with generally accepted auditing standards and, accordingly, included such tests of the accounting records and such other auditing procedures as we considered necessary in the circumstances.

In our opinion, the financial statements referred to above present fairly the financial position of XYZ Company as of December 3, 19x1, and the results of its operations and changes in its financial position for the year then ended, in conformity with generally accepted accounting principles applied on a basis consistent with that of the preceding year.

In connection with our examination, nothing came to our attention that caused us to believe that the Company was not in compliance with any of the terms, covenants, provisions, or conditions of sections XX to XX, inclusive, of the indenture dated July 21, 19x0, with ABC Bank. However, it should be noted that our examination was not directed primarily toward obtaining knowledge of such noncompliance.

COMPLIANCE WITH REGULATORY REQUIREMENTS —NEGATIVE ASSURANCE

We have examined the balance sheet of XYZ Company as of December 31, 19x1, and the related statements of income, retained earnings, and changes in financial position for the year then ended, and have issued

---

our report thereon dated March 5, 19x2. Our examination was made in accordance with generally accepted auditing standards and, accordingly, included such tests of the accounting records and such other auditing procedures as we considered necessary in the circumstances.

In connection with our examination, nothing came to our attention that caused us to believe that the Company had failed to comply with the limitation and increased investment requirement in section 993(d) (2) and (3) of the Internal Revenue Code of 1954. However, it should be noted that our examination was not directed primarily toward obtaining knowledge of noncompliance with such requirements.

PART III

LETTERS OF RECOMMENDATION TO MANAGEMENT

CHAPTER 7

Client-Centered Letters of Recommendation

- Basic Introductory Paragraph
- Expanded Introduction
- General Management Letter
- Brief Business Advisory Letter
- Organization and Facilities
  - —Sufficiency of Working Capital
  - —Needed Improvement in Organizational Structure
  - —Developing an Up-to-Date Organizational Chart
  - —Need for Written Job Descriptions and Reviews
  - —Adjusting Organizational Structure for Future Growth
  - —Competitive Need to Automate Operations
  - —Providing for Adequate Record Storage
- Personnel and Payroll
  - —Need for Formal Personnel Records
  - —Summary of Travel Expenses
  - —Effective Control over Vacation and Sick Pay
  - —Reason for Annual Vacation Policy
  - —Keeping Exemption Forms (W-4) for All Employees
  - —Signed Authorizations for Payroll Deductions

- **Budgeting and Forecasting**
  - —Necessity for Long-range Planning
  - —Budgeting to Control Costs and Expenses
  - —Forecasting and Budgeting to Improve Profits
  - —Using Current Rates to Measure Operations
  - —Monthly Preparation of Balance Sheets
- **Cash Receipts and Disbursements**
  - —Need for Written Procedures Manual
  - —Separation of Duties in Processing Cash Receipts
  - —Achieving Maximum Control over Cash Receipts
  - —Need for Supporting Vouchers
  - —Necessity for Clear-cut Invoice Cancellation
  - —Using Manual Signatures on Checks
  - —Security Requirements for Check-writing Materials
  - —Documents to Be Prenumbered and Accounted For

The letter that accompanies a formal audit report and contains suggestions to management for improving procedures, operations, and controls is sometimes called a *management letter,* sometimes a *business advisory letter,* sometimes a *letter of recommendation.* In this book the terms are used interchangeably.

A management letter is essentially a report addressed to the chief executive of a company. It brings to the attention of management whatever significant matters were noted in the audit procedure. It also makes recommendations for action. The management letter is a carefully prepared analysis of problems, concentrating on topics within the firm's area of expertise—accounting, auditing, tax, management.

The writer of a management letter must first identify present and potential problem areas within the company; then assemble the information needed to document them; and finally, present the information in an understandable way, proposing improvements in each instance, based on experience.

A management letter, if it is to be useful, must be client-centered. It must recognize the needs and difficulties facing management and be responsive to them. If the time and cost of implementing certain improvements are too high—however desirable the improvements are—it must point out that fact.

The chapter begins with two model introductions to management letters. An introduction is important, because a management letter has to bridge the gap from the audit report itself to the accompanying recommendations. The chapter then presents parts of two complete letters, primarily to show format. After that—in both this chapter and in the next one—there are a great many model paragraphs dealing with specific, recurring problems that auditors notice. The collection of paragraphs is extensive but not exhaustive. You should find some paragraphs that will fit directly into your own letters. Others you will have to adapt. The paragraphs are grouped into broad categories for ease of access and use.

BASIC INTRODUCTORY PARAGRAPH

During our regular examination of the financial statements of [name of company] for the period ended [date], we reviewed the company's accounting procedures and system of internal control. Our primary purpose in making the examination was to enable us to form an opinion concerning the company's accounts. Consequently, we would not necessarily discover all weaknesses that might exist in the system. Our examination did reveal the following areas, however, where we believe significant improvements could be made.

EXPANDED INTRODUCTION

Our examination of your financial statements for the year ended [date] revealed various weaknesses in your accounting procedures and internal controls, as well as certain other problems relating to your operations and personnel.

We have already discussed our observations with you, and we know that in some cases you have taken the needed corrective measures. Nevertheless, since each of the problems noted requires management review and evaluation, we are presenting this written summary.

As you know, our examination was conducted mainly to enable us to express an opinion on the financial statements of [name of company], and accordingly would not necessarily disclose all weaknesses that may exist.

This letter includes only comments of major importance on which no action has so far been taken.

GENERAL MANAGEMENT LETTER

The main reason for including this letter is to show an appropriate format for a complete letter of recommendation. Since the introduction used here varies from the preceding two, this letter also offers an alternate way to begin.

YOUR LETTERHEAD

[Date]

INSIDE ADDRESS

[Salutation]:

In connection with our examination of the financial statements of [name of company] for the year ended [date], we made a thorough study of your accounting procedures and system of internal controls. In addition, we observed your company's organization, policies, and operating methods.

As a result of this examination, we would like to present a number of recommendations for consideration by management. These suggestions are based primarily on the work done during our audit engagement, and we do not wish to imply that they cover every possible weakness. Nevertheless, we do think that they deserve your careful evaluation.

1. *Separation of Financial Duties.* At the present time [name of employee] is in charge of every stage of nearly every financial transaction. [She/He] handles cash receipts, makes bank deposits, approves purchase orders, and posts the general ledger. Good internal control requires that no one person be assigned all these duties. We recommend that certain of [name of employee]'s duties be reassigned to other available personnel.

2. *Prompt reconciliation of bank accounts.* We noted that the company's bank accounts are not being reconciled promptly. It is important to make prompt reconciliation in order to discover any clerical errors involving cash transactions or any misuse of funds. As indicated above, this reconciliation should be performed by personnel not involved in handling cash receipts or cash disbursements.

[other numbered paragraphs as needed]

If you or other members of your management team have any questions concerning these recommendations, we would welcome the opportunity to discuss them with you.

[Closing],

____

YOUR SIGNATURE

____

BRIEF BUSINESS ADVISORY LETTER

Here is another general letter of recommendation.

YOUR LETTERHEAD

[Date]

INSIDE ADDRESS

[Salutation]:

During our audit, we discovered some areas that merit your attention.

CASH MANAGEMENT

The average daily bank balance was extremely high; in excess of $140,000 over the last six months of the year. Because of this, the company has considerable cash sitting idle.

We recommend that you discuss the cash position with your banker and develop a means of transferring idle cash from checking to savings; transfers often can be accomplished by a phone call. Also, you should determine the amount of "float" to manage cash even better. This can be accomplished by noting the dates you mail checks and comparing them to the clearing dates on the bank statements. Large payments to [name of company], for instance, may give you a one-week float.

Implementation of our suggestions will take some time on your part. However, there is a tremendous benefit to be gained. The company could pay for most of our audit fee from the interest it earns.

EMPLOYEE STOCK OWNERSHIP PLAN

We briefly discussed with you the possibility of setting up an employee stock ownership plan (ESOP). There are numerous tax advantages available to both the seller and the management people acquiring the stock. If you are interested in pursuing this, we would be pleased to have someone from our tax department discuss the various alternatives. This is one of the few areas in which both the seller and the buyer can obtain real benefits.

BARTER CREDITS

The company has approximately $100,000 in barter credits remaining. When using the credits, it is imperative to determine the fair market values of the assets you receive. If you acquire an asset from a company that has published list prices, it is fairly easy to determine its value. But if you acquire land or used equipment from a nondealer, for example, the value might be more difficult to determine. If the value is not readily determinable, you might need to have the asset appraised to determine its worth.

MANAGEMENT PLAN

The company experienced a significant increase in volume this past year. If you anticipate future increases, plans should be developed to handle the additional volume. Plant capacity, availability of low-cost labor, along with marketing and administrative matters should be considered. We suggest that you work with key personnel to develop a business strategy that considers both short- and long-term goals and objectives. Part of this planning would include reviewing the labor force and cost of plant expansion.

If you are interested in developing a plan, we can provide you with an outline of how to start the process and some key factors to analyze. We also have professionals in this area who would be pleased to work with you.

Companies are developing budgets and forecasts with greater frequency. We have worked with several clients in preparing monthly budgets for cash flow. Microcomputer technology makes the job relatively easy. The ability to forecast accurately has assisted these clients in managing their companies better.

We hope to have a long-lasting relationship with you and your organization. Should you wish to discuss the services we can provide in these or other areas, please call me.

[Closing],

____

YOUR SIGNATURE

____

ORGANIZATION AND FACILITIES

Sufficiency of Working Capital

As a result of our audit of your financial statements for the year ended December 31, 19x7, we would like to offer certain suggestions concerning the status of your working capital. Clearly, the corporation has been operating with too little working capital. It is essential that effective long-range plans be made to ensure that the corporation has a sufficient amount of working capital on hand in the future. One important point to keep in mind is this: Avoid becoming so involved in the technical definition of working capital (current assets minus current liabilities) that you forget that the most effective form of working capital is still cash in the bank.

As you know, one basic uncertainty in any effort to maintain a satisfactory working capital is how much to provide for federal income taxes. Your company will face this problem when your planning includes preparing month-end projected and actual financial statements, with your estimated tax liability being increased or decreased by the tax on the net profit or loss of each month. There are various ways to determine this tax liability, and I am enclosing a copy of an article in last month's [name of magazine] that summarizes them very well.

Needed Improvement in Organizational Structure

Our examination indicated that the responsibilities of office personnel were not clearly defined. Improvement will be necessary if there is to be a smooth flow of work and adequate internal control. We recommend the preparation of an up-to-date organizational chart and a set of written procedures to portray individual responsibilities accurately and to show reporting relationships.

Developing an Up-to-Date Organizational Chart

Efficient operating performance depends to a large extent upon a well-structured organization. An organizational chart, accompanied by clearly defined responsibilities for management, spells out reporting and operating requirements and helps ensure that each person fully understands his or her duties. We recommend that [name of company] develop an up-to-date organizational chart with adequately defined responsibilities.

Need for Written Job Descriptions and Reviews

Current personnel policies were developed at a time when the company was much smaller and the interaction of employees was relatively informal. In view of the changed nature of the company, we suggest that certain specific guidelines be prepared.

For all salaried positions, we recommend that you (a) define job responsibilites and issue written job descriptions, (b) specify individual standards and performance goals, and (c) on an annual basis, review individual performance against those standards and goals.

In our judgment, the best way to accomplish the first two matters is to have each superior and subordinate work together on them. In this way there is agreement that the responsibilities are appropriate, the job descriptions are accurate, and the standards and goals are attainable.

Adjusting Organizational Structure for Future Growth

The organizational structure of [name of company] has not kept pace with the growth of the company. We recommend that you study your existing organizational structure with an eye toward accommodating future growth. At the same time, you should try to reduce the amount of officer involvement in routine matters. This will provide officers with more time than they now have to define company goals and make plans for meeting them.

A new organizational chart will be needed. Job responsibilities and reporting channels must be clearly defined. The chart should be designed to eliminate overlapping responsibilities and duplication of effort and, consequently, to avoid confusion among executives and supervisors.

Competitive Need to Automate Operations

Over the past year there seems to have been little improvement in plant operations. Outdated machinery and lack of automated equipment appear to be principal causes of this. While competitors—particularly those overseas—have made rapid strides in plant automation, [name of company] has relied on trying to increase individual employee productivity. That has worked to some extent, but it has not allowed the company to keep pace with its competition. We recommend that management seriously consider increased plant automation, even if the initial cost seems high in comparison with the salaries of the current work force.

Providing for Adequate Record Storage

A number of record-storing inadequacies came to our attention during the examination:

1. In our tests of the perpetual inventory records, we failed to locate those from September 19x5.
2. General ledgers, journal entry books, and other records are not clearly marked.
3. The record-storage area is cluttered, with records stacked on top of (or in front of) other records.

Quite apart from the unbusinesslike appearance of the area, we found it time-consuming and frustrating to locate records. We recommend that the record-storage area be cleaned, organized, and maintained efficiently, with all records clearly marked and easily accessible.

PERSONNEL AND PAYROLL

Need for Formal Personnel Records

The company does not maintain formal personnel records on its employees. We recommend that such records be developed and maintained. They are a valuable information source that serve a variety of purposes, including:

- Making salary adjustments
- Determining employee eligibility for the retirement plan
- Notifying next of kin in an emergency
- Answering questions that relate to an employee

We suggest that the five items listed below should be included in each employee's personnel file.

1. Completed job application form
2. Form or card containing the following basic employee information:
   a. Full name
   b. Date of birth
   c. Date of original employment
   d. Home address
   e. Home telephone number
   f. Person to contact in case of emergency
3. Current, signed W-4 tax withholding form
4. Form or forms authorizing specific payroll deductions
5. Current salary authorization form indicating effective date of most recent salary adjustment

Summary of Travel Expenses

During our recent examination of your financial statements, we discovered that your procedures in regard to travel and entertainment expenses need to be improved. Specifically, we recommend that employees' expense reports be accompanied by supporting documentary evidence of disbursements, whenever possible. These documents include hotel receipts, transportation ticket stubs, restaurant receipts of $25 or more, and other paid bills.

We further recommend that the accounting department prepare a monthly report summarizing for each employee the total amount of his or her travel, entertainment, and other reimbursable expenses, together with those expenses paid directly by the corporation. The summary should be presented to the respective employees for their approval and then submitted to the appropriate senior departmental administrative officer for review. These summaries should then be submitted to the treasurer.

Effective Control over Vacation and Sick Pay

Current procedures provide no accurate way to control the amount of vacation pay and sick pay that salaried employees receive. We suggest that new payroll reporting procedures be developed, requiring all vacation and sick days to be noted. A cumulative record of this information should also be kept.

Reason for Annual Vacation Policy

We understand that some employees have been in the habit of not taking annual vacations. As a part of good internal control, you should insist that all personnel in positions of trust take regular annual vacations. While these employees are away on vacation, their duties should be delegated to other employees. This policy of mandatory annual vacations should be strictly enforced.

Keeping Exemption Forms (W-4) for All Employees

We were unable to find the exemption certificates (W-4) for some employees. Your payroll records should be reviewed, and adequate documentation should be provided for all payroll deductions.

Signed Authorizations for Payroll Deductions

Company policy requires that all authorizations for payroll deductions be maintained in employee personnel files. We could not find some of these signed forms. Moreover, in a few instances the number of exemptions indicated on the forms did not agree with the number of exemptions being used to figure withholding taxes. We recommend a thorough review of the personnel files to ensure that all signed authorizations for deductions exist and are up-to-date.

BUDGETING AND FORECASTING

Necessity for Long-range Planning

Although [name of company] controls current operations by means of a budget, there is no formal long-range planning. It is easy for a company to overlook long-range planning because of the pressures of immediate concerns. Yet long-range planning, the process by which a company defines its objectives and formulates plans and policies for reaching these objectives, is as important a management tool as budgeting.

We suggest that management prepare a five-year forecast of sales and expenses. In doing so, you will (a) establish goals, (b) analyze the company's present markets and try to anticipate and react to changes in these markets, (c) identify attractive new markets, and (d) prepare research and development objectives, including an estimate of cost and likely benefits for each objective.

Along with the operating forecast of sales and expenses, you should develop a five-year cash-flow forecast to plan your borrowing requirements or the investment of surplus cash.

Budgeting to Control Costs and Expenses

Up to now the company has not used budgets to help control costs and expenses. Since the budgeting process forces the individuals responsible for expenditures to justify those expenditures, it is one of the best ways of keeping costs under control. More efficient use of capital results when managers forecast minimum cash requirements. We recommend that a system of budgeting be instituted for the purpose of cost control.

Forecasting and Budgeting to Improve Profits

We believe that the company would benefit from the development of a system of forecasting and budgeting. By intelligently planning future activities and making regular measurements of the success with which those plans are carried out, management is in a better position to determine the most profitable course for the business to follow and to develop a program that holds the company to that course.

In the future, the company should prepare annual budgets that include monthly figures on income and expenses. In connection with these, the company should develop cash forecasts that include monthly figures on receipts and disbursements. The monthly financial statements can then present comparative figures, for the month and the year to date, showing actual amounts compared with budgeted amounts.

Using Current Rates to Measure Operations

Labor rates and overhead costs may change considerably over the length of a long-term contract. Under the present system, however, these rates and costs are figured according to the terms of the original bid. This system does not work satisfactorily because operations are being judged and supervisors evaluated not under current conditions but under conditions that existed some time earlier. We recommend that current estimated rates be used to measure operations and evaluate personnel.

Monthly Preparation of Balance Sheets

Management has not been receiving operating results until a month or more after the end of the reporting period. Even then, the information is not always accurate, and year-end adjustments have had to be made. Balance sheets for the corporation are prepared only infrequently. Timely review is essential. We recommend that balance sheets be prepared monthly so that management will have the information needed for decision making, compliance with loan agreements, and judgments on the status of the corporation.

CASH RECEIPTS AND DISBURSEMENTS

Need for Written Procedures Manual

Some progress has been made toward the completion of a policies and procedures manual. We believe that work on this manual should be expedited so that objectives and responsibilities will be clearly defined for all employees. It is especially important that the manual include all significant functions involving the expenditure of company money, such as accounting, finance, purchasing, production, material control, and maintenance. Because of the benefits that stem from having written policies and procedures, we recommend that this project be assigned a high priority and that it be completed, if possible, before the end of the year.

Separation of Duties in Processing Cash Receipts

During our examination of the financial statements of [name of company], we noted a weakness in the manner of processing the cash received. At the present time, the same person who receives the checks and supporting documents also posts the cash received to the cash receipts journal and the individual accounts receivable cards. A different person should perform each of these tasks.

As you pointed in our discussions, the limited number of accounting personnel in your company makes it difficult to segregate these duties completely for the purpose of internal control. However, we have a suggestion that we think will help. The office manager should receive the checks and supporting documents when the mail is distributed. He should deposit the checks daily and give the supporting documents, together with a tape of the checks, to the accounts receivable bookkeeper. When the accounts receivable bookkeeper has posted all the items to the cash receipts journal and the individual accounts receivable cards, he or she should reconcile the total postings to the tape supplied by the office manager.

Achieving Maximum Control over Cash Receipts

Under your current system, mail is opened, sorted, and distributed by the bookkeeper. Cash receipts go directly to the cashier, who prepares deposits, posts remittances to customers' ledger accounts, prepares and mails monthly statements to customers, and sometimes reconciles the bank account.

We recommend that the secretary make a list of receipts included in incoming mail before the receipts are forwarded to the cashier. This list should then be compared to the receipts copy of the deposit slip, which should also be returned to the secretary, who files the deposit slips. With a limited number of qualified employees, it is difficult to separate all the cash receipt duties. However, management should constantly reappraise all employees, as well as its own practices, to achieve the maximum control possible.

Need for Supporting Vouchers

Our recent examination of your financial statements revealed a serious deficiency in the lack of documentation for the business promotion expenses claimed as deductions. We extended our usual tests so as to verify the accuracy of the amounts charged to the business promotion account. However, a much more systematic method than you now have is needed to show whom you entertained, where you entertained, when you entertained, and the business purpose of the entertainment. Consistent use of the standardized form that we discussed will serve this purpose well and will greatly simplify future audits.

Necessity for Clear-cut Invoice Cancellation

During out examination, we noted that a number of invoices submitted for payment were not stamped "Paid," or otherwise effectively cancelled, at the time of payment. Your employees should be advised that all documents must be effectively cancelled to prevent their possible resubmission.

Using Manual Signatures on Checks

At present the company uses a facsimile plate signature on all checks. Although this practice saves time, it is generally true that checks requiring manual signatures receive more careful scrutiny than ones that do not, and thus cash is controlled more closely. We recommend that manual signatures be used on all checks except those disbursed from the payroll account. We recommend, too, that dual signatures be required on all checks of $500.00 or more, and that the data supporting each check be examined by at least one person prior to signing.

Security Requirements for Check-writing Materials

During our examination, we noted that signature plates and unused checks are kept in an unlocked drawer. Signature plates should be kept in a locked drawer or cabinet in one location when they are not in the signature machine. Unused checks should be kept under lock and key in a different location and should be disbursed by the controller.

Documents to Be Prenumbered and Accounted For

The best method of document control is to have key documents, including the following ones, prenumbered and accounted for:

- Sales invoices
- Purchase orders
- Vouchers
- Shipping documents
- Receiving documents
- Checks
- Credit memos
- Debit memos

While prenumbering is important, accounting for each prenumbered document is equally important. Some prenumbered documents are presently used but are not accounted for. Occasionally, voided or unused documents are discarded without adequate supporting information.

CHAPTER 8

Key Paragraphs in Management Letters

- **Purchasing and Payments**
  - **—Formalizing Purchasing Procedures**
  - **—Need for Competitive Bids**
  - **—Making Full Use of Purchasing Agent**
  - **—Minimizing Discrepancies in Accounts Payable**
  - **—Need to Reconcile Vendor Statements**
- **Inventory and Warehousing**
  - **—Using Receiving Report Forms**
  - **—Eliminating Weaknesses in Inventory Control**
  - **—Consistency in Figuring Inventory**
  - **—Criteria for Determining Obsolescence**
  - **—Need for Accurate Perpetual Inventory**
  - **—Installing a Cost Accounting System**

- **Sales and Collections**
  - —Improved Method of Sales Forecasting
  - —Reviewing Special Price Offers
  - —Approval of Credit Memoranda
  - —Ways to Collect Past-Due Accounts
  - —Controlling Delinquent Receivables
- **Computers and Data Processing**
  - —Need for Company Policy on Personal Computers
  - —Replacing Inadequate Inventory Software Program
  - —Improving Computer Security
  - —Desirability of Adequate Software Backup
  - —Need for Manual of Operating Procedures
- **Assets and Liabilities**
  - —Desirability of Fixed Assets Ledger
  - —Adequacy of Insurance Coverage
  - —Standardizing Depreciation Policies
  - —Suggestions for Investing Idle Cash

PURCHASING AND PAYMENTS

Formalizing Purchasing Procedures

The purchasing procedures of [name of company] need to be reviewed. At present they are very informal. Even though purchase-order forms do exist, they are seldom used. Generally speaking, prices are approved only during the office manager's check of invoices. We recommend that the purchasing procedures be reviewed and that a more formal system of purchasing procedures be considered.

Need for Competitive Bids

Despite the fact that purchased materials represent nearly half the product cost of most items, [name of company] does not use competitive bids for most of the materials purchased. Sometimes the engineering department or the customer has specified one particular vendor. Often a long-standing relationship has been established with a vendor, even though comparable parts or materials are available from other vendors.

We recommend that competitive bids be obtained whenever practical. This should be done for both newly specified materials and for items presently purchased without competitive bids from existing vendors. Only in this way can the company be assured that it is receiving the lowest possible prices for materials that meet [name of company]'s exacting standards.

Making Full Use of Purchasing Agent

As a consequence of expansion, [name of company] has added a purchasing agent to its staff. But since old ways die hard, the purchasing function is still not as centralized as we believe it should be. Greater centralization of purchasing will help to avoid unauthorized purchases and will assure desired purchasing standards, such as obtaining competitive prices where practicable.

We recommend that the purchasing agent issue all purchasing orders and that authorized personnel use a purchase requisition to notify the purchasing agent of the need to make a purchase. We further recommend that the purchasing agent be given greater discretion in the choice of suppliers as he becomes increasingly familiar with the company.

Minimizing Discrepancies in Accounts Payable

During our examination, we mailed requests for confirmation to all vendors in the accounts payable ledger asking them to confirm balances as of June 30, 19x5. Of the 218 confirmations we received, 96 indicated that the stated amount was incorrect. While in-transit payments and disputed balances will account for some exceptions, the percentage of exceptions in this audit (44 percent) was abnormally high.

A number of the discrepancies seem to have arisen out of a failure to enforce company policy with regard to the routing of invoices. Vendors were occasionally paid twice, for example, because a manager had approved both an original invoice and a duplicate.

At the present time, checks are returned to the accounts payable department for mailing after they have been signed. Internal control is most effective when checks are mailed by someone other than an accounts payable clerk. We suggest that a secretary mail the checks after they have been signed. The accounts payable department should advise this secretary of any necessary attachments or enclosures.

Need to Reconcile Vendor Statements

Vendor statement balances are not being reconciled to the details of accounts payable. This makes the location of errors unnecessarily difficult and decreases the likelihood of prompt follow-up in cases of nonpayment. We recommend establishing a procedure for the periodic reconciliation of vendor statements.

INVENTORY AND WAREHOUSING

Using Receiving Report Forms

Company policy requires the use of receiving reports to verify the receipt of goods. Nevertheless, receiving report forms are not always being prepared. Sometimes packing slips are used as receiving reports, but not all shippers include them. A uniform system is needed for reporting the receipt of goods. We recommend using prenumbered receiving report forms, with packing slips (when available) attached as additional support. This system provides a record of goods received, whereby receipts of goods are matched with purchase orders and with vendors' statements. It also supplies a record of when the merchandise was received. Assuming that control over these forms is enforced, prenumbering provides an effective, easy-to-use means of reporting the receipt of goods.

Eliminating Weaknesses in Inventory Control

Our examination showed that the company incurred substantial book-to-physical-inventory losses during the year. These losses point to weaknesses in inventory control, cost accounting, and materials handling. We recommend a thorough examination of your inventory policies and practices—a study documented by flow charts and memoranda. The review should relate your cost-accounting system to production control procedures. Its goal should be to develop improved procedures and controls to reduce inventory losses in the future.

Consistency in Figuring Inventory

Our recent audit revealed certain shortcomings that suggest the desirability of tightening accounting controls. Most of these matters have been discussed with [name of executive], who has indicated that he [she] is taking steps to improve the situation.

The physical inventory was taken in board feet, linear feet, square feet, and pieces. In many instances, two or more types of count were used in the same categories. There were certain items to which metric measures were applied. This lack of consistency makes inventory taking unduly complex and the completed inventory records difficult to assess. We suggest that a standard unit of measurement be used within each category.

Criteria for Determining Obsolescence

The method being used to determine inventory obsolescence and overstock situations is informal. It depends upon an intimate knowledge of the various products, and only a few officers and employees possess this knowledge.

We believe that a better approach would be to prepare written guidelines that set forth specific criteria for the determination and valuation of obsolete and overstocked items. These criteria might include (a) the desired inventory levels for each product, (b) a determination, based on reasonable sales forecasts, of the expected monthly or yearly usage of each product, and (c) the adoption of a reasonable method of valuing inventory in excess of the desired levels.

Need for Accurate Perpetual Inventory

The company maintains no perpetual inventory records, making it difficult and time-consuming to find quantities on hand. Moreover, items are stored in different locations, which adds to the difficulty. We recommend that a perpetual inventory system be established to control inventory. Since many items in the inventory can be easily converted to personal use, this system should also help the company to detect pilferage.

Installing a Cost Accounting System

[Name of company] does not have a system for gathering or recording cost-accounting information. There are many advantages in having meaningful cost information, one of which is the help it can give you in quoting appropriate prices on new business. We recommend that you develop a basic cost-accounting system.

Many different types of systems exist, varying in their particulars and in their degrees of complexity. A number of them could do the job for you. We have not made a detailed study of your operation, but we believe that a relatively simple job-order or production-order actual-cost system would be a significant improvement over your present system. This would essentially require the gathering and recording of actual per-order costs of materials and labor, along with direct manufacturing expenses, and an overhead factor figured in for each department involved in the process.

SALES AND COLLECTIONS

Improved Method of Sales Forecasting

The sales forecasts of [name of company] indicate dollar amounts only. We recommend that future sales forecasts show not only dollar amounts but also projected unit sales broken down by product. This method of forecasting supplies the information necessary for early and effective production planning. It also provides better criteria for keeping inventories at optimum levels.

Reviewing Special Price Offers

The company maintains an approved price catalog that lists all standard products. Sometimes, however, the company is asked to produce variations on its standard products. These variations require special prices. At present the new prices are negotiated with the customer, without review by a second responsible person to determine their propriety or profitability. To improve internal control in this area, we recommend that a second responsible person in the sales department review any price that does not come directly from the approved price catalog.

Approval of Credit Memoranda

A number of credit memoranda do not show evidence of approval by an authorized person in the accounting department. Evidently, approval has sometimes been given orally. We recommend that all credit memoranda over a prescribed amount, perhaps $1,000, require signed approval by the controller.

Ways to Collect Past-Due Accounts

[Name of company] faces a pressing problem in the collection of past-due accounts. As of December 31, 19x6, you were owed approximately $415,500 in accounts over one year old. Little has been done to collect these overdue accounts, as revealed by the fact that as of December 31, 19x5, you were owed a similar amount in past-due accounts. It is important that progress be made in reducing the size of these very old account balances.

We recommend that you expand your credit department to deal with these old accounts. Since you do not want to (and should not) reduce your efforts in collecting current accounts, such an expansion appears to be the best solution. In some cases, the additional clerical workers will have to analyze the makeup of past-due accounts prior to making a collection effort. If special analysis is required, personnel from the accounting department should be made available on a temporary basis.

Controlling Delinquent Receivables

We noted a significant number of delinquent receivables at December 31, 19x7, indicating that receivables could benefit from more stringent controls. It is important to identify and react to such overdue accounts in a timely manner. To that end, we recommend that the controller prepare a monthly statement for management covering all accounts over $1,000 that have been delinquent for more than 60 days. This statement will be cumulative. Each item added to it during the current month should be shown separately and explained briefly.

COMPUTERS AND DATA PROCESSING

Need for Company Policy on Personal Computers

An increasing number of executives are acquiring personal computers for use in their own divisions or departments. Since no company policy exists in this regard, various brands are being purchased. Different computers have different capabilities and run different software. The consequence is that incompatible equipment is being acquired throughout the company. In the future, if networking is attempted, as it probably will be, some of the equipment now being added without central control will prove to be unusable. We recommended that the company establish a policy regarding the purchase of personal computers, stating specifically what can and cannot be acquired.

Replacing Inadequate Inventory Software Program

When the company was started in 19x8, it purchased a custom-designed inventory program for use on its IBM-compatible computer. The program, despite many modifications, still does not work properly. Far from reducing the amount of time required to check and maintain inventory, the program has increased it. We recommend that the company discard this custom-designed software and replace it with an off-the-shelf inventory program appropriate to its needs.

Improving Computer Security

More and more of the company's records are being maintained in its computer system. Efficiency is improved by this move toward computerization, but inadequate attention has been paid to security. Password codes exist that are intended to allow access only to information appropriate to the specific user. However, little control has been exercised over the passwords themselves, with the consequence that many employees seem to have access to information that should not be available to them. We recommend that new password codes be assigned and that stricter security measures be employed to keep the codes secret, as they are intended to be.

Desirability of Adequate Software Backup

Although employees are aware of the need for maintaining backup disks of company records, they are lax in keeping up to date with this disk backup. The consequence is that at any given time certain important information could be irretrievably lost, in the event of a system crash. This is too risky a gamble to take. We recommend that daily backup of disks be made an absolute requirement and that a person be put in charge of seeing that no exceptions occur.

Need for Manual of Operating Procedures

The ever-expanding use of the computer system at [name of company] has occurred mainly under the direction of two employees. These employees are the company's only experts on the computer system. If they were to leave, the result would be a period of uncertainty and turmoil. We recommend that these employees, working with others as necessary, prepare a manual of operating procedures for the computer system. This manual should be usable by anyone moderately familiar with computers but having no special knowledge of the programs now in use at [name of company].

ASSETS AND LIABILITIES

Desirability of Fixed Assets Ledger

Our examination indicated that [name of company] does not maintain a fixed assets ledger. In a company of your size, it is customary accounting procedure to maintain such a ledger, and we recommend that you do so.

A fixed assets ledger properly developed and maintained will benefit your company in two ways: First, it will reduce the risk of your losing valuable assets, and second, it will enable you to determine the most favorable methods of depreciation for tax purposes.

Adequacy of Insurance Coverage

Our examination included a review of the adequacy of the company's insurance coverage. The amount of coverage selected seems to have been entrusted entirely to the insurance agency, and it does not appear that company officials have reviewed the matter recently, nor that there is a policy of periodic review.

The present amount of coverage appears to be inadequate. The amounts of coverage for real and personal property represent original costs, not replacement costs. We therefore recommend that management investigate the whole area of its insurance coverage. We suggest, specifically, that consideration be given to increasing the amounts of property coverage to cover current replacement costs.

Standardizing Depreciation Policies

Company policy is to follow accounting practices that conform to federal income tax regulations. We recommend that the following practices be standardized:

- That federal income tax guidelines be followed for useful-life categories of depreciable assets.
- That no items costing less than $300 be capitalized, to avoid detailed accounting for minor fixed-assets purchases.
- That fully depreciated equipment not in use be eliminated from the records.

Suggestions for Investing Idle Cash

We recommend that you consider investing certain idle-cash funds in U.S. government securities. Specifically, we noted the following:

1. Throughout 19x9 the balance in your organization's Bond and Interest Fund checking account never fell below $138,850. Had that minimum balance been invested in U.S. Treasury bills, it would have produced more than $14,000 in income. Since you can accurately determine the cash requirements of this particular fund, it should be possible for you to make even larger temporary investments during the year.
2. Your Building Reserve Fund totaling $11,910 has remained unchanged for more than five years. We recommend that you either invest these funds or transfer them to another account where they can be used.

CHAPTER 9

Financial Services and Estate Planning

- Engagement to Set Up Financial Accounting System
- Fund Raising Engagement for Small Business Client
- Feasibility Study for Office Building
- Projected Financial Statements for Proposed Venture
- Interim Progress Report on Pricing of Products
- Covering Note for Business Advisory Letter
- Paragraphs on How to Maximize Cash Position
- Paragraphs on Improving Collection of Accounts Receivable
- Engagement Letter for Business Planning Session
- Approach Letter Regarding Personal Financial Planning
- Notice of Talk on Personal Financial Planning
- Engagement Letter for Estate Planning
- Letter Concerning Client's Personal Goals
- Checklist for Real Estate Holdings
- Letter Dealing with Continuation of Family Business
- Checklist for Estate Administration and Probate

The services covered by the letters in this chapter can be viewed as extensions of the services that accountants have typically provided. Whether the client is an individual or a business, offering advice on financial and tax matters has been a common procedure, not usually subject to a separate engagement. However, when the scope or nature of the work is such that special or additional effort is required, then a separate engagement is indicated.

Letters in the first part of this chapter deal with such matters as setting up a financial accounting system, helping a small business client obtain financing, conducting a feasibility study, and advising the client on how to improve the collection of accounts receivable. Two letters have to do with personal financial planning, a new and largely untapped field for accountants.

The second part of the chapter contains a number of letters on estate planning. As the letters show, modern estate planning is a team effort, usually involving the client, an attorney, a banker or investment adviser, an insurance agent or adviser, and an accountant. Because the estate plan is essentially a legal transaction, a lawyer ordinarily heads the team. However, accountants are increasingly being asked to help clients plan their estates, and the accountant who has experience and knowledge in the field can provide this service.

Both personal financial planning and estate planning have received rather poor press in recent years, mainly because unqualified practitioners—*not* accountants, as a rule—have tried to cash in on the public's growing awareness of its need for help in these areas. The two fields have clear growth potential, and they are ones in which accountants can make significant professional contributions. To do so can be both an opportunity and a challenge.

ENGAGEMENT TO SET UP FINANCIAL ACCOUNTING SYSTEM

This is basically a proposal letter for a specific management advisory services engagement. When signed by the client, it serves as the engagement letter.

YOUR LETTERHEAD

[Date]

INSIDE ADDRESS

[Salutation]:

Thank you for the opportunity of meeting with you and your management team and discussing your need to receive more timely and accurate accounting information. This letter summarizes our discussion and outlines the kind of assistance we propose to offer.

Our understanding of the situation is this: [name of company] has expanded rapidly over the past five years. One new division has been added through acquisition, and another has been created within the company. Expansion has strained the resources of management to the point where monthly financial reports have been late, with the result that management has sometimes been obliged to act on outdated information.

You therefore wish to establish a comprehensive financial accounting system that will give management the information it needs when it needs it. We believe that the following three items must be added if [name of company] is to have a viable financial accounting system:

1. Weekly performance reports that specify revenues, expenses, and key operating statistics
2. Detailed cost reports
3. Comparable performance and cost reports from each division

These three items, properly prepared and monitored, should lead to clear-cut improvement. They should:

- Improve profits through more effective cost control
- Allow management to see the effects of financial decisions earlier

- Give management the ability to respond rapidly to business trends
- Provide more accurate recording of expenses in the periods in which they occur
- Alert management quickly to excess expenditures

This engagement involves analyzing your present financial accounting system, determining the specific needs of management, and proposing a new and improved design. In regard to this design, we will submit samples of the proposed reports, flow diagrams of the proposed system, an analysis of projected costs, and an implementation schedule.

Upon completion of our study, we will present our findings and recommendations in a written report.

During this study, we will expect to talk with your personnel on a cooperative basis in order to gain an intimate knowledge of your present system and future requirements.

Our fee for this service will be billed at our standard rates plus out-of-pocket expenses. We estimate that the fee, not including out-of-pocket expenses, will range between $11,000 and $13,500. Invoices will be presented for monthly payment.

If this proposal meets with your approval, please sign one copy of this letter in the space below and return it to us. A duplicate copy of the proposal is enclosed for your files.

We look forward to working with you.

[Closing],

____

YOUR SIGNATURE

____

Approved:
By:______________________________ Date_______________
[Name of client]

FUND RAISING ENGAGEMENT FOR SMALL BUSINESS CLIENT

Prior to drafting this letter, you will have held one or more meetings with senior management so that you will know, at a minimum, the nature and history of the company, its organization and personnel, its products and market, its bank and bankers, and its cash problems and plans for growth.

YOUR LETTERHEAD

______________________ [Date]

INSIDE ADDRESS

____

[Salutation]:

This letter confirms the terms of the engagement as we discussed them on [date] in regard to obtaining new funds for [name of company].

We will study the financing needs of [name of company] and the basis for those needs. We will then suggest the source of funds that seems most appropriate under the circumstances, specifying the amount needed and the best method or methods of financing.

To ensure the most persuasive presentation possible to the financing source, we will assist you in preparing a business plan and any other documents that may be necessary. We will assist you in presenting the plan to the financing source and in negotiating terms.

We will also help you to prepare the financing or funding proposal package (i.e., the documents) needed for an effective presentation.

For your part, we expect you to supply all requested financial records and data and to work cooperatively with us in preparing the business plan and the financing package.

As we discussed when we met, you understand that our role is solely one of advising and assisting you in obtaining funds. We will make every effort on your behalf, but we can offer no assurance that the requested funds will be obtained.

We can begin work immediately upon your signing this letter. Assuming the ready availability of company financial records and data and the full cooperation of your personnel, we expect to complete the engagement in about eight weeks.

This engagement will be complete when all needed documents are submitted and the presentation to the funding source has been made. If funds are not obtained through this presentation, you may wish us to continue our efforts with other possible funding sources. If so, please notify us in writing, and we will extend the engagement for that purpose.

The engagement can be terminated at any point, by notification of either party, if circumstances arise that make it impossible to complete the engagement successfully.

Our fee for this engagement will be based on our regular rates plus out-of-pocket expenses. You will be billed each month, and the invoices will be due and payable upon presentation.

If this letter accurately sets forth your understanding of the services we are to provide, please sign in the space below and return one copy to us, retaining the other copy for your files.

[Closing],

____

YOUR SIGNATURE

____

Approved:
By: ______________________________ Date ______________
[Name of client]

FEASIBILITY STUDY FOR OFFICE BUILDING

In this letter, the practitioner grants the client permission to submit the final report to an unspecified bank or insurance company to obtain financing.

YOUR LETTERHEAD

[Date]

INSIDE ADDRESS

[Salutation]:

This letter is to confirm our understanding of an economic feasibility study that [name of accounting firm] will conduct for a proposed two-story office building at [location of proposed building].

On [date] we will meet with you to review plans for the building, including architectural sketches and any other relevant information. After this meeting, we will proceed as follows:

- Inspect the site to analyze its suitability for the proposed building. This inspection will include both the specific site and the general area surrounding it.
- Conduct a market survey of [name of city or other locale] to estimate the potential demand and the present and projected competition for this kind of building.
- Estimate the viability of the building in terms of existing types of buildings and facilities, lease rates, and levels of occupancy.
- Project the operating income and expenses for three levels of vacancy: 5 percent, 15 percent, 25 percent. We will then submit a written report estimating the economic feasibility of the project based on a maximum investment of [$ amount].

In the report, we will indicate the sources of information we have used during the study and will make clear the assumptions on which our study is based. Since the accuracy of predictions concerning future economic conditions are speculative, our estimates and projections must be regarded as tentative. We will not express an opinion on the report and the financial projections.

The report and financial projections will be for the information of [name of client]. No reference to the report or its contents are to be made in any document or agreement without our prior consent in writing. The one exception to this provision is that the report may be submitted to a bank or insurance company to help in obtaining financing.

Our fee for this feasibility study will be based on our regular rates plus out-of-pocket expenses. We estimate that the fee will not exceed $4,000 and the out-of-pocket expenses will not exceed $500. We ask that one half of the fee ($2,000) be paid upon the signing of this agreement. The balance is payable upon delivery of the report.

If you wish us to conduct this study, we can start within two weeks of your signing the agreement and will expect to submit our report no later than six weeks thereafter.

If the terms of this letter are satisfactory, please sign the original in the space provided and return it to us, along with a check for $2,000, as specified above. Please keep the copy of the letter for your files.

[Closing],

____

YOUR SIGNATURE

____

Approved:
By: ____________________________ Date ____________
[Name of client]

PROJECTED FINANCIAL STATEMENTS FOR PROPOSED VENTURE

Since this engagement is concerned with financial projections, the engagement letter requires a disclaimer.

YOUR LETTERHEAD

[Date]

INSIDE ADDRESS

[Salutation]:

This letter confirms the terms of our engagement to prepare and review projected financial statements for [description of proposed venture].

We will prepare projected statements of income and cash flow for the first three years of proposed operations and a related projected statement of income and losses reportable for tax purposes. Our estimates, assumptions, and projections will be based on information that you supply. We will test computations, discuss this venture with company management, and use whatever other procedures we believe are necessary.

The projected financial statements will be based on estimates, assumptions, and projections. Since the reliability of the projections depends on future events, their accuracy cannot be guaranteed. Accordingly, we will not express an opinion on the projected statements.

Our report and its projections are intended for the information and use of the management of [name of client company]. No reference to them will be made in any registration statement, prospectus, loan agreement, or other agreement or document.

Our fee for this engagement will be based on our regular rates plus out-of-pocket expenses. You will be billed each month, and the invoices will be due and payable upon presentation.

If these arrangements are in accordance with your understanding, please sign the original copy of this letter in the space provided and return it to us. The copy is for your files.

[Closing],

____

YOUR SIGNATURE

____

Approved:
By: ______________________________ Date ______________
[Name of client]

INTERIM PROGRESS REPORT ON PRICING OF PRODUCTS

This engagement involves a study of the pricing of the client company's products. Early in the engagement, the practitioner became aware of a situation that she felt should be mentioned immediately. This letter explains the situation. The contents of the letter will be a part of the final report but may be modified as a consequence of the client's reaction.

YOUR LETTERHEAD

[Date]

____

INSIDE ADDRESS

____

[Salutation]:

Although our final report on the pricing of your company's products is not yet complete, we believe it is worthwhile to mention one matter that has come to our attention.

It does not appear that [name of company]'s pricing policies are in line with industry standards. To take a single but representative example: Your word processing software program, *Wordwise,* is priced at $49.95. It is evidently a versatile, full-featured package, and judging by recent reviews is the equal of any on the market. Yet no competing word processing program sells for less than $79.95, and the current market leaders sell for $235.00 and $245.00.

In our preliminary discussions, we touched on management's policy regarding pricing. Our understanding at the time was that, while you wish to compete on the basis of price, you do not intend to price your products drastically below comparable competing products.

The questions raised are these:

1. How were the present list prices of your products determined?
2. Do you periodically evaluate your competition by analyzing competitors' pricing policies, assessing their products, and determining their market share?
3. Is there an effective customer feedback system that gives you an indication of how your prices are viewed by buyers?
4. Have you done research that indicates probable difficulty with significantly higher prices than you now charge?

We will make specific recommendations in our final report, but we thought it would be useful to raise these questions now since their answers may affect what we suggest later.

We look forward to hearing from you.

[Closing],

____

YOUR SIGNATURE

____

COVERING NOTE FOR BUSINESS ADVISORY LETTER

The letter that follows this two-paragraph covering note is a detailed report on how to improve profitability and increase the financial strength of the client company.

YOUR LETTERHEAD

[Date]

INSIDE ADDRESS

[Salutation]:

As part of our audit of your financial statements for 19x9, it is our pleasure to provide you with the comments on the following pages to help make your business more profitable and increase your financial strength. Our comments were discussed with appropriate officers and employees of [name of client company], and their input was useful in developing this letter.

We sincerely appreciate the courtesy and cooperation extended to us by officers and employees of [name of company] during our audit and while formulating these comments and suggestions. We will be pleased to discuss our recommendations at your convenience and assist you in implementing them.

[Closing],

YOUR SIGNATURE

PARAGRAPHS ON HOW TO MAXIMIZE CASH POSITION

These paragraphs are part of the business advisory letter introduced by the previous model.

To maximize your cash position, we recommend that you prepare a monthly cash forecast matching inflows and outflows, based on information contained in the company's budget. Once cash needs are identified, we suggest that you invest excess cash in highly liquid government securities, money market funds, or short-term certificates of deposit. If a cash shortage is identified, attempt to speed up receivable collections, sell inventory faster, pay expenses slower, or arrange for short-term loans. Analyze customer payment patterns to determine if payments can be obtained more quickly. One possibility is to establish a discount policy, if the benefits will exceed the costs and the possible loss of sales from requiring customers to pay earlier. A microcomputer program is an efficient way to develop these forecasts and modify them as needed. We would be pleased to help you select the appropriate microcomputer and software package.

Prepare a weekly statement of cash receipts and disbursements to highlight potential cash drains and cash resources. This also will provide information to modify the monthly cash forecasts as needed.

Consider adopting a lock-box system for cash collections. Under this system, customers mail checks to a post office box (called a "lock box"). You then authorize the bank to open the lock box at least once a day. The bank opens the customers' envelopes, copies the checks, and attaches each check copy to the invoice. The checks are deposited in your account and the check copies and invoices are mailed to you for processing. Once the funds are collected, the bank wires the money to a central collection bank where funds will be invested for you.

These are the advantages of a lock-box system:

1. You get your money faster. The maximum time that checks are in the mail is one or two days (rather than several days for checks drawn on out-of-state banks).
2. Record-keeping is easier.
3. It is a good internal-control device.

The principal disadvantage of a lock-box system is its cost in bank fees. The cost of maintaining the system should be compared with the additional revenue generated by collecting and investing cash more quickly.

Take advantage of appropriate purchase discounts. These discounts usually result in substantial savings. For example, based on a vendor's terms of 2 percent/10 days, net 30 days, the company loses a 2 percent discount by holding cash an extra 20 days. (Never pay before the 10th day!) In effect, by not taking discounts, the company is paying 36 percent interest (2 percent × 360/20 days) on 30-day credit purchases. It usually is cheaper to borrow funds—for example, a line of credit or a working capital loan—to take advantage of discounts than it is to let them lapse.

PARAGRAPHS ON IMPROVING COLLECTION OF ACCOUNTS RECEIVABLE

These paragraphs are part of the business advisory letter introduced by the model on page 201.

To maximize the collection of accounts receivable, we recommend using standard criteria to judge customers' character, ability to pay (liquidity), financial strength (net worth), and collateral when evaluating new or marginal accounts. In determining standard criteria, weigh marginal credit costs against marginal profits on increased sales. The optimal credit period is the point at which marginal profits offset the costs of carrying the additional accounts receivable. Likewise, the optimal discount period is the point at which the costs of offering discounts offset the profit on increased sales.

Prepare monthly aging analyses of accounts receivable and of accounts written off. We recommend that a listing of past-due accounts be prepared by the computer and all accounts outstanding over 30 days be followed up monthly. The credit manager should review all balances over $25,000. Smaller balances should be followed up by his assistant.

Identify the causes of write-offs to help evaluate the effectiveness of credit and collection policies, to prevent premature and fraudulent write-offs, and to make sure that accounts written off are not repeat offenders.

Analyze returns and allowances to determine if there are abuses by either company personnel or customers. Meet with customers who repeatedly request adjustments. Try to resolve the problem with them. If a satisfactory resolution cannot be worked out, it may be more economical to stop doing business with the customer.

ENGAGEMENT LETTER FOR BUSINESS PLANNING SESSION

A small business may want you or your firm to conduct a business planning session with the ultimate goal of maximizing profits.

YOUR LETTERHEAD

________________ [Date]

INSIDE ADDRESS

____

[Salutation]:

This letter confirms our understanding of the services we will perform for [name of company].

On September 22, 19x0, [name of partner] and I will meet with [names of company participants, including president and controller] in the conference room of our office at [location].

Because of prior audit engagements, we have [name of company]'s financial statements for the past several years. It would be helpful if, sometime before the meeting, you could furnish us with the last three years' sales figures for your various product lines as well as a current organizational chart.

Our function at the meeting will be to oversee it and to provide information and suggestions that seem useful and appropriate. Within one week following the meeting, we will submit to [name of company] a summary of the meeting along with any recommendations that we believe will assist you in your goal of maximizing profits.

If this letter accurately sets forth your understanding of the services we are to perform, please sign the original in the space provided and return it to us, retaining the copy for your files.

[Closing],

____

YOUR SIGNATURE

____

Approved:
By: ________________ Date ________
[Name of client]

APPROACH LETTER REGARDING PERSONAL FINANCIAL PLANNING

Personal financial planning is a growth business. Thousands of insurance agents, stockbrokers, and bankers offer the service, as do an increasing number of accountants. There has been considerable controversy over personal financial planning (PFP), because its lack of regulation has attracted some unethical practitioners. Nevertheless, it is a needed service, and no one has more technical expertise in it than an experienced accountant. The letter on page 207 is designed to inform present clients about the availability of the service.

YOUR LETTERHEAD

[Date]

INSIDE ADDRESS

[Salutation]:

For the past several years, our firm has assisted certain clients in their personal financial planning. Since many other clients who might benefit from this service are not aware of it, I would like to take a moment to outline what we can offer in this area.

Personal financial planning (PFP as it is often called) is a total financial planning service. We evaluate the client's financial status and goals and devise an overall financial plan, with periodic review, to help him or her meet those goals.

The service involves these five steps:

1. Collecting and evaluating all relevant data on the client's current financial status
2. Identifying the client's financial goals and objectives, with attention to any problems that may exist
3. Developing a written plan, with alternatives, that will achieve the goals and objectives
4. Implementing the plan
5. Reviewing the plan periodically, updating it when needed

As you probably know, this kind of service is offered by other professionals and by some financial institutions. You may already have a personal financial plan. If not, and if you would like to discuss this service further, please let me know.

[Closing],

YOUR SIGNATURE

NOTICE OF TALK ON PERSONAL FINANCIAL PLANNING

One way to make the public aware of the fact that your firm offers personal financial planning is to make it the topic of a speech or seminar. This can get your message across in an informative way without overt advertising.

YOUR LETTERHEAD

[Date]

INSIDE ADDRESS

[Salutation]:

This is just a note to let our clients know that Dwight Orr, a senior partner in our firm will be speaking on Friday, October 17, at 8:00 P.M. in Grey Auditorium at Halsey Community College. His topic is "Personal Financial Planning—What's It All About?"

Mr. Orr's talk is part of the weekly Public Information Series that the college is sponsoring. The talk will last approximately one hour, and admission is free.

Our firm has received so many requests for information about personal financial planning that we thought it might be helpful to mention Mr. Orr's talk. He will explain PFP in some detail and will suggest the various options that exist.

If the topic interests you, we urge you to consider attending.

[Closing],

YOUR SIGNATURE

ENGAGEMENT LETTER FOR ESTATE PLANNING

Estate planning is a complex field, but it offers the knowledgeable practitioner an excellent opportunity for client promotion and development. Because estate planning is complicated, the recommendations that are made are sometimes jargon-filled and bewildering to clients, who may not understand the financial benefits they have gained. Try to make the savings clear to the client as the engagement progresses. Here is a basic engagement letter for estate planning.

YOUR LETTERHEAD

________________________ [Date]

INSIDE ADDRESS

____

[Salutation]:

This letter is to confirm our understanding of the estate planning engagement that we discussed on [date].

The services we perform for you will involve analyzing and reviewing your estate plan and will include the following: We will:

1. Meet with you to assemble all pertinent information concerning the present circumstances of your estate. You will receive a checklist prior to this meeting that will help you gather the needed data.
2. Prepare a schedule of the distribution of your present estate assets and your projected estate tax liability under present conditions.
3. Make specific recommendations on ways to save on estate taxes and probate costs. In addition to these tax recommendations, we will make any other suggestions that may help you realize your personal or family estate-planning goals.
4. Prepare a schedule, based on the implementation of our recommendations, indicating your tax liability under the new plan, figured on the basis of the present situation and current law.

5. Obtain and coordinate any special assistance needed in the planning of your estate and in putting our recommendations into effect.

Our fee, charged at our standard billing rate, plus out-of-pocket expenses will be based upon the amount of time required to complete the engagement. We estimate the total fee at approximately [$ amount]. Payment is due upon presentation of our invoice.

If this letter accurately sets forth your understanding of our arrangements, please sign the original in the space provided and return it to us, retaining the copy for your files.

It is a privilege to have been chosen for this engagement. If you have questions regarding any of the points in this letter, please call me and I will try to answer them.

[Closing],

____

YOUR SIGNATURE

____

Approved:
By: ______________________________ Date ____________
[Name of client]

LETTER CONCERNING CLIENT'S PERSONAL GOALS

This letter is intended to get the client thinking about what he or she hopes to achieve by estate planning. It precedes a personal meeting in which the same questions will be asked. The person who heads the estate planning team—whether an accountant or a lawyer—is the one to ask these questions. Typically, such questions would be asked by a lawyer since many of the answers affect present or future provisions of a will.

YOUR LETTERHEAD (OR ATTORNEY'S)

[Date]

____

INSIDE ADDRESS

____

[Salutation]:

Prior to our meeting on [date], you will find it helpful to go over the following questions which will be discussed at that time. There is no need to respond to this letter, or even to write down the answers, but it has been my experience that this kind of preparation can save time and result in more specific answers than are obtained on an impromptu basis.

1. At what age do you expect to retire? Will you have any dependents at that time? If so, who?
2. Other than dependents, what will be your financial obligations upon retirement? Mortgage(s)? Other loans?
3. What income will you need during retirement to meet your dependents' needs and other financial obligations?
4. Do you have particular post-retirement interests or goals that will require special consideration? Hobbies? Travel? Other?
5. What sources of income will you have upon retirement? Investments? Pension? Social Security? Other?
6. If you have substantially more retirement income than you need, who should receive the excess?

7. In the event of your death, what income will your widow [or widower] require for living expenses? Maintenance of residence? Will she [he] be able to handle her [his] own money? If not, what provisions should be made?
8. Do any of your children have continuing or special needs? Education? Wedding expenses? Physical or mental disability? Lack of income? Establishment of business? Other?
9. When should children receive substantial amounts of capital?

I look forward to seeing you on [date].

[Closing],

____

YOUR SIGNATURE
(OR ATTORNEY'S)

____

CHECKLIST FOR REAL ESTATE HOLDINGS

Checklists are a convenient way to assemble the data needed in estate planning. The preceding letter is based on a checklist that the accountant (or lawyer) uses when meeting with the client. There are other useful checklists covering bank accounts, stocks and bonds, stock options, life insurance, mortgages and notes, profit sharing and pension plans, tangible personal property, miscellaneous assets, miscellaneous liabilities, and so on. These lists are for office use and are not usually sent to the client. Consequently, they are not included in this book. For illustrative purposes, however, this real estate checklist is included. (Note that the checklist is for one parcel only. You [or the lawyer] would have to go over the checklist with the client for each parcel of real estate owned.)

REAL ESTATE

1. Specific location
2. Brief physical description
3. Type of use (residential or commercial)
4. Date of purchase and original cost
5. Form of ownership
6. If joint owners, list contributions of each owner
7. If multiple owners, list names, addresses, and ownership shares
8. Mortgages
    a. Amount of each mortgage
    b. Name and address of each mortgage holder
    c. Amount of monthly payment on each mortgage
    d. Interest rate on each mortgage
    e. Duration of each mortgage
9. Other liens
    a. Amount of each lien
    b. Name and address of each lien holder
10. Fire, title, and other insurance
    a. Kind of insurance
    b. Name and address of insurer
    c. Policy number
    d. Amount of insurance

11. Annual income from rental property
    a. Gross rental income
    b. (minus) Taxes
    c. (minus) Depreciation
    d. (minus) Interest
    e. (minus) Other expenses
    f. Net rental income
12. Estimated current value; basis of estimate

LETTER DEALING WITH CONTINUATION OF FAMILY BUSINESS

One important aspect of the estate plan for an owner of a family-owned business is whether the business is to continue after the client's death.

YOUR LETTERHEAD (OR ATTORNEY'S)

_______________ [Date]

INSIDE ADDRESS

____

[Salutation]:

When we meet to review your estate plan on [date], I would like to go over the question of whether your business, [name of business], is or is not to be continued beyond your lifetime. This question has many ramifications, and I hope you will have a chance to think about them, and ideally to discuss them with your spouse and others in your family, so that we will have a solid basis on which to make some estate-planning decisions.

Please think about these questions:

- Do you have employees, relatives, or others who are willing and able to manage and maintain the business?
- Are there employees, relatives, or others who might be interested in buying the business interest from your estate? If so, are they in a financial position to make the purchase?
- Will continuation of the business provide greater income to your beneficiaries than would disposition of it?
- If the business is continued, will there be enough cash available to pay taxes and administrative expenses and to see the business through the transitional period?
- Does continuation of the business seem reasonable in view of the rest of the estate plan? For instance, will ownership be fragmented by the terms of the will?

- Are the beneficiaries, including minors, likely to be able to succeed in carrying on the business? In particular, is your spouse temperamentally suited to be involved in its continuation?

These are by no means the only important questions, but they provide a starting point. The answers to many of them are speculative, of course, but an estate plan must include provisions on this important matter.

[Closing],

____

YOUR SIGNATURE
(OR ATTORNEY'S)

____

CHECKLIST FOR ESTATE ADMINISTRATION AND PROBATE

This checklist was designed for use by an attorney, and the "you" in it is more logically an attorney than an accountant. In fact, however, no single individual is likely to have all the skills required of an estate planner. An estate planner should know the law regarding wills, trusts, estates, and taxes. He or she should understand accountancy, the administration of fiduciary portfolios, and insurance. Small wonder that estate planning is usually a team effort.

ESTATE ADMINISTRATION AND PROBATE

1. Do you have the name, address, and phone number of client's
   - attorney(s)
   - physician(s)
   - banker(s)
   - insurance advisor(s)
   - investment advisor(s)
2. Can client or spouse supply basic documents on the family, such as
   - birth certificates
   - marriage certificates
   - tax returns
3. Should client's safe deposit box be closed and its contents transferred to a box in the name of another person?
4. Should receivables from family members be forgiven? from business associates?
5. Can out-of-state assets be transferred to another person, to a trust, or returned to this state so as to avoid separate administration?
6. Can client transfer partnership interests to another member of the family?
7. Should a revocable trust be executed and implemented?
8. Is client a fiduciary, or does client hold any assets as a trustee or nominee of another person?
9. If client is a fiduciary, can he or others change the fiduciary at this time?

PART IV

TAX-RELATED CORRESPONDENCE

CHAPTER 10

Better Tax Return Preparation Letters

- Letter Advising Client to Compile Tax Data
- Reminder on Filing Tax Forms
- Items Needed for Payroll Tax Returns
- Instructions for Filing IRS Declaration of Estimated Tax
- Letter to Client's Prior Tax Accountant
- Client's Letter of Authorization
- Request for Tax Data from Client's Internal Accountant
- Letter Asking for Details on Deductible Expenses
- Informing Client of Changes in Tax Law
- Letter to IRS for Qualification of Retirement Plan
- Note to IRS on Final Partnership Return
- Explanatory Note to State Requesting Refund Due
- Notice of Termination of Business

Federal and state tax laws have historically been lengthy, complex, and ever-changing. You would expect the taxes of huge multinational corporations to require expert and meticulous preparation. But even individual income taxes had become a somewhat esoteric subject by the 1980s, and a very time-consuming one for the average person. Not surprisingly, millions of people began relying on accountants or other tax specialists to prepare their individual returns.

Even though clients do not prepare their own returns, they naturally want to know about the tax changes that affect their businesses and that impact on them personally. Even in a year with no changes in the tax laws—an unlikely year indeed—clients still need to be reminded when tax time is approaching. And of course some kind of transmittal letter must accompany any completed tax form that goes to the client. In other words, there is a good deal of correspondence involved in tax accounting.

The model letters in this chapter are designed to guide you in drafting letters that will remind clients about tax deadlines, help them in assembling tax data, inform them of changes in tax laws, and, in general, aid them in any matters involving taxation. The letters are also intended to convey the message, either directly or indirectly, that you value each client's business and look forward to a continuing relationship in the future.

LETTER ADVISING CLIENT TO COMPILE TAX DATA

A brief letter serves to remind clients that tax time is approaching. The accompanying checklist indicates items needed to prepare the individual returns.

YOUR LETTERHEAD

[Date]

INSIDE ADDRESS

[Salutation]:

You will want to begin soon to gather the information needed for preparing your 19x8 federal and state income tax returns. To assist you, I am enclosing a checklist that you will find helpful in assembling the data. The checklist may remind you of important items you might otherwise overlook.

Once the information has been gathered—as soon as possible after the end of the year—please bring it or send it to my office. If you would like to set up an appointment in advance, please give me a call.

Best wishes for the holidays.

[Closing],

YOUR SIGNATURE

REMINDER ON FILING TAX FORMS

This letter specifies the federal and state forms regarding payroll that must be filed by the end of the year. It provides a handy checklist for the client.

YOUR LETTERHEAD

[Date]

INSIDE ADDRESS

[Salutation]:

This is a note to advise you that a number of forms regarding payroll must be filed at the end of the year. These forms include:

Employer's Quarterly Federal Tax Return (941)
Employer's Annual Federal Unemployment Tax Return (940)
New Jersey Unemployment and Disability Contribution Report (UC27)
New Jersey Employer Report of Wages Paid (WR30)
Wage and Tax Statements (W-2)
Federal Transmittal of Income Tax Statements (W-3)
New Jersey Transmittal of Income Tax Statements (NJW-3)

If you want us to prepare these returns for you, please get in touch with us immediately so that we can advise you of what information we will need from you.

[Closing],

YOUR SIGNATURE

ITEMS NEEDED FOR PAYROLL TAX RETURNS

A checklist like the one that follows serves two purposes. First, it helps the client assemble the necessary items. Second, it makes your own efforts more efficient by ensuring that everything you need will reach you in time.

YOUR LETTERHEAD

____________________ [Date]

INSIDE ADDRESS

____

[Salutation]:

In order to make it easier to file your payroll tax returns for the quarter ending March 31, 19x5, this letter provides a list of the items we will need. Please bring or mail the listed items to our office no later than April 8, 19x5.

Period covered: January 1, 19x5 to March 31, 19x5
Due date of returns: April 30, 19x5

________ Payroll sheets with all figures for the quarter totaled. (Be sure that the total net pay plus the total deductions equals the total gross for each employee.)

________ FICA/federal withholding deposits made during the quarter. (Please include the dates on which they were deposited.)

________ Form 941 (Quarterly Federal Return)

________ Form UC27 (Quarterly Contributions Report)

________ Form WR-30 (State of New Jersey Wage Reporting System)

We hope this list will be of assistance to you. If you have any questions, please give us a call. We will be happy to help.

[Closing],

____

YOUR SIGNATURE

____

INSTRUCTIONS FOR FILING IRS DECLARATION OF ESTIMATED TAX

A letter of this kind is a convenient reminder to the taxpayer of the due dates and installment amounts of his or her estimated federal income tax. Where applicable, a similar letter can be used to list estimated state income taxes.

YOUR LETTERHEAD

[Date]

INSIDE ADDRESS

[Salutation]:

Your 19x6 U.S. Declaration of Estimated Tax is $456 and may be paid in full or in the installments shown below.

If you expect your income, deductions, or exemptions to change substantially from those listed on the attached worksheet, an amended declaration will probably be needed.

You should not file any voucher which indicates that no payment is due.

Voucher Number	*Amount of Installment*	*Credit Applied*	*Net Amount to Be Paid*	*Due Date*
1	$114		$114	4/15/x6
2	114		114	6/15/x6
3	114		114	9/15/x6
4	114		114	1/15/x7

Make your check payable to "Internal Revenue Service" and include your Social Security Number and the words "19x6 Form 1040-ES" on the check. Attach the check to the voucher.

Each of the four vouchers and checks should be mailed on or before the dates listed above to:

Internal Revenue Service Center
Holtsville, New York 00501-2222

If you have any questions about this return, or about future tax planning, please call our office at [phone number].

[Closing],

YOUR SIGNATURE

LETTER TO CLIENT'S PRIOR TAX ACCOUNTANT

It is good practice to send the following letter to the prior accountant immediately upon receipt of the signed engagement letter from your new client. At the same time this letter is sent, the new client should send a letter of authorization (on the client's letterhead) for the release of any or all records that you, as the new accountant, request. See the model letter on page 229. A fast and coordinated effort at the outset could save you time and headaches later.

YOUR LETTERHEAD

[Date]

INSIDE ADDRESS

[Salutation]:

We have been engaged by [name of client] to provide tax and accounting services. We understand that your firm previously served in that capacity.

If you know of any reason why we should not accept this engagement, please notify us immediately. Otherwise, so as to cause the least possible disruption to [name of client]'s business affairs, kindly forward to this office copies of all corporate, partnership, individual, and payroll tax returns, along with all supporting work papers and adjusting entries.

Thank you for your cooperation.

[Closing],

YOUR SIGNATURE

CLIENT'S LETTER OF AUTHORIZATION

The new client sends this letter at the same time that you send the preceding one.

CLIENT'S LETTERHEAD

_______________ [Date]

INSIDE ADDRESS

____

[Salutation]:

Please note that effective immediately we have engaged the accounting firm of [name of your firm]. This letter is your authorization to release all records that they may request.

Thank you for your past services and for your cooperation in this transfer.

[Closing],

____

CLIENT'S SIGNATURE

____

REQUEST FOR TAX DATA FROM CLIENT'S INTERNAL ACCOUNTANT

This letter is simply a reminder to the client company to send the usual material required for income tax preparation. The addressee is the chief accountant of the corporate client.

YOUR LETTERHEAD

[Date]

INSIDE ADDRESS

[Salutation]:

Once again the time for filing your 19x3 federal corporation income tax return is approaching. Therefore, please furnish us with schedules similar to the ones you provided last year. In view of the preparation time ordinarily needed, we would appreciate receiving these schedules no later than Monday, May 15, 19x7.

Thank you.

[Closing],

YOUR SIGNATURE

LETTER ASKING FOR DETAILS ON DEDUCTIBLE EXPENSES

Even though the client was asked to supply specifics in all relevant categories, you may find some information still missing, as here.

YOUR LETTERHEAD

[Date]

INSIDE ADDRESS

[Salutation]:

To complete your 19x9 federal and state income tax returns, we need detailed listings of your deductions in the following categories:

1. Charitable contributions: names of recipients and amounts contributed
2. Interest payments: to whom paid and amounts
3. Medical and dental expenses: to whom paid and amounts
4. Other deductible expenses: moving expenses, theft losses, safe-deposit box rental fee, etc.

Please bring this information directly to our office or send it by Express Mail as soon as possible so that we can complete your returns before the April 15, 19x0 deadline.

[Closing],

YOUR SIGNATURE

INFORMING CLIENT OF CHANGES IN TAX LAW

Federal income tax laws are constantly changing, sometimes moderately, sometimes drastically, and it is important to keep clients informed of these changes. The following letter is a model of its kind—but a model only, since it deals with a specific situation in the past.

YOUR LETTERHEAD

[Date]

INSIDE ADDRESS

[Salutation]:

During the past few weeks, Congress has discussed many new ideas involving changes in the tax law. If any or all of the changes are enacted, they will affect items to be deducted in 19x5 and the tax rates in effect during 19x5.

A general rule of thumb for a taxpayer with substantial taxable income is to defer all taxable income possible until 19x5 and pay all deductible expenses prior to December 31, 19x4. Doing so will take advantage of the likely changes in tax laws from 19x4 to 19x5.

We encourage you to pay all deductible expenses, such as real estate taxes, interest, contributions, tax-advisory service fees, rentals, and business-related items prior to the end of the year, while we know for certain what laws and regulations apply.

In line with maximizing your tax benefit, we are including with this letter a retainer statement for our services. Assuming that payment is made prior to December 31, 19x4, you will be able to take a larger deduction for 19x4 than will otherwise be possible. Of course, whatever amounts you pay will be applied toward actual services rendered, and any differences will be reconciled later.

If you have any questions about the changes taking place, or about your retainer statement, please feel free to contact us.

We wish you a happy holiday season and a prosperous new year.

[Closing],

YOUR SIGNATURE

LETTER TO IRS FOR QUALIFICATION OF RETIREMENT PLAN

This letter contains all the documents required for the Internal Revenue Service to reach a decision as to whether contributions to the plan will be tax deductible.

Internal Revenue Service
EP/EO Division
Post Office Box 1680
Newark, New Jersey 07101

[Salutation]:

SUBJECT: TRI-CITY SALVAGE COMPANY
[Employer Identification Number]

Enclosed are the following documents submitted on behalf of the taxpayer named above:

1. Retirement Plan and Trust
2. Form 5300 and applicable attachments
3. Form 2848, Power of Attorney
4. Executed Corporate Resolution
5. Notice to Employees

We request a determination that the plan is qualified under Section 401(a) of the Code, that the associated trust is qualified under Section 501(a) of the Code, and that, therefore, contributions by the taxpayer to the plan and trust will be tax deductible.

If you have any questions or require further information, please feel free to contact us.

[Closing],

____

YOUR SIGNATURE

____

NOTE TO IRS ON FINAL PARTNERSHIP RETURN

In part this is a transmittal letter, but it is more than that because it also informs the IRS of the termination of the partnership. Send this letter by certified mail, return receipt requested. Be sure to label the return as being FINAL.

YOUR LETTERHEAD

[Date]

Internal Revenue Service
1040 Waverly Avenue
Holtsville, New York 00501

[Salutation]:

SUBJECT: FAR ACRES DEVELOPMENT COMPANY
[Tax Identification Number]
Attached notice and Form 1065

You will find attached a copy of the final return filed for this partnership for the calendar year ended 19x5.

Please note that 19x4 was the last year of active business for the partnership. The assets were distributed to the two partners, and they continued to operate the business as two separate, sole proprietorships.

If you have any questions on this matter, please let me know.

[Closing],

____

YOUR SIGNATURE

EXPLANATORY NOTE TO STATE REQUESTING REFUND DUE

When explaining an oversight on their part to the IRS or state or local tax authorities, both tact and specificity are called for, as shown by this letter.

YOUR LETTERHEAD

[Date]

State of New Jersey
Division of Taxation
CN 244
Trenton, New Jersey 08646

[Salutation]:

SUBJECT: FITTS, GEORGE L. & MARGARET C.
[Social Security Numbers]
Unrefunded overpayment, 19x3 NJTT-203

The taxpayers named above moved from New York State to New Jersey in 19x3. All required tax forms, city, state, and federal, were filed before April 15, 19x4.

Line [number] on form NJTT-203 shows an overpayment of [$ amount], which the taxpayers requested to be refunded. As of this date, they have not received the refund.

I enclose complete copies of 19x3 NJ 1040NR and related NJTT-203. You will notice that the taxpayers submitted a check for [$ amount] along with these two returns. I enclose a copy of the canceled check and copies of their W-2 forms.

Please review this matter and expedite the refund at your earliest convenience.

[Closing],

YOUR SIGNATURE

NOTICE OF TERMINATION OF BUSINESS

Most states have a fixed set of forms necessary to advise them of the termination of a business. In the absence of such forms, this letter should serve the purpose.

YOUR LETTERHEAD

[Date]

State of New Jersey
Sales and Use Tax
CN 260
Trenton, New Jersey 08646

[Salutation]:

SUBJECT: PENNEVER INDUSTRIES CORP.
[Tax Identification Number]

This is to advise you that the above corporation has ceased all activities effective June 1, 19x9, and has paid all sales and use taxes through that date.

Please place this corporation on inactive status.

If you require additional information, do not hesitate to contact me.

[Closing],

YOUR SIGNATURE

CHAPTER 11

Tax Transmittal Letters

- All-Purpose Tax Transmittal Letter
- General Purpose Transmittal for Form 1040
- Individual Letter to Filer of Form 1040, Tax Owed
- Individual Letter to Filer of Form 1040, Refund Due
- Combined Federal and State Transmittal, "Boxed" Format
- Combined Federal and State Transmittal, Open Format
- Happy Face/Sad Face Federal and State Transmittal
- U.S. Estimated Tax Payments with Checklist
- U.S. Fiduciary Income Tax Transmittal
- Alternate Form for U.S. Fiduciary Income Tax Return
- Form for Sending Client Application for Tax ID Number
- Transmittal for U.S. Partnership Tax Return
- Alternate Form for U.S. Partnership Tax Return
- Transmittal for U.S. Corporation Tax Return
- Alternate Form for U.S. Corporation Tax Return
- Transmittal for U.S. Short-form Corporation Tax Return
- U.S. Corporation Estimated Tax Payments
- State Corporation Tax Return
- State Corporation Estimated Tax Payments
- Transmittal Letter for Form 1139 (Corporate Refund)
- Transmittal Letter for Form 5500-C (Pension Plan)

Tax transmittal letters are as varied as the fifty states. A complete collection of them, involving all state and local tax forms, as well as federal tax forms, would fill many volumes. The collection in this chapter is a representative sample, mainly focused on common federal tax forms.

The purpose of a tax transmittal letter is to convey essential information that the client needs in order to file properly the returns enclosed with it. Generally speaking, this information includes the kind of tax, the due date of returns, the amount of refund or payment due, the person who should sign the returns, and the place where they should be sent.

Since this is cut-and-dried information—much the same for each client—the practice of using form letters as tax transmittals began a long time ago. The use of form letters is still widespread for all kinds of federal, state, and local taxes, whether the returns are filed by an individual, a fiduciary, a partnership, or a corporation. With the advent of word processing, however, it has become possible (but unnecessary in many cases) to send separately typed transmittals with some or all tax returns.

Regardless of how you want to reproduce transmittal letters, you should find a number of useful models in this chapter. The wide variety of styles included should also help you in designing the specific forms you will need for your own practice.

ALL-PURPOSE TAX TRANSMITTAL LETTER

The advantage of an all-purpose letter is that it can be used to accompany any kind of tax return. The disadvantage is that since it is so general you have to add a great deal of specific information each time it is used.

INSTRUCTIONS FOR FILING

____

FORM __________________
YEAR ENDED __________________

CLIENT'S NAME____

The attached return must be signed and dated by ________ as indicated on the ________ page(s) of the return. File with ______________________ on or before ______________________________________.

Total tax due $________, with return, or payments may be made as follows:
(Please enter Social Security Number or Tax Identification Number on check.)

____

____

____

____

____

The attached copy of the return is for your files.

Dated: ______________________________

[NAME OF ACCOUNTANT OR ACCOUNTING FIRM]

GENERAL PURPOSE TRANSMITTAL FOR FORM 1040

The following transmittal, like many others in this chapter, is designed to be used as a printed or photocopied form. The required information can be easily added to it by hand or by typewriter.

YOUR LETTERHEAD

[Date]

____

INSIDE ADDRESS

____

[Salutation]:

Attached is Form 1040, U.S. Individual Income Tax Return, for 19____. The copy stamped "Client's Copy" is for your records. The return should be signed (joint returns by husband and wife), dated, and mailed to Internal Revenue Service Center, [city, state, and ZIP] no later than________________. The item indicated below applies to your return:

( ) A check (enter your Social Security Number on the check) payable to "Internal Revenue Service" for $_______ should accompany the return.

( ) No tax is due; no refund will be received.

( ) The overpayment of $________ will be refunded.

( ) The overpayment of $________ was applied to your estimated tax to the extent of $________; the balance, if any, will be refunded.

The item indicated below applies to your estimated tax for 19____.

( ) Based on the information in your income tax return, estimated tax payments are not required. Please notify us of any significant changes in employment or income.

( ) At your request, estimated tax payments were not prepared.

( ) Estimated tax payments should be made. A separate letter explains your estimated tax.

[Closing],

____

YOUR SIGNATURE

____

INDIVIDUAL LETTER TO FILER OF FORM 1040, TAX OWED

This is a form letter that can be typed separately for each client or used as a shell document in a word-processing system (see Chapter 17).

YOUR LETTERHEAD

[Date]

INSIDE ADDRESS

[Salutation]:

SUBJECT: INSTRUCTIONS FOR FILING 19xx U.S. INDIVIDUAL INCOME TAX RETURN

Please sign the original return at the bottom of page 2, Form 1040. You [*or* Both of you] should sign your full name[s].

Your 19xx U.S. Individual Income Tax Return shows a balance due of [$ amount]. Make your check payable to "Internal Revenue Service." Include your Social Security Number and the words "19xx Form 1040" on the check. Attach the check to the bottom of page 1, Form 1040.

The enclosed tax return has been prepared from data submitted to us. It should be reviewed before filing.

Mail the signed return, along with the check, on or before April 15, 19xx to:

INTERNAL REVENUE SERVICE CENTER
[CITY, STATE, ZIP]

If you have any questions about this return, or about future tax planning, please call our office at the number shown above.

[Closing],

YOUR SIGNATURE

INDIVIDUAL LETTER TO FILER OF FORM 1040, REFUND DUE

This letter is a variation on the preceding one. If used in a word-processing system, it can be conveniently divided into two shell documents—one for a full refund, the other for a refund applied against next year's estimated tax.

YOUR LETTERHEAD

[Date]

INSIDE ADDRESS

[Salutation]:

SUBJECT: INSTRUCTIONS FOR FILING 19xx U.S. INDIVIDUAL INCOME TAX RETURN

Please sign the original return at the bottom of page 2, Form 1040. You [*or* Both of you] should sign your full name[s].

Your 19xx U.S. Individual Income Tax Return shows a refund owed you of [$ amount]. This overpayment will be refunded to you in full. [*or:* This overpayment has been applied to your estimated tax for 19xx. *Optional, if applicable:* This overpayment has been applied to your estimated tax to the extent of [$ amount]; the balance will be refunded.]

The enclosed tax return has been prepared from data submitted to us. It should be reviewed before filing.

Mail the signed return on or before April 15, 19xx to:

INTERNAL REVENUE SERVICE CENTER
[CITY, STATE, ZIP]

If you have any questions about this return, or about future tax planning, please call our office at the number shown above.

[Closing],

YOUR SIGNATURE

COMBINED FEDERAL AND STATE TRANSMITTAL, "BOXED" FORMAT

Four separate items are included with this letter. Ruled lines around the instructions for each of the four items help to clarify the transmittal.

YOUR LETTERHEAD

[Date]

INSIDE ADDRESS

[Salutation]:

ENCLOSED ARE YOUR 19x6 INCOME TAX RETURNS AND 19x7 ESTIMATED TAX VOUCHERS. THE RETURNS SHOULD BE SIGNED AND DATED BY BOTH HUSBAND AND WIFE. MAIL YOUR RETURNS ON OR BEFORE APRIL 15, 19x7.

WE HAVE ENCLOSED MAILING ENVELOPES FOR YOUR CONVENIENCE IN FILING YOUR RETURNS.

SPECIFIC FILING INSTRUCTIONS ARE AS FOLLOWS:

FEDERAL INCOME TAX RETURN:

MAIL TO: INTERNAL REVENUE SERVICE CENTER
HOLTSVILLE, NEW YORK 00501

ENCLOSE YOUR CHECK FOR $________ PAYABLE TO: INTERNAL REVENUE SERVICE. INCLUDE YOUR SOCIAL SECURITY NUMBER ON THE CHECK.

FEDERAL ESTIMATED TAX VOUCHERS:

SEPARATELY MAIL VOUCHER 1 OF FORM 1040-ES by April 15, 19x7.

MAIL TO: INTERNAL REVENUE SERVICE CENTER
HOLTSVILLE, NEW YORK 00501

ENCLOSE YOUR CHECK FOR $_______ PAYABLE TO:
INTERNAL REVENUE SERVICE. INCLUDE YOUR SOCIAL SECURITY NUMBER AND THE WORDS "ESTIMATED TAX PAYMENT" ON YOUR CHECK.

RETAIN VOUCHERS 2, 3, AND 4 IN YOUR FILES AND MAIL TO THE ABOVE ADDRESS ON OR BEFORE THE DATES INDICATED.

FOR YOUR REFERENCE WE HAVE LISTED ALL ESTIMATED TAX PAYMENTS AND THEIR DUE DATES BELOW. VOUCHERS REQUIRING NO PAYMENT SHOULD NOT BE FILED.

VOUCHER NO. 1 BY 4/15/19x7 $_______
VOUCHER NO. 2 BY 6/15/19x7 $_______
VOUCHER NO. 3 BY 9/15/19x7 $_______
VOUCHER NO. 4 BY 1/15/19x8 $_______

NEW JERSEY INCOME TAX RETURN:

MAIL YOUR STATE RETURN ON OR BEFORE APRIL 15, 19x7.

MAIL TO: STATE OF NEW JERSEY
DIVISION OF TAXATION
INCOME TAX - CN 111
TRENTON, NEW JERSEY 08645

ENCLOSE YOUR CHECK FOR $_______ PAYABLE TO: STATE OF NEW JERSEY - TGI

NEW JERSEY ESTIMATED TAX VOUCHERS:

SEPARATELY MAIL VOUCHER 1 OF THE DECLARATION OF ESTIMATED TAX BY APRIL 15, 19x7. ENCLOSE YOUR CHECK FOR $________ PAYABLE TO: STATE OF NEW JERSEY - TGI

MAIL TO: STATE OF NEW JERSEY
DIVISION OF TAXATION
CN 222
TRENTON, NEW JERSEY 08646

RETAIN VOUCHERS 2, 3, AND 4 IN YOUR FILES AND MAIL TO THE ABOVE ADDRESS ON OR BEFORE THE DATES INDICATED.

FOR YOUR REFERENCE WE HAVE LISTED ALL ESTIMATED TAX PAYMENTS AND THEIR DUE DATES BELOW.

VOUCHER NO. 1 BY 4/15/19x7 $________
VOUCHER NO. 2 BY 6/15/19x7 $________
VOUCHER NO. 3 BY 9/15/19x7 $________
VOUCHER NO. 4 BY 1/15/19x8 $________

PLEASE REVIEW THESE RETURNS FOR COMPLETENESS AND ACCURACY.

WE SINCERELY APPRECIATE THE OPPORTUNITY TO SERVE YOU. PLEASE CONTACT US IF YOU HAVE ANY QUESTIONS CONCERNING THE TAX RETURNS.

COPIES OF THE COMPLETED RETURNS ARE ENCLOSED FOR YOUR FILES. WE SUGGEST THAT YOU RETAIN THESE COPIES INDEFINITELY.

[Closing],

____

YOUR SIGNATURE

____

COMBINED FEDERAL AND STATE TRANSMITTAL, OPEN FORMAT

The following transmittal serves the same purpose as the preceding one. The main difference is in format. This transmittal is less telegraphic; it reads more like a regular letter.

YOUR LETTERHEAD

[Date]

____

INSIDE ADDRESS

____

[Salutation]:

Enclosed are your 19x7 individual income tax returns.

Your federal return (Form 1040) shows a refund of $________.

Your federal return (Form 1040) shows a balance due of $________. Please make your check payable to "Internal Revenue Service" and attach it to your federal tax return. Be sure to write your Social Security Number on the check.

Your California return (Form 540) shows a refund of $________.

Your California return (Form 540) shows a balance due of $________. Please make your check payable to "Franchise Tax Board" and attach it to your state tax return. Be sure to write your Social Security Number on the check.

Income averaging (Schedule G) was used on your federal return, resulting in a tax saving of $________.

Income averaging (Schedule G) was used on your state return, resulting in a tax saving of $________.

Your 19x8 federal estimated tax vouchers (Form 1040-ES) are also enclosed. On each date indicated, please make a check payable to "Internal Revenue Service," attach it to the due voucher, and mail it to the address shown below.

April 15, 19x8 .... $________

June 15, 19x8 .... $________

September 15, 19x8 .... $________

January 15, 19x9... $________

Mail federal estimated tax payments to:

INTERNAL REVENUE SERVICE CENTER
FRESNO, CALIFORNIA 93888

Include your Social Security Number and the words "Estimated Tax Payment" on your checks.

Your 19x8 California estimated tax vouchers (Form 540-ES) are also enclosed. On each date indicated below, please make a check payable to "Franchise Tax Board," attach it to the due voucher.

April 15, 19x8 .... $________

June 15, 19x8 .... $________

September 15, 19x8 .... $________

January 15, 19x9... $________

Mail state estimated tax payments to:

FRANCHISE TAX BOARD
540-ES UNIT
SACRAMENTO, CALIFORNIA 95867

Include your Social Security Number and the words "Estimated Tax Payment" on your checks. If state voucher 4 is paid in December 19x8, it can be used as an itemized deduction on your 19x8 federal return.

Be sure to fund your IRA to the full amount of $________ by the due date of your return.

Please sign and date each return in the space provided. The returns should be mailed in the attached pre-addressed envelopes on or before the due dates. Complete copies of the returns are enclosed for your records.

[Closing],

____

YOUR SIGNATURE

____

HAPPY FACE/SAD FACE FEDERAL AND STATE TRANSMITTAL

Much shorter and considerably more informal than most tax transmittals, this form contains less detailed information than others in this chapter. It may nevertheless be appropriate, and even ideal, in some circumstances.

YOUR LETTERHEAD

[Date]

FILING INSTRUCTIONS

TO:______________________________

1. Please review your returns: Social Security Numbers, number of dependents, etc.
2. Sign and date the returns. Spouse must sign.
3. Retain copy for your files.

REFUND

FEDERAL $________
STATE $________

TAX DUE

FEDERAL $________
STATE $________

4. This return has been prepared from information furnished by you. It is possible that your financial position will change during the year. Therefore, in regard to your Declaration of Estimated Tax, you should review your income prior to quarterly due dates so that an amended estimate may be filed, if required.
5. Additional instructions:

If you have any questions, please contact me.

[Closing],

YOUR SIGNATURE

U.S. ESTIMATED TAX PAYMENTS WITH CHECKLIST

The checklist at the end of this letter covers four common situations or contingencies. As many as three of them could apply to any given taxpayer.

YOUR LETTERHEAD

[Date]

____

INSIDE ADDRESS

____

[Salutation]:

Attached is Form 1040-ES, U.S. Estimated Tax Payment Voucher for 19x6. The forms should be separated and mailed to Internal Revenue Service Center, [city, state, ZIP], along with a check (enter your Social Security Number on the check) payable to "Internal Revenue Service," as follows:

April 15, 19x5	$________
June 17, 19x5	$________
September 16, 19x5	$________
January 15, 19x6	$________

The checked item or items below apply to your estimated tax:

( ) The estimated tax payments are based on your prior year's tax to protect from underpayment penalties. Please notify us if your income is significantly reduced.

( ) The estimated tax payments are based on your projection of income. Because these payments total less than your prior year's tax, you may be subject to underpayment penalties.

( ) The estimated tax payments are based on federal withholding tax of at least $________.

( ) Overpayment of $________ on your 19x4 federal income tax return was applied to reduce the estimated tax.

[Closing],

____

YOUR SIGNATURE

____

U.S. FIDUCIARY INCOME TAX TRANSMITTAL

YOUR LETTERHEAD

_______________ [Date]

INSIDE ADDRESS

____

[Salutation]:

INSTRUCTIONS FOR FILING

U.S. FIDUCIARY INCOME TAX RETURN (Form 1041)
.... for the year ended _______________

DUE DATE: File the return no later than _______________

MAILING INSTRUCTIONS: (Be sure postage is adequate.)

The return must be signed and dated by the fiduciary. Mail the return to:
INTERNAL REVENUE SERVICE CENTER
[CITY, STATE, ZIP]

U.S. FEDERAL INCOME TAX PAYABLE WITH THIS RETURN: $ [amount]
Balance of tax may be paid in full or as follows:

[date due]	$_______
[date due]	_______
[date due]	_______
[date due]	_______
Total	$_______

U.S. FEDERAL INCOME TAX OVERPAYMENT
.... (which will be refunded) $_______________

We recommend that you mail your tax return by certified mail with return receipt requested. If you have any questions about the filing of your return or payments, please let us know.

[Closing],

____

YOUR SIGNATURE

____

ALTERNATE FORM FOR U.S. FIDUCIARY INCOME TAX RETURN

This transmittal serves the same purpose as the previous one but differs from it in format.

YOUR LETTERHEAD

INSTRUCTIONS FOR FILING
U.S. FIDUCIARY INCOME TAX RETURN (Form 1041)
FOR THE YEAR ENDED________

TAXPAYER:________________________ DATE:__________

DUE DATE	The enclosed return must be filed on or before __________________.
TAX DUE OR REFUND DUE	Total federal income tax .... $________ Tax previously paid or withheld ..... $________ Balance due .... $________ Overpayment (will be refunded) .... $________ Balance of tax may be paid in full on ____[date]____, or as follows: __[date due]__ .... $________ __[date due]__ .... ________ __[date due]__ .... ________ __[date due]__ .... ________ $________
SIGNATURE	The return must be signed and dated by the fiduciary at the bottom of page 1.
MAILING INSTRUCTIONS	Make checks payable to Internal Revenue Service. The signed return and remittance, if any, should be mailed to: INTERNAL REVENUE SERVICE CENTER [CITY, STATE, ZIP]

We will gladly furnish any additional information with respect to the attached return.

[Closing],

____

YOUR SIGNATURE

____

FORM FOR SENDING CLIENT APPLICATION FOR TAX ID NUMBER

Every partnership, corporation (including S corporations), estate, or trust must have an employer identification number (EIN). A sole proprietor who pays wages to one or more employees also needs an EIN. So does a sole proprietor who pays any excise taxes, including those for alcohol, tobacco, or firearms.

YOUR LETTERHEAD

____________________ [Date]

INSIDE ADDRESS

____

[Salutation]:

Since you are a sole proprietor who pays wages to another person, federal income tax regulations require that your employer identification number be shown on your returns.

Our records do not indicate that you have been assigned a number. Consequently, we are enclosing an application for an employer identification number (Form SS-4). This form should be signed, dated, and then mailed to the Internal Revenue Service Center in the attached envelope.

Please let us know the number that has been assigned to you so that we can include it on your future tax returns.

[Closing],

____

YOUR SIGNATURE

____

Encl.
Number assigned: 22-________

TRANSMITTAL FOR U.S. PARTNERSHIP TAX RETURN

In this letter the checklist concerns the handling of the partners' Schedule K-1's.

YOUR LETTERHEAD

[Date]

____

INSIDE ADDRESS

____

[Salutation]:

Attached is Form 1065, U.S. Partnership Return of Income, for the year ended ________. The copy stamped "Client's Copy" is for your records.

The return should be signed by a general partner, dated, and mailed to Internal Revenue Service Center, [city, state, ZIP], no later than __________.

The partners' copies of Schedule K-1, Partner's Share of Income, Credits, Deductions, etc., have been handled as follows:

( ) At your request, K-1's were mailed directly to the partners.

( ) K-1's were retained in our office to be used in preparing the partners' individual income tax returns.

( ) K-1's are enclosed with this letter and should be distributed to the partners.

[Closing],

____

YOUR SIGNATURE

____

ALTERNATE FORM FOR U.S. PARTNERSHIP TAX RETURN

This transmittal letter serves the same purpose as the previous one but differs from it in format.

YOUR LETTERHEAD

______________________________ [Date]

INSIDE ADDRESS

____

[Salutation]:

INSTRUCTIONS FOR FILING

U.S. PARTNERSHIP INCOME TAX RETURN (Form 1065)
..............................for the year ended________________

DUE DATE: File the return no later than________________

MAILING INSTRUCTIONS: (Be sure postage is adequate.)

The return must be signed and dated by a partner or member duly authorized so to act.

Mail the return to:
INTERNAL REVENUE SERVICE CENTER
[CITY, STATE, ZIP]

U.S. PARTNERSHIP INCOME TAX DUE: No tax is due with respect to these returns since the income is reported by the partners individually.

We recommend that you mail your tax return by certified mail and request a return receipt. If you have any questions about the filing of your return, please let us know.

[Closing],

____

YOUR SIGNATURE

____

TRANSMITTAL FOR U.S. CORPORATION TAX RETURN

YOUR LETTERHEAD

[Date]

____

INSIDE ADDRESS

____

[Salutation]:

Attached is Form 1120, U.S. Corporation Income Tax Return, for the year ended ________. The copy stamped "Client's Copy" is for your records.

The return should be signed by an officer, dated, and mailed to Internal Revenue Service, [city, state, ZIP], no later than ________. The item indicated below applies to this return:

( ) A check (enter your employer identification number on the check) payable to your depository bank for $______, accompanied by a Federal Tax Deposit Coupon (please mark 1120 and 4th Quarter), should be deposited at the bank no later than ________.

( ) No tax is due; no refund will be received.

( ) The overpayment of $______ will be refunded.

( ) The overpayment of $______ was applied to your estimated tax to the extent of $______; the balance, if any, will be refunded.

The item indicated below applies to the corporation's estimated tax for the year ending____________:

( ) Based on the information in the income tax return, estimated tax payments are not required. Please notify us of any significant changes in income.

( ) At your request, estimated tax payments were not prepared.

( ) Estimated tax payments should be made. A separate letter explains your estimated tax.

[Closing],

____

YOUR SIGNATURE

____

ALTERNATE FORM FOR U.S. CORPORATION TAX RETURN

This transmittal letter serves the same purpose as the previous one but differs from it in format.

YOUR LETTERHEAD

[Date]

INSIDE ADDRESS

[Salutation]:

INSTRUCTIONS FOR FILING

U.S. CORPORATION INCOME TAX RETURN (Form 1120)
..............................for the year ended________________

DUE DATE: File the return no later than________________

MAILING INSTRUCTIONS: (Be sure postage is adequate.)

The return must be signed and dated by an officer of the corporation.

Mail the return to:
Internal Revenue Service Center
[City, State, ZIP]

U.S. Federal Income Tax Due.......................... $__________

DO NOT REMIT PAYMENTS TO THE INTERNAL REVENUE SERVICE

All payments must be deposited at an authorized commercial bank depository or a federal reserve bank or branch, along with a Federal Tax Deposit Coupon, properly marked. The *balance* of the tax due *must be paid in full* when the return is due to be filed.

We recommend that you mail your tax return by certified mail and request a return receipt. If you have any questions about the filing of your return or payments, please let us know.

U.S. FEDERAL INCOME TAX OVERPAYMENT .... $__________

Amount credited to 19____ estimated tax __________

Refund due you .... __________

U.S. CORPORATION ESTIMATED INCOME TAX for the year ended ________ is due as follows:

First payment	[date due]	$__________
Second payment	[date due]	__________
Third payment	[date due]	__________
Fourth payment	[date due]	__________
	Total	$__________

[Closing],

____

YOUR SIGNATURE

____

TRANSMITTAL FOR U.S. SHORT-FORM CORPORATION TAX RETURN

YOUR LETTERHEAD

[Date]

INSIDE ADDRESS

[Salutation]:

INSTRUCTIONS FOR FILING

U.S. SHORT-FORM CORPORATION INCOME TAX RETURN (Form 1120-A) ....for the year ended________

DUE DATE: File the return no later than________

MAILING INSTRUCTIONS: (Be sure postage is adequate).

The return must be signed and dated by an officer of the corporation.

Mail the return to:
INTERNAL REVENUE SERVICE CENTER
[CITY, STATE, ZIP]

U.S. FEDERAL INCOME TAX DUE .... $________

DO NOT REMIT PAYMENTS TO THE INTERNAL REVENUE SERVICE

All payments must be deposited at an authorized commercial bank depository or a federal reserve bank or branch, along with a Federal Tax Deposit Coupon, properly marked. The *balance* of the tax due *must be paid in full* when the return is due to be filed.

U.S. FEDERAL INCOME TAX OVERPAYMENT .... $________

Amount credited to 19___ estimated tax .... ________

Refund due you .... ________

We recommend that you mail your tax return by certified mail and request a return receipt. If you have any questions about the filing of your return or payments, please let us know.

[Closing],

YOUR SIGNATURE

U.S. CORPORATION ESTIMATED TAX PAYMENTS

YOUR LETTERHEAD

[Date]

____

INSIDE ADDRESS

____

[Salutation]:

U.S. Corporation Estimated Tax payments are required for the year ending ________. These payments should be made as follows:

1. Make a check payable to your authorized depository bank. Enter your employer identification number on each check.
2. Attach the check to a federal tax deposit coupon. Write "1120" on the coupon, as well as the appropriate quarter as indicated below (e.g., "1120 — 3rd Quarter").
3. Deposit the check and coupon at the bank.

The item or items indicated below apply to the estimated tax:

( ) The estimated tax payments are based on the prior year's income and tax so as to protect the corporation from underpayment penalties. Please notify us if income is significantly reduced.

( ) The estimated tax payments are based on your projection of income and tax. Because this amount is less than the prior year's income and tax, you may be subject to underpayment penalties.

( ) Overpayment of $________ on the U.S. Corporation Income Tax Return was applied to reduce the estimated tax.

[Closing],

____

YOUR SIGNATURE

____

STATE CORPORATION TAX RETURN

The following form, with slight modifications, should be usable in most states.

YOUR LETTERHEAD

____________________ [Date]

INSIDE ADDRESS

____

[Salutation]:

INSTRUCTIONS FOR FILING

CALIFORNIA CORPORATION FRANCHISE TAX RETURN (Form 100)

FOR THE YEAR ENDED________

TAXPAYER:____________________ Date:__________

DUE DATE	The enclosed return must be filed on or before ________.
TAX DUE OR REFUND DUE	\$________ payable to the Franchise Tax Board in full. \$________ will be refunded to you by the state of California.
SIGNATURE AND DATE	An officer of the corporation must sign and date the return at the bottom of page 1.
MAILING	Mail the return and a check, if required, to: FRANCHISE TAX BOARD SACRAMENTO, CALIFORNIA 95857

We will gladly furnish any additional information with respect to the attached return.

[Closing],

____

YOUR SIGNATURE

____

STATE CORPORATION ESTIMATED TAX PAYMENTS

Requirements for this transmittal may vary somewhat from state to state. The sample below relates to California.

YOUR LETTERHEAD

[Date]

____

INSIDE ADDRESS

____

[Salutation]:

CALIFORNIA CORPORATION ESTIMATED TAX (Form 100-ES)
. . . . for year ending ____________

Installment payments must be made in accordance with the following schedule:

Overpayment applied		$__________
First payment	[date due]	$__________
Second payment	[date due]	$__________
Third payment	[date due]	$__________
Fourth payment	[date due]	$__________
Total payments		$__________

Each payment should be accompanied by a payment voucher. An officer of the corporation should sign and date the voucher where indicated. Mail vouchers to:

FRANCHISE TAX BOARD
SACRAMENTO, CALIFORNIA 95857

Envelopes for these returns are enclosed for your convenience.

Please contact us if you have any questions.

[Closing],

____

YOUR SIGNATURE

____

TRANSMITTAL LETTER FOR FORM 1139 (CORPORATE REFUND)

A corporation that has sustained a net operating loss (NOL) may secure prompt administrative action by filing an application on Form 1139 for tentative carryback of NOL.

YOUR LETTERHEAD

____________________ [Date]

INSIDE ADDRESS

____

[Salutation]:

INSTRUCTIONS FOR FILING

Attached is Federal Form 1139.

1. The original of this form should be signed and dated, where indicated, by an officer of the corporation.
2. There is no tax due with this form.
3. *Do not* attach Form 1139 to your income tax return. Submit it separately.
4. Form 1139 must be filed within one year after the year in which the net operating loss, net capital loss, or unused investment credit arose, but only after the return for such year is filed.
5. Mail the signed copy of this form to:

   INTERNAL REVENUE SERVICE CENTER
   [CITY, STATE, ZIP]

A copy of the completed form is enclosed for your files.

[Closing],

____

YOUR SIGNATURE

____

TRANSMITTAL LETTER FOR FORM 5500-C (PENSION PLAN)

Annual returns for each funded plan of deferred compensation must be filed with the IRS (Code Sec. 6058). Form 5500 is used for plans with 100 or more participants. Form 5500-C is used for plans with fewer than 100 participants.

YOUR LETTERHEAD

[Date]

PERSONAL AND CONFIDENTIAL

INSIDE ADDRESS

[Salutation]:

SUBJECT: GOVERNMENT FORM 5500-C FOR PENSION PLAN YEAR BEGINNING AUGUST 1, 19x4

We enclose two copies of the following forms, one for filing and the other for your records:

(a) Form 5500-C
(b) Schedule P
(c) Schedule B
(d) Summary Annual Report Notice to Employees

Please sign and date both copies of items (a) and (b) and mail the originals, along with item (c), to:

INTERNAL REVENUE SERVICE CENTER
[CITY, STATE, ZIP]

In order to avoid the assessment of late filing penalties, the forms should be mailed in time for receipt by May 15, 19x6.

A copy of the enclosed Notice to Employees, item (d), should be distributed to each participant no later than June 15, 19x6.

If you have any questions, or if we can be of any assistance, please do not hesitate to call.

[Closing],

YOUR SIGNATURE

CHAPTER 12

Letters Concerning Tax Returns and IRS Tax Audits

- Reason for Late Filing of Tax Returns
- Request for Credit for IRS Payment Already Made
- Request for Correction of Taxpayer's Account
- Request for Status of Taxpayer's Account
- Resolving a Continuing Problem with the IRS
- Request for Abatement of Penalties Assessed on Underpayment
- Explanation and Request for Abatement of Penalties
- Correcting Errors Made by Previous Accountant
- Asking the IRS How to Proceed with Problem Resolution
- Apology for Late Reply to Notices
- Letter Clarifying Status of Taxpayer
- Eliminating State Taxpayer Registration Number
- Humorous Letter Explaining a State Tax Mistake
- Relaying IRS Agent's Request for More Data
- Postponement of Audit to Obtain Documents
- Letter Asking Client for Information for Tax Exam
- Letter Summarizing Results of Tax Examination
- Notification of Acceptance of Form 1040 as Filed
- Recommendation That Client Accept Deficiency
- Letter Advising Client to Sign Waiver

Although the Internal Revenue Service is seldom regarded as one of America's beloved institutions, and although horror stories about it abound, it is nevertheless staffed by people, not machines. No machine, after all, can read a letter. When you write a letter to the IRS—even when the letter is addressed to that impersonal, two-line, no-street destination—it will be read by a human being.

Your correspondence to the Internal Revenue Service should be concise and tactful. It should display sound professional judgment. The approach and tone of a letter to the IRS (as with any other letter) can make a significant difference. The specific type of correspondence obviously helps to determine what is appropriate. A letter in response to a computer-generated, unmatched 1099 Notice will differ considerably from one sent directly to a named revenue agent relating to an audit.

Since a sizable percentage of letters to the IRS go to an unknown recipient, you lack the advantage that familiarity with your reader can offer. You often have to write in a void, trying to anticipate responses, hoping that what you say will have the desired effect. This is not easy, but it can be done, as the letters in this chapter show.

The letters here, as throughout the book, were obtained from accountants across the country. They are (or were) successful letters, but no one can predict what will succeed at any given time under any given set of circumstances, particularly with the IRS. A letter that works brilliantly on one occasion may fail dismally on another. You should keep that in mind whenever you write to the IRS, and whenever you use or adapt the letters in this chapter.

REASON FOR LATE FILING OF TAX RETURNS

The following letter explains in some detail the circumstances that led to late filing. Its purpose is to try to convince the IRS to waive the penalties that have been assessed. Different circumstances would call for different particulars, but this is a good model of a letter that succeeded.

YOUR LETTERHEAD

[Date]

Internal Revenue Service
Holtsville, New York 00501

[Salutation]:

SUBJECT: LAKEVIEW FLORISTS
22-*******
DLN******

The taxpayer named above has received the attached notices indicating that certain penalties have been assessed.

It should be noted that this is a new business started in 19x4 by Mr. and Mrs. William Hathaway. Not long after its start-up, Mr. Hathaway passed away unexpectedly. This event had a profound effect on Mrs. Hathaway, who has had to take over in his absence. Because of certain financial commitments that had been made prior to Mr. Hathaway's untimely death, she had no choice but to proceed with the venture.

Mrs. Hathaway's unfamiliarity with the running of a business resulted in her late filing of these returns. In view of the circumstances that led to this unintentional late filing and Mrs. Hathaway's ignorance of the law regarding it, we request that consideration be given to abating the penalties assessed.

We hope you will consider this matter favorably.

[Closing],

____

YOUR SIGNATURE

____

Enclosures
cc: Mrs. Edith Hathaway

REQUEST FOR CREDIT FOR IRS PAYMENT ALREADY MADE

Very little needs to be explained in this letter, since it simply accompanies a photocopy of a check proving that the uncredited payment was made.

YOUR LETTERHEAD

[Date]

Internal Revenue Service
Holtsville, New York 00501

[Salutation]:

SUBJECT: NICOLL-LAMPERT COMPANY
22-*******
DLN******
Form 941: Dec. 31, 19x6

Regarding this notice, you will find enclosed a copy of the front and back of the above-named taxpayer's canceled check representing payment of the amount shown as being due.

Please look into this matter and give proper credit to the taxpayer's account.

Thank you.

[Closing],

YOUR SIGNATURE

REQUEST FOR CORRECTION OF TAXPAYER'S ACCOUNT

This letter is similar to the preceding one. Here, however, the taxpayer has received a number of notices.

YOUR LETTERHEAD

[Date]

Internal Revenue Service
Holtsville, New York 00501

[Salutation]:

SUBJECT: DAVID A. KASSIAN, INC.
22-*******
DLN******

Mr. Kassian has received the notice indicated above.

We enclose photocopies of the front and back of the canceled checks used in payment of the Form 941 tax liability for the quarter ended March 31, 19x5.

Please correct the taxpayer's account.

Also, please note that this taxpayer, who is very careful to make his tax deposits on time, receives a notice almost every quarter. You can see from the copies of his canceled checks that he shows his employer identification number, quarter, and form number clearly and makes his deposits at his bank using the proper deposit slip.

[Closing],

____

YOUR SIGNATURE

____

Enclosures
cc: Mr. David A. Kassian

REQUEST FOR STATUS OF TAXPAYER'S ACCOUNT

The main difference between this and the two previous letters is that in this one the accountant asks the IRS not only to credit a payment (in fact, an overpayment) but also to report on the status of the account.

YOUR LETTERHEAD

[Date]

Internal Revenue Service
Holtsville, New York 00501

[Salutation]:

SUBJECT: SONDRA FEIBELMAN
22-*******
DLN******

The taxpayer above has received the referenced notice and forwarded it to me.

Enclosed is a copy of the front and back of the canceled check used to pay the liability referred to in this notice. As you will see, the taxpayer actually overpaid this liability.

Please compare your records against the enclosed documentation and advise of the status of this taxpayer's account.

Thank you.

[Closing],

YOUR SIGNATURE

Enclosures
cc: Ms. Sondra Feibelman

RESOLVING A CONTINUING PROBLEM WITH THE IRS

This letter and its enclosures follow a telephone call and attempt to straighten out a long-standing problem.

YOUR LETTERHEAD

[Date]

Internal Revenue Service
Problem Resolution Office
Attn: Ms. Greene
Newark, New Jersey 07102

Dear Ms. Greene:

SUBJECT: L.G. KIRTLAND, INC.
22-*******
DLN******
Form 941: Dec. 31, 19x7

In accordance with your request, I am enclosing all previous correspondence to and from the Internal Revenue Service regarding the taxpayer named above.

As I indicated to you during our telephone conversation of [date], the Form 941 balance you show of [$ amount] comes from the June 30, 19x5 quarter. Apparently this balance has been carried forward by the Internal Revenue Service because the June 30, 19x5 return was not marked "FINAL." Payment against this liability is supported by the enclosed copies of the front and back of canceled checks.

L.G. Kirtland, Inc. performed engineering and surveying services. When Mr. Kirtland, the president, died unexpectedly on May 22, 19x5, all activities of this business ceased. The last payroll the corporation paid was in June, 19x5.

We have been attempting to resolve this misunderstanding for nearly two years. After discussing the situation with you, I feel confident the matter will be closed shortly.

Please let me know if you have any further questions.

[Closing],

YOUR SIGNATURE

Enclosures
cc: [Attorney for Mr. Kirtland's estate]

REQUEST FOR ABATEMENT OF PENALTIES ASSESSED ON UNDERPAYMENT

Form 2210 (individuals) or Form 2220 (corporations) should be used to explain the reason for underpayment of the current year's tax and to request abatement of penalties if the taxpayer qualifies under one of the specified exemptions. This letter can serve as a transmittal of either Form 2210 or Form 2220.

YOUR LETTERHEAD

[Date]

Internal Revenue Service
Holtsville, New York 00501

[Salutation]:

SUBJECT LINE

We respectfully request abatement of assessed penalties in the amount of [$ amount] regarding the above-named taxpayer.

We base this request on exception one, prior year's tax, and enclose Form 2220.

Your consideration of this request is appreciated.

[Closing],

YOUR SIGNATURE

EXPLANATION AND REQUEST FOR ABATEMENT OF PENALTIES

This letter contains a detailed explanation of the situation that led to the problem and penalties.

YOUR LETTERHEAD

[Date]

Internal Revenue Service
Holtsville, New York 00501

[Salutation]:

SUBJECT: BOSNIA CONSTRUCTION COMPANY
22-*******
DLN******
Form 941: Quarters ended 3/31/19x7
6/30/19x7
9/30/19x7

We have received your notice indicated above, and it brings a significant discrepancy to our attention.

The taxpayer's payroll tax account was not credited for any of the federal payroll tax deposits made during the first three quarters of 19x7. Attached are copies of the front and back of canceled checks representing FICA and federal withholding deposits made during the first quarters of 19x7. A summary of payments and payroll tax liabilities follows:

Quarter	*Liability per Form 941*	*Deposits per canceled checks*
3/31/19x7	[$ amount]	[$ amount]
6/30/19x7	[$ amount]	[$ amount]
9/30/19x7	[$ amount]	[$ amount]

Underpayment	[$ amount]
Overpayment on 12/31/19x7 (Form 941 attached)	[$ amount]
Balance due (check enclosed)	[$ amount]

For the first nine months of 19x7, the taxpayer had engaged an accounting firm from [city, state] and instructed that firm to advise the taxpayer of all federal and state filing and deposit requirements and to prepare all federal and state payroll tax returns. For whatever reason, some of the deposits as calculated by these former accountants were incorrect.

Acting in good faith and following the accountant's instructions, the taxpayer made these deposits exactly as instructed (and on time, I might add).

It is, and always has been, this taxpayer's practice to comply with all federal and state tax regulations. When the taxpayer received your notice, this office was immediately contacted; hence this letter along with the necessary documentation and taxpayer's check.

On the basis of the facts presented here, we respectfully request abatement of all penalties and interest.

Thank you for your fair consideration.

[Closing],

____

YOUR SIGNATURE

____

Enclosures
cc: Mr. R.T. Phelps, Bosnia Construction Company

CORRECTING ERRORS MADE BY PREVIOUS ACCOUNTANT

The IRS will consider abatement of penalties based on reasonable cause—but there is no clear-cut definition of *reasonable cause.* The following letter explains a situation that should qualify—but there are no guarantees.

YOUR LETTERHEAD

[Date]

Internal Revenue Service
Holtsville, New York 00501

[Salutation]:

SUBJECT LINE

In regard to the taxpayer named above, the following items are enclosed:

1. Duly executed power of attorney (Form 2848)
2. Taxpayer's check #1683 payable to the Internal Revenue Service in the amount of $400.

This taxpayer entrusted his former accountant with all financial aspects of his business since its inception. Late in 19x4 it became more and more difficult for the taxpayer to contact his accountant. When the taxpayer learned that his accountant was institutionalized for an alcohol problem, he immediately contacted this office. In January 19x6, I began to rectify the errors committed by the former accountant.

I have made my client aware of the filing and reporting requirements set forth by the Internal Revenue Service, and he has assured me of his intent to comply.

Kindly credit the enclosed $400 to the taxpayer's past-due payroll tax account and forward to me an analysis of that account. At this time, based on the facts stated, I respectfully request abatement of all penalties that have been assessed.

Thank you for your consideration.

[Closing],

____

YOUR SIGNATURE

____

ASKING THE IRS HOW TO PROCEED WITH PROBLEM RESOLUTION

Many practitioners have experienced serious delays in resolving particular matters with the IRS even after intervention by the Problem Resolution Office. One frustrated accountant, after more than two years of correspondence, went right to the top in the district.

YOUR LETTERHEAD

[Date]

Mr. Aloysius J. Perry
District Director, Internal Revenue Service
970 State Street, Room 1660
Newark, New Jersey 07101

[Salutation]:

SUBJECT LINE

We have been in touch with your Problem Resolution Office in regard to this taxpayer since November 28, 19x4. Last week Problem Resolution sent us a form letter referring us to Taxpayer Service. Our understanding is that when problems of this kind continue to exist, the Problem Resolution Office is the appropriate authority.

Please advise us how we should proceed. I enclose copies of all previous correspondence.

[Closing],

YOUR SIGNATURE

APOLOGY FOR LATE REPLY TO NOTICES

With luck, you will never have to write a letter like this.

YOUR LETTERHEAD

[Date]

Chief of Taxpayers Assistance Section
Internal Revenue Service
Holtsville, New York 00501

[Salutation]:

SUBJECT LINE

I regret the late reply to your notices. I had extended the due date of this return, but prior to that date I was rushed to the hospital with a possible heart attack.

However, the two partners had been given their K-1's so that they could file their returns by the extended due date, which they did.

This oversight on my part is regrettable, but under the circumstances outlined above, I formally request abatement of the penalty.

Your favorable consideration of this request would be appreciated.

[Closing],

YOUR SIGNATURE

LETTER CLARIFYING STATUS OF TAXPAYER

This is the first of three letters dealing with problems involving state taxes.

YOUR LETTERHEAD

[Date]

State of New Jersey
Division of Taxation—Sales and Use Tax
CN 260
Trenton, New Jersey 08646-0260

[Salutation]:

SUBJECT LINE

The taxpayer named above has received the enclosed notice.

This taxpayer does not collect sales taxes and is not subject to use taxes. His name and assigned number should be removed from your rolls.

Although the taxpayer has written to you in the past to advise you of this, he continues to receive notices.

If you have any questions concerning this matter, please direct them to my attention. Thank you.

[Closing],

YOUR SIGNATURE

ELIMINATING STATE TAXPAYER REGISTRATION NUMBER

Keeping on top of small matters can sometimes prevent big problems later.

YOUR LETTERHEAD

[Date]

New York State Department of Labor
Unemployment Insurance Division
State Office Building Campus
Albany, New York 12240

[Salutation]:

SUBJECT LINE

This letter is in response to your "Report to Determine Liability Under the New York State Unemployment Insurance Law."

Please note that the only employee of the above-named taxpayer was his spouse. Any payments made to a spouse do not qualify as remuneration according to item 8a (6) of your Form A-100.1A(5-85). Therefore, this taxpayer is not subject to registration with your department.

Kindly correct your records to reflect this situation and eliminate his assigned taxpayer registration number. Thank you.

[Closing],

YOUR SIGNATURE

HUMOROUS LETTER EXPLAINING A STATE TAX MISTAKE

There are not too many occasions when an amusing letter is appropriate, but the following situation seems to be one of them. Even though the facts could be explained straight-forwardly, you can easily see why the accountant found the humorous approach impossible to resist.

YOUR LETTERHEAD

[Date]

Illinois Department of Revenue
Tax Processing Center
P.O. Box 4019
Springfield, Illinois 62702

Dear Mr. Computer:

SUBJECT LINE

My name is [name of client's son]. I am 10 years old, and I have a problem. You are trying to collect $489.17 from me, and I don't think I owe it. (See attached Form ITR-85, Final Notice Before Filing Lien.)

Let me try to tell you what happened. On September 25, 19x7, when I was eight years old, I sold some "listed securities." I had received the securities as a gift from my grandpa several years ago. My grandpa bought them on January 5, 19x1, and even though I wasn't around then, that became my "date of acquisition."

On my 19x7 Illinois return, I showed the sale, but because of the August 1, 19x9 valuation limitation, I adjusted the gain taxable in Illinois. And since the securities were "listed securities," I used the August 1, 19x9 value of the securities (as listed in one of those books) to limit my Illinois gain. To be honest with you, I didn't really do all that fancy stuff. My CPA [name and address of accountant] did it. He told me that he did everything the right way, and I believe him because he's been doing my return since I was just a little kid.

Well, anyway, in September 1978, you wrote me asking for $412.58 additional tax, because you thought this stock thing wasn't done the right way on my 1977 return. I am enclosing your letter to me dated September 20, 19x8, asking for more money and also indicating that I had not submitted an appraisal with the return. Well, Mr. [last name of accountant] said I do not need an appraisal since the stock was a "listed security." He said he put everything necessary on that Schedule D thing for 1978.

I was really confused, so I asked Mr. [last name of accountant] to call or write you. He said he had done both more than a year ago, and I am enclosing a copy of his letter to you dated October 31, 19x8, explaining the whole thing.

Gosh, I hope this letter and all the things stapled to it help you understand what my CPA did. I really don't want you to file a lien, because the only assets I have are my sled and my bike. I'm using the sled now, and I just got the bike from Santa Claus and haven't even used it yet. Please, Mr. Computer, tell me that everything is okay.

[Closing],

CLIENT'S SON'S SIGNATURE

Enclosures
cc: [Accountant]
[Father]

RELAYING IRS AGENT'S REQUEST FOR MORE DATA

This letter and the ones that follow deal with IRS examinations. In this case, the IRS agent has requested more information in regard to the examination.

YOUR LETTERHEAD

[Date]

Mr. Jay Loomis, Treasurer
The Woodworks, Inc.
3456 Commercial Drive
St. Paul, Minnesota 55101

Dear Mr. Loomis:

SUBJECT: IRS EXAMINATION OF THE WOODWORKS, INC.
FOR FISCAL YEARS ENDED 8/31/x7 AND 8/31/x8

Enclosed is a list of additional information that the Internal Revenue Service agent requires to complete his examination for the years indicated.

Please forward the material to me as soon as possible. In view of the amount of data requested, you may want to send it in by segments as it is assembled.

[Closing],

YOUR SIGNATURE

POSTPONEMENT OF AUDIT TO OBTAIN DOCUMENTS

It is not unusual to need additional time to gather appropriate information for an audit. The IRS should be given ample notice. Generally the IRS does not like to reschedule audits more than twice, but there seems to be no actual rule to that effect.

YOUR LETTERHEAD

[Date]

Internal Revenue Service
Wheaton Plaza South
Wheaton, Maryland 20902

Dear Mr. Loomis:

SUBJECT: DAVID AND VALERIE DIXON
[Social Security Number]

This letter is in reference to your letter of July 22, 19x5 (a copy of page 1 is attached), requesting my clients to appear on August 16, 19x5, at 1:15 p.m. for an audit of their 19x3 tax return.

Enclosed is a copy of a duly executed power of attorney Form 2848, authorizing me to represent the taxpayers before the Internal Revenue Service in this matter.

I have met with my clients and reviewed their records and tax returns. We noted that some records were missing, and I have therefore instructed my clients to obtain copies from various third parties. These documents will be needed to support certain items claimed on the 19x3 tax returns.

In order to have the audit process proceed efficiently, it would be best to meet with you when all relevant documents have been obtained. Therefore, I respectfully request a postponement of the audit appointment for about 30 days until the documents can be assembled.

Since I will be representing my clients in this matter, please call my office to arrange a convenient time to schedule the audit of their 19x3 tax returns.

Thank you for your cooperation in this matter.

[Closing],

____

YOUR SIGNATURE

LETTER ASKING CLIENT FOR INFORMATION FOR TAX EXAM

When questions arise in connection with a tax examination, a phone call may provide you with the answers. If the problem is tricky, however, or if there are a number of parts to it, you may want to raise the questions in a letter.

YOUR LETTERHEAD

[Date]

Ms. Deborah Stevens
313 Nazareth Hill Road
Barkley, Kentucky 41600

Dear Ms. Stevens:

SUBJECT: IRS EXAMINATION OF 19x7 TAX RETURN OF IVOR ASSOCIATES

A few questions have arisen in regard to this examination. I am writing to each of the partners of Ivor Associates in an attempt to clarify the situation. If you can supply answers to any or all of the following questions, I would appreciate hearing from you promptly.

1. The files relating to Ivor Associates' contract with the Southside Training Center are incomplete. The one-year contract was canceled after three months, but biweekly payments on it seem to have been made for five months thereafter. Can you supply some kind of written evidence to show why these payments continued?
2. No supporting evidence exists regarding the year-long rental of an IBM PC and Epson printer. It is my understanding that this equipment was used entirely for business purposes in various associates' homes throughout the year. Do you have (a) the rental papers for this equipment and/or (b) a log or other document showing your own individual use of the equipment?
3. The expense-account sheets that were submitted following your July convention in Aruba generally fail to name a person or persons and a business purpose under entertainment expenses. It may be too late to rectify this, but it is worth making the attempt. Please examine your own

records for the July convention and send me any missing specifics you find on entertainment expenses.

Since this tax examination is in the last stages of discussion, I hope you will send me your answers as quickly as possible. A favorable resolution of the issues in this examination will result in a considerable tax saving for Ivor Associates.

[Closing],

YOUR SIGNATURE

LETTER SUMMARIZING RESULTS OF TAX EXAMINATION

Occasionally you will have to report bad news. In this letter, the accountant tactfully informs her client that additional taxes plus interest are being assessed as a consequence of the tax examination.

YOUR LETTERHEAD

[Date]

Mr. Orrin Deutsch, President
MicroVenture Ltd.
14 Diskette Drive
Seaver, Massachusetts 02300

Dear Mr. Deutsch:

SUBJECT: IRS EXAMINATION OF 19x6 INDIVIDUAL TAX RETURN AND TAX RETURN FOR MICROVENTURE LTD.

My meetings with Mr. Brown, the Internal Revenue agent conducting this examination, have been concluded, and the results are as follows:

1. Except for Line 18 (partnership income), your individual return for 19x6 has been accepted as filed. However, its totals have been affected by the partial disallowance of two deductions on the MicroVenture partnership return, Form 1065, as explained below.
2. Despite attempts to substantiate the partnership's $7,200 deduction for travel and entertainment expenses, Mr. Brown, after much negotiation, declared that he had to disallow $4,500 of that amount. I tried without success to get him to consent to a smaller disallowance.
3. Mr. Brown also disallowed $600 of the $935 that the partnership claimed as charitable deductions. This disallowance was based on a lack of sufficient documentation.
4. No other changes were required on either the partnership return or your individual return. The $2,675 that the partnership claimed for repairs was allowed, notwithstanding the sketchiness of the receipts, as

was the $3,800 claimed for advertising on radio station WTWX, owned by your uncle.

5. I estimate that the loss of $5,100 in MicroVenture deductions will result in an additional tax on your personal return for 19x6 of approximately $1,420 plus interest.

If you have any questions concerning the results of this tax examination, please call me at any time.

[Closing],

____

YOUR SIGNATURE

____

NOTIFICATION OF ACCEPTANCE OF FORM 1040 AS FILED

This letter conveys the good news that the supporting data requested by the IRS, and submitted to the examining agent, have been accepted, resulting in acceptance of the return as filed.

YOUR LETTERHEAD

[Date]

INSIDE ADDRESS

[Salutation]:

We are pleased to inform you that the Internal Revenue Service has accepted your 19x8 Form 1040 as filed.

The IRS agent accepted in full the data that we had requested from you in support of your medical deduction.

[Closing],

YOUR SIGNATURE

RECOMMENDATION THAT CLIENT ACCEPT DEFICIENCY

A letter of this kind requires tact. The taxpayer is not likely to welcome the news that he or she owes money. Yet if that is the case, it must be conveyed to the client. The best you can do is to (1) present the outcome briefly and factually and (2) make clear that you believe acceptance of the deficiency is a sensible choice.

YOUR LETTERHEAD

[Date]

INSIDE ADDRESS

[Salutation]:

RE: 19x2 AUDIT

Enclosed you will find the examiner's revised report dated [date] concerning this audit. The report shows a balance due of [$ amount]. I suggest that you consent to this amount by signing at the bottom, in the place indicated, and remitting your check immediately.

All things considered, I am satisfied with the outcome of the audit. If you have any questions or disagree with any part of the report, please let me know as soon as possible.

[Closing],

YOUR SIGNATURE

LETTER ADVISING CLIENT TO SIGN WAIVER

Since the taxpayer has decided to accept the examiner's findings, it makes sense to sign the waiver so as to stop the accrual of interest.

YOUR LETTERHEAD

____________________ [Date]

INSIDE ADDRESS

____

[Salutation]:

Enclosed you will find Form 890, Waiver of Restrictions on Assessment and Collection of Deficiency in Tax, which was sent to us by the agent who was reviewing your case. The indicated deficiency is based on the settlement that we discussed on the telephone.

I suggest that you sign the waiver and return it to the agent as soon as possible. The effect of the waiver is to stop the accrual of interest 30 days after it is filed. The waiver is not a final agreement, and the settlement proposed by the agent is subject to review. Agents' reports, however, are usually accepted as submitted.

Soon after the waiver is filed, you will receive a deficiency notice. When you receive it, please make a copy of it and send the copy to us.

I have enclosed an additional copy of the waiver for your files, along with an addressed envelope that you should use in returning the signed original to the agent.

If you have any questions concerning this waiver, please let me know.

[Closing],

____

YOUR SIGNATURE

____

PART V

OFFICE OPERATIONS LETTERS

CHAPTER 13

Invoices, Fees, and Fee Collection

- Explanation of Billing Policies—Individual Income Tax
- Explanation of Billing Policies—Small Business
- Invoice Listing Services
- Accompanying Letter Explaining Invoice
- Detailed Request for Fee Increase
- Brief Letter Announcing Fee Increase
- Letter Explaining Increase in Amount Billed
- Confirmation of Oral Fee Agreement
- Answering a Complaint Concerning Fees
- Friendly Reminder Letter
- Reminder Letter on Overdue Amount
- Letter Referring to Unpaid Invoices
- Request for Payment of Overdue Fees
- Payment Request Tied to Performance
- Request to Arrange Payment Plan
- Promissory Note
- Urgent Request for Payment of Past Due Fees
- Letter to Attorney Confirming Fee Collection Agreement
- Thank-You Note for Payment of Overdue Bill

Fees and invoicing can be a delicate area for the accountant. You are selling a service, not manufacturing a product, and the time and effort you put into an engagement may not appear to be matched by anything tangible you can hand your client.

For example, if you are engaged to perform services in the sale of a business, you may spend many hours preparing correspondence, making phone calls, dealing with attorneys and other accountants. None of that time translates into much that the client can see or touch. When you present your bill, especially if it is a large one, you may wish you could hand the client something more solid—like the keys to a new sports car.

Even when you have carefully explained your billing rates and correctly estimated the amount of time needed, you may still have a twinge of doubt. You shouldn't. Your inventory is time. You are selling your expertise.

Clients often have short memories. After you explain your billing procedures—in person, by letter, or both—you will do well to keep your client informed of the time being spent as the engagement progresses. You may want to do this through in-progress billings or simply by means of oral reminders. In any case, you should invoice promptly at the conclusion of the engagement.

EXPLANATION OF BILLING POLICIES—INDIVIDUAL INCOME TAX

This is a detailed breakdown of fees and services. It can be used as the basis for a letter, or it can simply be reproduced as an enclosure.

YOUR LETTERHEAD

BILLING POLICIES FOR
INDIVIDUAL INCOME TAX RETURNS

We always welcome new clients in our practice, and we wish to explain fully the nature of our services and fees. Perhaps the most misunderstood aspect of our business is in the area of billing. This is due to a variety of reasons, but most often it stems from a lack of communication.

Our Fee Structure

We charge for our services based upon hourly rates plus our direct out-of-pocket costs. Our current hourly rates are as follows:

Partner	$125
Manager	80
Supervisor	65
Senior	45–50
Staff Accountant	35–45
Paraprofessional	25–35
Secretarial	20–30

These rates are comparable to those of other CPA firms in the area.

A typical Form 1040 tax return preparation would involve the following:

Preparation by Staff or Senior Accountant	6 hr	$240.00
Review by Manager or Supervisor	2 hr	130.00
Review by Partner	1/2 hr	62.50
Computer costs		50.00
Copy costs		5.00
Other costs		5.00
Total charges		$492.50

The fee shown above would ordinarily involve an existing client with itemized deductions and estimated tax requirements. Additional charges would be incurred for such items as these:

- State income tax returns
- Tax planning
- Projections
- Conferences with CPAs
- Telephone conferences
- Amended returns
- Special problems, such as business income, oil and gas income, lump-sum pension distributions, rental properties, employee business expenses, moving expenses, installment sales, sale of a personal residence

We usually bill for our services upon completion of the engagement. Our bills are payable upon receipt. A service charge of 1-1/2 percent per month is charged on all unpaid accounts over 30 days.

New Clients

A new client generally requires additional services. We need to gather background data, and a conference with a partner or with another CPA is often warranted.

Time must be spent in reviewing tax returns from prior years. This can result in the preparation of corrective, amended returns. Sometimes a new client has a unique tax situation that requires research in our extensive library, as well as an analysis by the team working on the return.

Our minimum fee for preparing an individual income tax return is $350. We request a retainer of this amount from all new individual income tax return clients.

Minimizing Our Fees

Our clients can help us keep preparation time to a minimum. The most important assistance comes from complete and orderly presentation of the data. We provide data sheets to help you in this regard.

Our Philosophy

We strive to provide the best possible professional service for a reasonable fee. We try to blend our technical expertise with the practicalities of each client's individual situation so as to achieve the best possible tax result for you.

EXPLANATION OF BILLING POLICIES—SMALL BUSINESS

In many ways, this explanation resembles the preceding one. However, its focus is on the preparation of partnership and corporation tax returns.

YOUR LETTERHEAD

BILLING POLICIES FOR
PARTNERSHIP AND CORPORATION TAX RETURNS

We always welcome new clients in our practice, and we wish to explain fully the nature of our services and fees. Perhaps the most misunderstood aspect of our business is in the area of billing. This is due to a variety of reasons, but most often it stems from a lack of communication.

Our Fee Structure

We charge for our services based upon hourly rates plus our direct out-of-pocket costs. Our current hourly rates are as follows:

Partner	$125
Manager	80
Supervisor	65
Senior	45–50
Staff accountant	35–45
Paraprofessional	25–35
Secretarial	20–30

Our major expenses involve personnel. We strive to maintain the best staff available; we therefore pay salaries which will attract such people. In addition, we must recover through fees our costs for library services, office equipment, and overhead. Our hourly rates are set with a view toward recovering all expenses plus a reasonable return on our investment. Our fee structure is comparable with those of other quality firms in this area.

A typical engagement for year-end tax preparation might involve the following:

Preparation by Staff or Senior Accountant	12 hr	$ 640.00
Review by Manager or Supervisor	4 hr	275.00
Review by Partner	1 hr	125.00
Typing costs		50.00
Computer costs		10.00
Copy costs		25.00
Other costs		10.00
Total charges		$1,135.00

The fee structure shown above would ordinarily involve an existing client with federal and state corporation income tax returns. Additional charges would be incurred for such items as these:

Individual income tax returns

Financial statements

Accounting and bookkeeping services

Tax planning

Projections

Conferences with partners or other CPAs

Telephone conferences

Amended returns

Special problems, such as pension plans, specialized accounting methods, consolidated returns, related corporations or entities, installment sales, related party accruals, interest-free loans, officer and employee life insurance programs, numerous asset additions, asset trade-ins or dispositions, personal use of business assets

We usually bill for our services upon completion of the engagement. Our bills are payable upon receipt. A service charge of 1-1/2 percent per month is charged on all unpaid accounts over 30 days.

New Clients

A new client generally requires additional services. We need to gather background data, and a conference with a partner or with another CPA is often warranted.

Time must be spent in reviewing tax returns from prior years. This can result in the preparation of corrective amended returns. Sometimes a new client has a unique tax situation that requires research in our extensive library, as well as analysis by the team working on the return.

Our minimum fee for preparing a corporate or partnership tax return is $500. We request a retainer of either the greater of one-half the estimated total or $500 from all new clients.

Minimizing Our Fees

Our clients can help us keep preparation time to a minimum. The most important assistance comes from complete and orderly presentation of the data. Complete books of account with the requested back-up documentation are essential; not having adequate information can be doubly costly. If we begin preparing the return and find the data incomplete, we must call or write for the missing information, set the job aside, and work on a different engagement. When the information arrives, we must start over again, refamiliarizing ourselves with the return and the data.

Our Philosophy

We strive to provide the best possible professional service for a reasonable fee. We try to blend our technical expertise with the practicalities of each client's individual situation so as to achieve the best possible tax result for you.

INVOICE LISTING SERVICES

Some accountants like to break down their invoices by hour for each service. Other accountants show total dollar amounts for each service. Still others prefer to show all services, then total the hours and show the dollar amount due.

YOUR LETTERHEAD

For Professional Services Rendered

Tax and accounting services to date, including various meetings, consultations, telephone conferences, contracts, accounting procedures, and federal and state registrations. Preparation of December 31, 19x5, quarterly and annual federal and state payroll tax returns:

Employer's Quarterly Federal Tax Return (941)
Employer's Annual Federal Unemployment Tax Return (940)
New Jersey Employer Report of Wages (WR-30)
Wage and Tax Statements (W-2)
Federal Transmittal of Income Tax Statements (W-3)
New Jersey Transmittal of Income Tax Statements (NJW-3)
Status report filed with N.J. Unemployment and Disability Agency
$800.00

Thank you.

ACCOMPANYING LETTER EXPLAINING INVOICE

If you have reason to think that the amount of the invoice will surprise your client, a letter of explanation may be in order.

YOUR LETTERHEAD

[Date]

INSIDE ADDRESS

[Salutation]:

Having concluded our engagement for fiscal 19x7, I have prepared your invoice at our usual rates. The invoice is enclosed.

Quite frankly, the charges are somewhat higher than I had anticipated. With the retirement of [name of internal accountant], the accounting procedures in your company suffered from certain irregularities and oversights that required a great deal of time to rectify. I believe this time was well spent and will ultimately save the company both time and money, but for this year it did increase the cost of our work.

After you have had a chance to review these charges, I would be happy to discuss them with you. I assure you that they were figured at our usual rates, and that the amount reflects the unexpected additional services required in 19x7.

[Closing],

YOUR SIGNATURE

DETAILED REQUEST FOR FEE INCREASE

If a fee increase is substantial and has not been previously agreed to, you may want to support it with facts and figures, such as those in this letter.

YOUR LETTERHEAD

[Date]

INSIDE ADDRESS

[Salutation]:

As we discussed on the phone, I am writing to request a fee increase for our auditing and tax accounting services. This increase is based in large part on your rapid expansion over the past few months.

Two years ago, when the present monthly fee schedule was established, your company was grossing less than $500,000 annually. Today, it is grossing more than $4 million and is growing fast. A consequence of this growth has been an ever-increasing amount of time devoted to servicing your account.

At the same time this has occurred, our costs have increased significantly. We are paying accountants about 25 percent more on average than we were two years ago, while our rent has gone up more than 33 percent.

For these reasons, I believe that an increase in our monthly retainer from [$ amount] to [$ amount] is not only justified, but absolutely essential.

If a further explanation of this request is needed, I would be pleased to meet with you at a mutually convenient time. As you know, I value you highly as a client and want to do nothing that might jeopardize a pleasant and beneficial relationship.

[Closing],

YOUR SIGNATURE

BRIEF LETTER ANNOUNCING FEE INCREASE

If a fee increase is modest and is not likely to create difficulties, a short note may be sufficient.

YOUR LETTERHEAD

________________ [Date]

INSIDE ADDRESS

____

[Salutation]:

In view of our rising costs and the steady increase in your company's business, we find it necessary to request a fee increase of [$ amount] per month for our accounting services.

We trust that you will agree to this modest increase, which will take effect January 1, 19x8.

[Closing],

____

YOUR SIGNATURE

____

LETTER EXPLAINING INCREASE IN AMOUNT BILLED

Even though your client is probably anticipating a higher bill, you may want to review the reason for it.

YOUR LETTERHEAD

[Date]

INSIDE ADDRESS

[Salutation]:

Enclosed is our invoice for services that we performed for you in the year ended December 31, 19x4.

The bill is slightly higher than last year's, as I believe you expected. Our hourly billing rates went up in April for the first time in more than three years, and these increases are reflected in the invoice. In addition, the work required on your profit-sharing trust was somewhat greater than last year because of changes in the plan made during the year.

If you have any further questions about the invoice, please let me know, and I will try to answer them.

[Closing],

YOUR SIGNATURE

CONFIRMATION OF ORAL FEE AGREEMENT

If an arrangement for fees is agreed upon in person or by telephone, you will want to confirm it by letter.

YOUR LETTERHEAD

[Date]

____

INSIDE ADDRESS

____

[Salutation]:

Let me summarize the results of our telephone conversation this morning regarding the agreed-upon fee arrangement for 19x0.

Beginning with January 1, 19x0, you will pay a retainer of [$ amount] per month, or [$ amount] per year. This amount will cover the annual audit and the preparation of corporate and individual federal and state income tax returns.

In June 19x0, we will meet to review our experiences with this arrangement. Throughout the year we will do everything possible to keep our charges to a minimum, including using the same personnel whenever possible and using your accounting department to assemble data.

Any work not covered by this letter will be billed separately at our usual rates.

I believe that this summarizes our understanding. If you have any questions, or if I have misstated some part of our agreement, please let me know.

[Closing],

____

YOUR SIGNATURE

____

ANSWERING A COMPLAINT CONCERNING FEES

No matter how carefully you explain your billing arrangements, there may be complaints. This letter deals tactfully with such a complaint.

YOUR LETTERHEAD

[Date]

INSIDE ADDRESS

[Salutation]:

This letter is in response to your telephone conversation with [name of staff member] concerning the amount billed to you in December. We have reviewed our audit procedures for this engagement as well as the time involved in carrying them out. Although the procedures used and the time charged were reviewed prior to billing, as is our custom, we did it once again to determine whether an error had been made.

Our review indicates that the work we performed was necessary and that it was completed efficiently. The amount billed, [$ amount], is slightly lower than the amount billed for the same engagement last year.

In reviewing our procedures, we compared them with the procedures we follow in auditing other service stations. The comparison shows that our work on your account required virtually the minimum amount of time for such an engagement. That was due in large part to your promptness and thoroughness in supplying the information we needed.

We value our association with you and hope it will continue. We try to be fair to all our clients by charging on the basis of the time involved, reducing the time to a minimum, and keeping our rates in line with those of other accounting firms in the area. Most of our clients recognize, without objection, that adjustments in our rates are sometimes made for charitable organizations.

We regret that you have a complaint about our bill. If you wish to discuss the matter in detail, please let me know so that a convenient time can be arranged for a meeting.

[Closing],

YOUR SIGNATURE

FRIENDLY REMINDER LETTER

When an amount becomes overdue, a brief letter may elicit payment.

YOUR LETTERHEAD

[Date]

INSIDE ADDRESS

[Salutation]:

Please note that our [date] billing to you for [$ amount] has not yet been paid.

We bring this to your attention in case it may have been overlooked.

[Closing],

YOUR SIGNATURE

REMINDER LETTER ON OVERDUE AMOUNT

A courteous letter can often bring results, particularly if it suggests an extension of time, if necessary, as this one does.

YOUR LETTERHEAD

[Date]

INSIDE ADDRESS

[Salutation]:

It is our pleasure to serve you, and we thank you for the opportunity.

However, the enclosed statement of your account as of the end of [month] shows an amount that became due some time ago.

We feel certain that you understand how important it is that every successful business organization keep its receivables up to date, and you can help us in this respect by sending us your payment within the next week.

If this is not possible, will you kindly tell us at the bottom of this letter the date on which we can expect payment, and return the letter to us.

Your cooperation will be greatly appreciated.

[Closing],

YOUR SIGNATURE

LETTER REFERRING TO UNPAID INVOICES

Since this letter involves a number of unpaid bills, its approach is more direct, and its tone is less congenial than in the two previous letters.

YOUR LETTERHEAD

[Date]

INSIDE ADDRESS

[Salutation]:

Let me call your attention to a number of invoices that we have sent you, but you have not paid. These include amounts totaling [$ amount] and going back to [date or dates].

We would appreciate your immediate attention to these invoices, and we hope you will advise us if you have any question as to the amounts involved.

If you are unable to pay the total amount due, we will consider making some satisfactory monthly payment arrangement with you, perhaps $100 a month.

We look forward to a prompt response. Thank you.

[Closing],

YOUR SIGNATURE

REQUEST FOR PAYMENT OF OVERDUE FEES

This is a more personal letter than some of the others. Nevertheless, it makes its point forcefully.

YOUR LETTERHEAD

[Date]

INSIDE ADDRESS

[Salutation]:

With some reluctance, I must ask that you review the age and amount of your indebtedness to us. You are one of our oldest and best clients, but we simply cannot continue to serve you in the absence of payment.

On [date], we offered you the choice of paying in installments, perhaps [$ amount] monthly, if that would help. At that time, you replied that you would pay the full amount promptly, yet we have received no payment for [length of time]. Clearly, an installment arrangement is preferable to nothing, and if you would like to reconsider such an arrangement, we are more than willing to discuss it.

We wish to settle this account amicably on some basis that will not unduly inconvenience you—but it must be settled.

We would prefer discussing this with you in person, but have been unable to reach you by phone. Please let us know your plans as quickly as possible.

[Closing],

YOUR SIGNATURE

PAYMENT REQUEST TIED TO PERFORMANCE

Here there are overdue fees that would have to be paid under any circumstances, but the writer uses a favorable tax settlement as a lever to induce payment.

YOUR LETTERHEAD

[Date]

INSIDE ADDRESS

[Salutation]:

Enclosed is our final invoice for services rendered in representing you before the Internal Revenue Service. The terms of your income tax settlement have been finally arranged. Within a few months you should receive your net refund from the IRS.

Meanwhile, I would like to remind you that several past invoices are overdue. I expect these bills to be paid before you receive your refund from the IRS.

May I point out that I have obtained unusually good results for you in this engagement. Indeed, the settlement is more than ten times greater than my total fee. In view of this, I hope you will not allow your overdue bills to persist.

If you have any reason to object to this request for payment, please let me hear from you. Otherwise, I shall expect full payment of the overdue invoices within the next ten days.

[Closing],

YOUR SIGNATURE

REQUEST TO ARRANGE PAYMENT PLAN

When one of your clients runs into cash-flow problems, you may be able to help the client (and yourself) by establishing a reasonable payment plan. In most cases you will want to see the client through this difficult period and continue the business relationship.

YOUR LETTERHEAD

[Date]

INSIDE ADDRESS

[Salutation]:

Enclosed please find a copy of your account with our office. As you can see, it is past due. Please contact me within the next ten days so that we can discuss a method of payment. I will be happy to accommodate any reasonable payment plan you suggest.

Thank you for your prompt attention to this matter.

[Closing],

YOUR SIGNATURE

PROMISSORY NOTE

In some instances a promissory note may be in order.

YOUR LETTERHEAD

[$ amount owed] [Date]

The undersigned hereby agrees that the services rendered for which the amounts are now due have been received and accepted for [name of client].

FOR VALUE RECEIVED, the undersigned promises to pay to the order of [name of accountant or accounting firm], in lawful money of the United States of America, the principal sum of [$ amount spelled out in capitals—followed by $ amount in numerals] with interest on the outstanding principal balance at 2 percent over [name of bank] prime lending rate determined at the first day of each month, payable in weekly installments of [$ amount] applying first to interest, then to principal, due on Friday of each week until paid in full.

All or any portion of the principal or interest hereof may be prepaid at any time.

____
personally

URGENT REQUEST FOR PAYMENT OF PAST DUE FEES

This is a final notice to the client when all previous efforts have failed.

YOUR LETTERHEAD

[Date]

INSIDE ADDRESS

[Salutation]:

We are enclosing a copy of your outstanding bill. Invoices are due and payable upon receipt. As of this date, we have not received payment for services rendered in October and December 19x5.

We feel that we have been more than fair in allowing this much time for payment. We must now ask that payment be made within the next ten days or we will have no choice but to turn your account over to our attorneys for collection.

If circumstances make it impossible for you to make full payment, we will be happy to set up a payment schedule with you. If you wish to do this, please contact us immediately.

[Closing],

YOUR SIGNATURE

LETTER TO ATTORNEY CONFIRMING FEE COLLECTION AGREEMENT

If all else fails and you have to take legal action to collect overdue fees, you will want to have a written agreement with your attorney. The following letter spells out the terms of the attorney's involvement.

YOUR LETTERHEAD

[Date]

INSIDE ADDRESS

[Salutation]:

As we discussed this morning, I am writing to confirm our agreement under which you are to receive one fourth (25 percent) of all monies that you collect from [name of client] on their indebtedness to us, totaling [$ amount].

We have already furnished you with the details of the indebtedness. In support of your collection efforts, we are prepared to sue and will supply whatever details and court testimony may be required.

As you know, we wish you to proceed promptly. It is difficult to set an equitable time limit in a contingent collection contract of this kind, but we believe that three months should allow you sufficient time to collect.

Therefore, unless a court action becomes necessary, we reserve the right to cancel this arrangement with respect to any part of the indebtedness that has not been collected by [date] or has not been scheduled for installment payments (which may extend beyond that date).

Payment is to be made directly to us by check from [name of client]. We will pay your commission by our check as soon as sufficient time has elapsed for [name of client]'s check to clear.

To indicate your acceptance of the terms stated in this letter, please sign one copy of the letter and return it to us.

[Closing],

YOUR SIGNATURE

Approved
By:______________________ Date__________
[Name of attorney]

THANK-YOU NOTE FOR PAYMENT OF OVERDUE BILL

Depending on circumstances, you may want to acknowledge receipt of an overdue payment.

YOUR LETTERHEAD

[Date]

INSIDE ADDRESS

[Salutation]:

Thank you for your letter of [date] and the accompanying check. Our receipted invoice is enclosed.

We understand the reason for the delay and appreciate your efforts to expedite payment. A check, though late, is always welcome!

[Closing],

YOUR SIGNATURE

CHAPTER 14

Employee Relations Letters

- Response to Inquiry About Employment
- Letter Inviting Applicant for an Interview
- Letter Stating That No Position Is Open
- Letter Noting That Résumé Will Be Kept in Active File
- Request for Second Interview with Desirable Candidate
- Letter Offering Position with Firm
- Confirmation of Offer of Position
- Letter to Candidate Who Has Declined Offer
- Rejection Letter
- Letter Requesting Postponement of Jury Duty
- Request for Employee to Be Excused from Reserve Meeting
- Letter Advising of Salary Increase
- Congratulations on Outstanding Work
- Best Wishes on Employee's Marriage
- Congratulations on Birth of Child
- Get-Well Note to Hospitalized Employee

A large accounting firm needs many more letters concerning employees than a small firm or an individual practitioner does. In general, the smaller the firm the fewer the recruitment letters you will have to write, and the less internal correspondence you will have to produce.

Even so, you may occasionally have to write letters to, or on behalf of, people within the firm. If you do, you will find that they tend to be routine in their content—the kinds of letters that can make good use of existing models such as the ones in this chapter.

RESPONSE TO INQUIRY ABOUT EMPLOYMENT

This is a general response to a general inquiry. It does not suggest a formal interview but merely a visit to the office at the candidate's convenience.

YOUR LETTERHEAD

[Date]

INSIDE ADDRESS

[Salutation]:

Thank you for your recent letter in which you inquire about the possibility of employment with our firm. We are always interested in young persons with outstanding qualifications in the accounting field, and we would be pleased to meet with you at your convenience.

We are a small firm with a varied practice. Because of our size, we do not always have open positions, although we have added one accountant during the past year and expect to add more. It has been our observation that a young person who enters this firm can gain experience rapidly and can assume responsibility much earlier than would be possible in a larger organization.

In any case, we would be delighted to discuss the matter at greater length when you visit us. Please let us know a day or two in advance so that we will be expecting you.

[Closing],

YOUR SIGNATURE

LETTER INVITING APPLICANT FOR AN INTERVIEW

When a position is open, you may want to set up a number of interviews. The following letter also asks for the necessary supporting documents.

YOUR LETTERHEAD

[Date]

INSIDE ADDRESS

[Salutation]:

Thank you for your inquiry concerning employment with our firm. Your resume is excellent, and we would like to consider you as one of the candidates for the position we have open.

If you would like to visit our office, please telephone [name of person] at [telephone number] to arrange for an interview. While you are here, we will try to give you a thorough picture of what the firm does and, specifically, what you would do were you to join us.

In addition to your resume, which we already have, we would appreciate receiving a transcript of your college grades as well as the enclosed application form completed in your own handwriting.

We look forward to meeting you soon.

[Closing],

YOUR SIGNATURE

LETTER STATING THAT NO POSITION IS OPEN

If there are no available positions, you may wish to send a very brief letter to applicants.

YOUR LETTERHEAD

[Date]

INSIDE ADDRESS

[Salutation]:

Thank for your recent letter expressing an interest in joining our firm.

At present we have no openings, nor do we anticipate any in the near future.

We are sorry that our response cannot be more positive. We appreciate your having considered us, and we wish you well in your search for an appropriate position.

[Closing],

YOUR SIGNATURE

LETTER NOTING THAT RÉSUMÉ WILL BE KEPT IN ACTIVE FILE

You may occasionally get an application that you would like to consider, but you have no position open at the moment. Rather than sending an outright rejection, you may want to explain the situation briefly.

YOUR LETTERHEAD

[Date]

INSIDE ADDRESS

[Salutation]:

Thank you for your interest in [name of firm]. If we had a position open at the moment, your excellent résumé would prompt us to invite you for an interview. However, we will not be doing any hiring for at least the next few weeks.

Our employment decisions are based on the firm's long-range objectives. Among the factors considered are current clientele, anticipated growth, and staff turnover.

We will keep your résumé on file for three months. If, during that period, a job opening should develop, we will get in touch with you immediately.

Thank you again for your interest in our firm.

[Closing],

YOUR SIGNATURE

REQUEST FOR SECOND INTERVIEW WITH DESIRABLE CANDIDATE

When you are giving serious thought to hiring a candidate, you will probably want to extend an invitation to meet for a second interview.

YOUR LETTERHEAD

[Date]

INSIDE ADDRESS

[Salutation]:

It was a pleasure meeting you recently, and I would like to have the opportunity to visit with you again. This would give both of us a chance to become better acquainted.

If you remain interested in pursuing a career with our firm, please call me at [telephone number] to set up an appointment. If I am not in the office when you call, please talk to [name of secretary]. She knows my schedule and can make the necessary arrangements.

I look forward to seeing you again soon.

[Closing],

YOUR SIGNATURE

LETTER OFFERING POSITION WITH FIRM

This letter indicates the salary being offered and the projected first day of employment. It also asks for a decision by a specified date.

YOUR LETTERHEAD

[Date]

INSIDE ADDRESS

[Salutation]:

It is with great pleasure that I offer you the position with our firm that we discussed during our interview. All of us who met you were impressed with your background and enthusiasm.

Your beginning salary at our firm would be [$ amount] per month, plus overtime. As we discussed, we would expect you to begin work with us on or about [date].

We hope you agree that our firm offers you a promising and challenging career. Please let us know your decision by [date].

Naturally, we hope you will say yes, and we look forward with great anticipation to your working here. If you have any questions at all, please feel free to call us.

[Closing],

YOUR SIGNATURE

CONFIRMATION OF OFFER OF POSITION

If an offer of employment has been made orally, you will want to confirm it in writing.

YOUR LETTERHEAD

[Date]

INSIDE ADDRESS

[Salutation]:

All of us enjoyed meeting and talking with you on your recent visit to [name of firm].

This letter is to confirm our offer to join our firm, beginning on [date]. Your annual starting salary will be [$ amount].

You will find that the work here is varied and interesting, covering a wide range of clients and engagements. As a career opportunity, we firmly believe that a position with our firm is unsurpassed.

Please let us know your decision at your earliest convenience. If you have any questions, or if we can assist you in any way, let us know.

[Closing],

YOUR SIGNATURE

LETTER TO CANDIDATE WHO HAS DECLINED OFFER

If a candidate says no to a job offer, you may want to know why. Was a higher salary offered somewhere else? Did the atmosphere at another firm seem more congenial? A letter such as this one will sometimes furnish answers.

YOUR LETTERHEAD

[Date]

INSIDE ADDRESS

[Salutation]:

Thank you for your recent letter. I was disappointed that you decided not to join our firm, but all of us knew that with your qualifications you would have various options from which to choose.

Since you undoubtedly weighed those options carefully, I would be interested to learn what prompted you to take another offer. Salary? Working conditions? Personnel? If you could take a moment to write or call me, I would be most appreciative. Your comments will be held in strictest confidence.

Best wishes in your new position. All of us at [name of firm] believe you have a bright professional future.

[Closing],

YOUR SIGNATURE

REJECTION LETTER

There is no reason for a rejection letter to be either long or apologetic, but it should be tactful.

YOUR LETTERHEAD

[Date]

INSIDE ADDRESS

[Salutation]:

Thank you for the opportunity to talk with you about a position with [name of firm].

We regret that we are unable to offer you a position at this time.

The interest you showed in our firm was most gratifying, and we wish you every success in finding the right opening to advance your career.

[Closing],

YOUR SIGNATURE

LETTER REQUESTING POSTPONEMENT OF JURY DUTY

A judge may recognize the validity of this request and grant a postponement.

YOUR LETTERHEAD

[Date]

INSIDE ADDRESS

[Salutation]:

[Name of staff member] of this firm has just received a summons to serve as a grand juror beginning [date].

This timing creates a serious hardship for us, since [name of staff member] is now engaged in an audit that requires specialized knowledge and expertise. It is unlikely that we could complete the audit on time if [name of staff member] were to leave for jury duty on the date specified.

Therefore, we respectfully request that [name of staff member]'s jury duty be postponed until after [date acceptable to firm].

Thank you for your consideration.

[Closing],

YOUR SIGNATURE

REQUEST FOR EMPLOYEE TO BE EXCUSED FROM RESERVE MEETING

In some cases this request may have to be accompanied by an affadavit signed by a partner of the firm.

YOUR LETTERHEAD

[Date]

INSIDE ADDRESS

[Salutation]:

[Name of staff member] of this firm is a [rank] in the [name of reserve unit]. He is scheduled to attend a reserve meeting on [date].

Because of an extremely tight deadline on a major engagement, we have been forced to ask [name of staff member] to work on that date.

Consequently, we respectfully request that [name of staff member] be excused from attending the reserve meeting on [date].

Thank you for your consideration.

[Closing],

YOUR SIGNATURE

LETTER ADVISING OF SALARY INCREASE

When an employee has merited a salary increase, a brief letter may be in order. This kind of letter can be very short, since the information it conveys makes embellishment unnecessary.

YOUR LETTERHEAD

[Date]

INSIDE ADDRESS

[Salutation]:

In recognition of your professional performance during this past year, I am pleased to advise you that effective [date], your salary will be increased to the annual amount of [$ amount].

Thank you for your fine work, and best wishes for the future.

[Closing],

YOUR SIGNATURE

CONGRATULATIONS ON OUTSTANDING WORK

When a staff member has done something truly out of the ordinary, a note of this kind may be in order.

YOUR LETTERHEAD

[Date]

[Salutation]:

Congratulations on the superb job you did in representing [name of client] before the Internal Revenue Service.

Both [name of client] and [IRS agent] remarked on your thorough preparation and clear presentation in this highly complex tax matter. The client was delighted with the outcome, of course, and I was personally pleased and impressed with your performance.

Keep up the good work!

[Closing],

YOUR SIGNATURE

BEST WISHES ON EMPLOYEE'S MARRIAGE

This letter and the following one require some rewording if the employee is a female.

YOUR LETTERHEAD

[Date]

[Salutation]:

On behalf of all of us at [name of firm], I congratulate you on your forthcoming marriage and wish you and [first name of fiancée] a bright and happy future. May your lives together as Mr. and Mrs. [last name of employee] be rich and full.

[Closing],

YOUR SIGNATURE

CONGRATULATIONS ON BIRTH OF CHILD

YOUR LETTERHEAD

[Date]

[Salutation]:

Congratulations on the birth of your daughter! [Name of daughter] is fortunate indeed to be born into the [last name of employee] family. May the years ahead be bright and happy ones for all of you.

On behalf of all of us at [name of firm], I extend best wishes to you, your wife, and the newest member of your family.

[Closing],

YOUR SIGNATURE

GET-WELL NOTE TO HOSPITALIZED EMPLOYEE

YOUR LETTERHEAD

[Date]

[Salutation]:

This is just a note to let you know that all of us here are thinking of you and praying for your speedy recovery.

What we want most is for you to follow your doctor's orders and do whatever is necessary to regain your health. That includes forgetting about the work at [name of firm] for the time being.

We look forward to your return when you are fully recovered. In the meantime, if there is anything we can do for you, please let us know.

[Closing],

YOUR SIGNATURE

CHAPTER 15

Image Building Through Public Relations

- Brochure Explaining Firm's Capabilities
- Letter Accompanying Newsletter
- Request to Reprint Article in Newsletter
- Advice to Staff on Public Relations
- Press Release to Local Newspapers
- Letter Inviting Press to Speaking Engagement
- Follow-up Letter on Media Coverage
- Letter to Editor Presenting Accountant's Viewpoint
- Letter Accompanying Article
- Welcome Letter to New Client
- Thanks for Recommending Client
- Letter Accepting Speaking Engagement
- Letter Declining Speaking Engagement
- Best Wishes on Opening New Business
- Congratulations on Appointment to Office
- Congratulations on Joining Organization
- Praise for Achievement in Community
- Congratulations on Promotion
- Congratulations on New Position
- Best Wishes on Retirement

Public relations means different things to different people. It can mean simply letting the public know what an accountant, or an accounting firm, does. To many people, the work of an accountant is rather mysterious. Accountants are generally viewed as competent professionals and as men and women of integrity. But as to what accountants actually *do*—that is not always clear to the community at large.

Anything that enlightens the public about accountancy is good public relations. Public relations, ideally, should not only *inform* the public factually, but it should also *enhance* the image of accountants. Specifically, it should enhance the image of you and your accounting firm. Good public relations on your own behalf will help bring in new clients and will bolster your image in the eyes of your present clients.

Yet public relations is not synonymous with self-promotion. An accountant or a firm may have high visibility and still be viewed in an unfavorable light. The point of PR is not merely to develop a public image, but also to develop a positive public image. This involves more than a bag of clever tricks. It involves performance. Genuine high regard must be earned. It is based on high standards, hard work, solid performance, and an enduring interest in clients and their well-being. The letters in this chapter convey those ideals.

No one is likely to notice good works that are *too* well hidden. To be known in the profession and among members of the business community, you have to make an effort. There are dozens of ways to promote good public relations. It's true that PR can be overdone, but the accounting profession is naturally conservative and has tended to underdo rather than overdo its image-building. In this chapter a number of proven public relations techniques are discussed or implied in the letters.

BROCHURE EXPLAINING FIRM'S CAPABILITIES

A brochure is very useful for a small accounting firm that wants to build its practice. It lets the business community know that your accounting firm exists and explains what services you offer. The brochure tells and *sells.* It can be developed either in-house or by an outside agency.

The brochure can be large or small, long or short, plain or illustrated, costly or inexpensive. The best way to start developing a brochure is by looking at brochures put out by other accounting firms. Most firms will send you a copy on request. Then decide what you want, and draw up plans for producing it.

This book cannot go into detail about brochures, but you will find excellent articles on the topic in professional journals and in more general publications. One that relates directly to accounting is Beryl C. Argall Stover's "Firm Brochures and Client Newsletters—Two Vital Marketing Tools," in the July 1981 issue of *The Practical Accountant.*

If you decide to do a brochure, you will begin with a few major headings. Here are the principal headings in an impressive brochure from Israeloff, Trattner & Co. of Valley Stream, New York:

- Why select Israeloff, Trattner & Co.?
- A history of growth and service
- Our most valuable asset is our people
- Our services:
  —Audit and accounting services
  —Tax services
  —Management services
- Our clients
- Affiliations and extended capabilities

The brochure is illustrated with a number of black-and-white photographs and is printed on high-quality, glossy paper. The text is written in an easy-to-read style. Here are some brief excerpts from the "Why select . . . " section:

- **Because We Know Your Business**
  And we know your problems and how to solve them. We've solved them before. . . .
- **Because We Provide a Personalized Service**
  We know it's important to you to have one person who knows your account intimately. . . .
- **Because We Provide a Full Range of Services . . .**
  . . . from basic accounting functions to highly specialized tax and management services engagements.

- **Because We Have Broad Experience in Business and Finance**
  We believe it's important for an accounting firm to be fully grounded in all aspects of business operations. . . .
- **Because We Offer a Team Approach**
  At Israeloff, Trattner & Co., we are prepared to bring in our own specialists in a team effort whenever you need special assistance. . . .
- **And Israeloff, Trattner & Co. Is Especially for You. . .**
  . . . if yours is a closely held company which typically requires the kind of personalized attention that is our hallmark.

LETTER ACCOMPANYING NEWSLETTER

If the size of your firm permits it, a monthly or quarterly newsletter is an excellent way to keep your firm's name before the public. The following letter accompanies the first issue that a client or other recipient receives.

YOUR LETTERHEAD

[Date]

INSIDE ADDRESS

[Salutation]:

Good morning!

We have added your name to our mailing list for the [name of newsletter], a quarterly publication that spotlights items of current interest or particular relevance to the business community.

This newsletter is distributed as a service to our clients and other interested businesspeople by [name of firm]. For the past [number of years] we have provided a broad range of tax, financial, and management advisory services to a wide variety of clients.

We have observed that many of the articles featuring CPAs in the local papers concentrate on the "Big Eight" or other large national firms. At [name of firm] we feel that the perspectives of a local firm are often more relevant to smaller businesses, which form the greatest portion of the total business community.

We hope that you find the newsletter useful, informative, and thought provoking. We also hope that if the occasion arises you will consider using the services of a local firm such as [name of firm].

[Closing],

YOUR SIGNATURE

REQUEST TO REPRINT ARTICLE IN NEWSLETTER

Sometimes you will find a published article that is ideal for your firm's newsletter. You may be able to get permission to reprint it. You should promise to include proper credit.

YOUR LETTERHEAD

[Date]

INSIDE ADDRESS

[Salutation]:

A number of us at [name of firm] were favorably impressed by the article [name and author of article] in the [date] issue of [name of publication].

Would you allow us to reprint this article in the [date] issue of [name of newsletter], published quarterly by our firm. Our newsletter, a copy of which is enclosed, is distributed free to approximately 700 clients and other interested people in the business community.

Thank you for considering this request. I can assure you that if permission is granted the material will be credited to you and properly acknowledged.

[Closing],

YOUR SIGNATURE

ADVICE TO STAFF ON PUBLIC RELATIONS

This is an internal memo intended to increase staff awareness of the need for good public relations.

YOUR LETTERHEAD

[Date]

TO: ALL STAFF

FROM: [YOUR NAME]

RE: PUBLIC RELATIONS

Surveys have shown that public perception of the accounting profession is generally favorable. However, many people do not fully understand what an accountant does or what services are available from a public accounting firm. I hope that each of you will take it upon yourself to help educate the business community and others about the capabilities, competence, and integrity of the members of the public accounting profession.

The local media should perceive our firm as a reliable authority (and a good one to consult) on accounting, auditing, or tax issues. To this end, I encourage you to think about ways to keep our firm's name before the public. Naturally, our day-to-day activities do not constitute news. What the media report are out-of-the-ordinary events. Over the years, the firm has routinely sent out press releases to announce a new office location, publication of our newsletter, newly hired staff members, night courses taught by members, promotions, and the like. Much more in the way of publicity is surely possible.

I have attached to this memo a copy of William J. Corbett's article, "Boosting the Profession with PR," published in the February 1986 issue of *Journal of Accountancy,* which I hope you will read at your convenience. If the article suggests to you some effective new ways for [name of firm] to enhance its public image, please let me know. Our firm is already well known in [name of community], but it can and should be even better known.

PRESS RELEASE TO LOCAL NEWSPAPERS

You should write a press release in such a way that it can be published intact as a complete article. If you do, it may be printed without change or with only minor editing. Of course, a newspaper or magazine is under no obligation to use what you send them. A press release, like the fictitious one below, is usually headed "For Immediate Release" or "Press Release."

For Immediate Release

Delano Greene, CPA, a member of the accounting firm Ballou & Schmidt, has written a new book for young adults in a series called *Career Awareness* published by Ligon-Rice, Inc. Mr. Greene's book is entitled, *Accounting: Is It For You?*

A prepublication reviewer in *Publishers Digest* writes that the book "is a clear, compelling picture of what life is like as a public accountant. It discusses the skills needed for the job and provides the young reader with all he or she needs to know to make a preliminary decision about accounting as a possible career. Mr. Greene obviously loves his profession and is able to convey the challenge and vitality of a job that on the surface may seem rather unexciting to children."

Mr. Greene, a native of Brooklyn, has been associated with Ballou & Schmidt for the past nine years. Prior to that, he was on the Boston staff of Holmes, Freeman, and Christie. Although this is his first book, Mr. Greene is well-known locally for his monthly column on taxes in the Orrville *Globe*. He has also written a number of articles for professional journals.

"The main audience for my book," says Mr. Greene, "will be school children. My publisher expects it to sell primarily to school libraries and public libraries. Therefore, you won't see it in bookstores." The book is available in a hardcover library binding directly from Ligon-Rice, Inc., 800 Silver Parkway, Galveston, Texas 77550, for $9.95 postpaid.

LETTER INVITING PRESS TO SPEAKING ENGAGEMENT

If you think a speaking engagement warrants press coverage, you can write to (or phone) the local newspaper, giving enough information to allow the editor to decide.

YOUR LETTERHEAD

[Date]

INSIDE ADDRESS

[Salutation]:

J. Arnold Schmidt, CPA, a senior partner in the accounting firm of Ballou & Schmidt, will address the Young Presidents Club of Fitchburg next Thursday at 7:30 P.M. in Gould Auditorium, McHale University. His topic is "The Rise of Computer Crime."

You may want to have a reporter cover this talk for a number of reasons. One is that indictments were recently handed down in Morrow County against three high-level executives of the Berkon Corporation, charging them with computer fraud involving millions of dollars. Another is that Mr. Schmidt was recently named to Governor Egan's blue-ribbon panel on how to deal with the growing problem of computer crime. Still another is that on June 14 Mr. Schmidt will appear on the *Wake Up, New Jersey* television show, along with Attorney General Dwight Gavin, to discuss this important topic.

A transcript of Mr. Schmidt's talk will be available to the press at the time of his speech.

[Closing],

YOUR SIGNATURE

FOLLOW-UP LETTER ON MEDIA COVERAGE

If you receive radio or TV coverage, whether requested or not, you may want to send a thank-you note to remind the station of your firm's participation and your willingness to cooperate in the future.

YOUR LETTERHEAD

[Date]

INSIDE ADDRESS

[Salutation]:

Let me thank you for arranging the interview yesterday with Laura Tedesco, CPA, a tax expert in our firm. I hope that your viewers found her remarks on the proposed changes in the state sales tax law to be helpful and enlightening.

Be assured that members of our firm are ready at any time to share their expertise on tax or financial matters with your reporters and your station's viewers. I am pleased that WEIR sought the views of our firm, and of Ms. Tedesco personally, on this subject of urgent concern to the businesspeople in the state.

[Closing],

YOUR SIGNATURE

LETTER TO EDITOR PRESENTING ACCOUNTANT'S VIEWPOINT

The press can be both a friend and a foe. If a particularly objectionable article, feature, or cartoon appears in your local newspaper, you can help set the record straight by writing a thoughtful letter to the editor.

YOUR LETTERHEAD

[Date]

INSIDE ADDRESS

Dear Editor:

As a Certified Public Accountant, a sole practitioner engaged in a small tax and accounting practice in Elm City, I take strong exception to Fred Nellen's editorial cartoon that appeared on September 28 on the *Clarion-Call*'s editorial page.

We all know that Congress, whatever its intent, did not simplify the tax code. My fellow practitioners and I will now have to spend a great deal of time and money to educate ourselves on the complex changes in the regulations so as to serve our clients and members of the general public who look to us for advice.

Your editorial cartoon depicts the CPA, the tax attorney, and other hardworking professionals in a highly unfavorable light. Readers are to conclude, I assume, that we "sharks" in your cartoon are feeding off the public and giving society nothing in return. I cannot accept that unfair conclusion, and neither should your readers.

I have devoted many years of my life to becoming a CPA, have spent thousands of dollars to computerize my office, and have educated myself on a continuing basis to better serve my clients. The consequence, I believe, is that my clients pay the least amount of taxes required under the law. Far from picturing myself as a "shark," I see myself as a fighter against excessive taxation, government waste, and the frightening accumulation of federal debt.

The people who might more accurately be shown as sharks are the members of Congress who are spending us into debt for generations to come. To cover their profligacy, they ballyhooed a "tax reform" bill that became, for most people, simply a tax increase in disguise.

Your cartoonist is entitled to his editorial point of view, but it distresses me that the public may be willing to accept this unflattering image of accountants while continuing to picture Congress as a group of brave Horatios at the bridge. Such a view of reality makes very little sense.

[Closing],

YOUR SIGNATURE

LETTER ACCOMPANYING ARTICLE

Sometimes an article is so appropriate for a certain client that you may want to send the client a photocopy of it. Not only is this a good public relations gesture, but it may also have a beneficial effect on a specific engagement.

YOUR LETTERHEAD

[Date]

INSIDE ADDRESS

[Salutation]:

As you recall, the last time we talked I suggested a way you might consider for financing the college educations of your three children. What I recommended was a spousal remainer trust, which I tried to explain in some detail.

Today as I was glancing through the latest issue of *The Practical Accountant*, I saw an article by Craig J. Langstraat entitled, "The Spousal Remainer Trust: Its Advantages and Disadvantages as a Tool for Financing a Child's Education." I am enclosing a copy of the article with this letter. Not only does it reinforce what I said about this kind of trust, but it also includes a great deal of additional information that may be useful to you.

[Closing],

YOUR SIGNATURE

WELCOME LETTER TO NEW CLIENT

If your proposal has been accepted from among many submitted, you may want to send a brief letter welcoming the new client.

YOUR LETTERHEAD

[Date]

INSIDE ADDRESS

[Salutation]:

We are pleased to learn that you have accepted our proposal for the audit of the books and records of the School District of Davis County for the year ended December 31, 19x3.

We appreciate the confidence you have shown in us and are looking forward to working with you.

[Closing],

YOUR SIGNATURE

THANKS FOR RECOMMENDING CLIENT

When an outside recommendation brings you a new client, a brief note of thanks is in order.

YOUR LETTERHEAD

[Date]

INSIDE ADDRESS

[Salutation]:

Thank you very much for suggesting that Ms. Caren Drew get in touch with our firm. We appreciate the confidence you have shown in us and will do our best to merit your recommendation.

[Closing],

YOUR SIGNATURE

LETTER ACCEPTING SPEAKING ENGAGEMENT

Speaking before business and professional groups is an excellent way to gain recognition within the community.

YOUR LETTERHEAD

[Date]

INSIDE ADDRESS

[Salutation]:

Thank you for your kind invitation to speak before the Kiwanis Club at your July 14 luncheon meeting in the Regency Room of the Sheraton Centre. I accept with pleasure.

As you suggested, I will deal with the topic of business ethics. The title of my talk, which I believe you need for inclusion in your newsletter, is "Yes, It's Legal, But Is It Right?"

I look forward to getting to know you and the members of your group better.

[Closing],

YOUR SIGNATURE

LETTER DECLINING SPEAKING ENGAGEMENT

Despite the advantages of public-speaking appearances, you may sometimes have to respond to an invitation with a tactful refusal.

YOUR LETTERHEAD

[Date]

INSIDE ADDRESS

[Salutation]:

Thank you for your invitation to speak at the August meeting of the Northwestern Association of Accountants. I regret that prior commitments make it impossible for me to accept.

The topic that you asked me to present, "MAS in the Small Accounting Firm," is of great interest to me, as it is to many of our Association members. Have you considered either Bill Gerrold of Oak Knoll or Myron Katz of Pacifica as possible speakers? Both are knowledgeable specialists and excellent speakers on this topic.

Best wishes for your meeting. I only wish I could be there and speak to the group.

[Closing],

YOUR SIGNATURE

BEST WISHES ON OPENING NEW BUSINESS

Each new business is a potential new client. This letter is a direct but discreet bid for consideration as the company's accounting firm.

YOUR LETTERHEAD

[Date]

INSIDE ADDRESS

[Salutation]:

On behalf of [name of your firm], I extend our congratulations on the opening of your new business venture. We wish you every success as you undertake this new activity.

Starting a new business in the complex business environment of today is not easy. It is imperative that business owners enlist the aid of a team of professional advisors in order to minimize risk and maximize success.

At [name of firm] we have served businesses such as yours for more than [length of time]. We provide our clients with a broad array of services, including accounting, tax, and management advisory services. We can assist you in setting up your initial accounting/management information systems, including computerization, if that is indicated.

We hope that your new venture is both personally and financially rewarding. We also hope that [name of firm] can play a part in your success.

[Closing],

YOUR SIGNATURE

CONGRATULATIONS ON APPOINTMENT TO OFFICE

Since public relations consists essentially of keeping your name favorably in public view, the appointment of a new public official often warrants a congratulatory note.

YOUR LETTERHEAD

[Date]

INSIDE ADDRESS

[Salutation]:

On behalf of [name of your firm], I extend our congratulations on your appointment as Superintendent of Schools of Lake City.

I hope that you will find your new position to be both personally and professionally rewarding and that in the future we will have an opportunity to meet in person.

Best wishes for your continued success.

[Closing],

YOUR SIGNATURE

CONGRATULATIONS ON JOINING ORGANIZATION

When a company fills a position that has relevance to your role as an accountant or accounting firm, it is a good policy to welcome the new person. The company may already be a client, or it may be one that you would like to have as a client.

YOUR LETTERHEAD

[Date]

INSIDE ADDRESS

[Salutation]:

On behalf of [name of your firm], I extend our congratulations on your appointment as [name of position] with [name of company].

I hope that you find your new position to be both personally and financially rewarding and that in the future we will have an opportunity to meet in person.

Best wishes for your continued success.

[Closing],

YOUR SIGNATURE

PRAISE FOR ACHIEVEMENT IN COMMUNITY

When a client or a client's employee (or a nonclient, for that matter) has made a significant contribution to the community, you may want to write a congratulatory note.

YOUR LETTERHEAD

[Date]

INSIDE ADDRESS

[Salutation]:

On behalf of the partners and staff at [time of your firm], I would like to congratulate you for serving as fund-raising chairman for the new Ridge County Hospice.

Your willingness to serve in this capacity demonstrates your concern for and dedication to the community. Your achievement in putting the fund over the top is clear evidence of the kind of competence that has helped make [name of addressee's company] so successful.

You sacrificed a great deal of personal time to do this job, but many people will benefit in the years ahead.

[Closing],

YOUR SIGNATURE

CONGRATULATIONS ON PROMOTION

If someome you have been associated with receives a promotion, you will want to offer congratulations. Your closeness to the person will affect the tone and details of the letter.

YOUR LETTERHEAD

[Date]

INSIDE ADDRESS

[Salutation]:

Everyone here was delighted to hear of your promotion to [new title]. We have enjoyed our long and friendly association with you, and we join your many other friends and associates in wishing you the best in your new position.

[Closing],

YOUR SIGNATURE

CONGRATULATIONS ON NEW POSITION

Although a letter of congratulations is often short, it should be prompt, natural, specific, and enthusiastic.

YOUR LETTERHEAD

[Date]

INSIDE ADDRESS

[Salutation]:

This morning in the *Daily Herald* I saw the announcement of your promotion to Vice-President, Finance, at Wynn-Swift, Inc.

Congratulations! Should I tell you that I was expecting it? You clearly deserved the promotion, and I felt it was only a matter of time before you got it.

No one is more qualified than you to take on this responsible and demanding job. I wish you every success in your new position.

[Closing],

YOUR SIGNATURE

BEST WISHES ON RETIREMENT

The retirement of a person you have come to know well is an occasion that calls for a friendly expression of feelings.

YOUR LETTERHEAD

[Date]

INSIDE ADDRESS

[Salutation]:

The news that you will be retiring in June prompts me to write you this note. It goes without saying that I wish you happiness and fulfillment in the years ahead.

More than that, I want to tell you how much I have enjoyed our long association, which goes back to that day (eons ago, wasn't it?) when I first met you at Algonquin Foods, Inc. Since that day, I cannot recall having worked with a more pleasant, thoughtful, and dedicated person. To me, you represent the best in a fine company, and I will miss your presence.

I know that your retirement will be an active one, and I'm sure you will pursue some new and exciting ventures. Best wishes in whatever you do—and don't forget to visit us when you have an opportunity.

[Closing],

YOUR SIGNATURE

CHAPTER 16

Time-Saving General Transmittal Letters

- Letter of Transmittal for Adjusting Entries
- Letter of Transmittal for Fiscal Closing
- Transmittal of Draft Audit for Comments
- Transmittal of Audited Financial Statements
- Transmittal of Unaudited Financial Statements
- Letter Accompanying Annual Report to Stockholders
- Transmittal of Printed Annual Report
- Transmittal of Working Papers Used for Annual Report
- Letter Transmitting Notice About Employee Benefit Plan
- Letter Transmitting Pension Fund Report
- Letter Transmitting Pension Plan Amendment
- Transmitting Letter of Recommendations to Management
- Letter to Bank Supporting Proposed Plant-Expansion Mortgage
- Transmittal to Bank of Financial Statements re Mortgage
- Transmitting Copies of Prior Correspondence
- Letter Accompanying Accounting Report to Partners
- Transmittal of Special Report to Stockholders

A straight transmittal letter is usually nothing more than a covering note for the main document being sent to the client—a report, a tax return, copies of prior correspondence. Transmittals for tax returns are a separate, large category of letters. Models of tax transmittals appear in Chapter 11.

Many transmittal letters are brief form letters requiring only the insertion of names, dates, and other easily added information. Such letters can be stored in a word-processing system or, lacking that, can be photocopied or preprinted.

Some transmittal letters have to be written to fit specific circumstances. It may be that what is being sent has to be explained, interpreted, or amplified. In such cases a form letter will be of no use unless you can add the needed information at the end.

What you need to transmit depends on the nature of your accounting practice and the needs of your clients. Every transmittal letter, however, should perform these two basic functions: (1) It should introduce the document or documents it accompanies; and (2) It should (by means of a carbon or photocopy) provide you with a record of the transmittal.

LETTER OF TRANSMITTAL FOR ADJUSTING ENTRIES

YOUR LETTERHEAD

[Date]

INSIDE ADDRESS

[Salutation]:

For your convenience, we have enclosed [number] adjusting entries prepared for the period ended [date].

Kindly acknowledge receipt of this letter and sign below to indicate that the adjusting entries have been posted to your general ledger.

Please return the signed copy to us in the self-addressed envelope we have provided. The second copy of the letter is for your files.

[Closing],

YOUR SIGNATURE

Identification block

To: [Your name and address]

Adjusting entries accompanying this letter have been posted to our general ledger.

Signed____________________________ Date______________

LETTER OF TRANSMITTAL FOR FISCAL CLOSING

YOUR LETTERHEAD

[Date]

INSIDE ADDRESS

[Salutation]:

For your convenience, we have enclosed [number] adjusting entries prepared as of the close of your fiscal year.

Kindly acknowledge receipt of this letter and sign below to indicate that the adjusting entries have been posted to your general ledger.

Please return the signed copy to us in the self-addressed envelope we have provided. The second copy of the letter is for your files.

[Closing],

YOUR SIGNATURE

Identification block

To: [Your name and address]

Adjusting entries accompanying this letter have been posted to our general ledger.

Signed________________________

TRANSMITTAL OF DRAFT AUDIT FOR COMMENTS

YOUR LETTERHEAD

____________________ [Date]

INSIDE ADDRESS

____

[Salutation]:

Enclosed is a draft of the audited financial statements and other financial information concerning the retirement income plan for employees of [name of client company] for the year ended December 31, 19x7.

We would appreciate any comments that you may wish to make before we issue the report.

[Closing],

____

YOUR SIGNATURE

____

TRANSMITTAL OF AUDITED FINANCIAL STATEMENTS

YOUR LETTERHEAD

[Date]

INSIDE ADDRESS

[Salutation]:

We are enclosing six copies of your audited financial statements for the year ended December 31, 19x5, along with our opinion on them.

[Closing],

YOUR SIGNATURE

TRANSMITTAL OF UNAUDITED FINANCIAL STATEMENTS

YOUR LETTERHEAD

[Date]

INSIDE ADDRESS

[Salutation]:

In accordance with the terms of our engagement, we are enclosing five copies of your unaudited financial statements for the year ended December 31, 19x5.

[Closing],

YOUR SIGNATURE

LETTER ACCOMPANYING ANNUAL REPORT TO STOCKHOLDERS

YOUR LETTERHEAD

[Date]

INSIDE ADDRESS

[Salutation]:

Enclosed are two copies of your Annual Report to Stockholders for the fiscal year ended [date].

We have manually signed the Accountant's Report included therein.

[Closing],

YOUR SIGNATURE

TRANSMITTAL OF PRINTED ANNUAL REPORT

YOUR LETTERHEAD

[Date]

INSIDE ADDRESS

We received ten printed copies of your 19x8 Annual Report today.

As you requested, we are returning six of these copies to you immediately. In them we have manually signed our opinion appearing on page [number].

[Closing],

YOUR SIGNATURE

TRANSMITTAL OF WORKING PAPERS USED FOR ANNUAL REPORT

YOUR LETTERHEAD

[Date]

INSIDE ADDRESS

[Salutation]:

As you requested, I am enclosing photocopies of our working papers used in the preparation of your annual report to [recipients of report] for the year ended December 31, 19x9.

[Closing],

YOUR SIGNATURE

LETTER TRANSMITTING NOTICE ABOUT EMPLOYEE BENEFIT PLAN

YOUR LETTERHEAD

[Date]

INSIDE ADDRESS

[Salutation]:

As we discussed earlier today, I am enclosing a Notice to Interested Parties. This notice should be posted no later than February 18, 19x5, in a conspicuous place for all employees to read.

If an employee should ask to review the application being made to the Internal Revenue Service, please *separate from the application the Form 5302 attachment showing individual salaries and benefits. Form 5302 is not open to public inspection.*

[Closing],

YOUR SIGNATURE

LETTER TRANSMITTING PENSION FUND REPORT

YOUR LETTERHEAD

[Date]

INSIDE ADDRESS

[Salutation]:

We have prepared the Annual Report and Annual Statement of [name of pension fund] for calendar year 19x8.

The accounting and other data contained in the report and statement were obtained from the records maintained at your pension fund office. The amount of the Reserve for Benefits Not Insured was determined and supplied by [name of actuarial firm].

Page [number] of the Report and page [number] of the Statement both require the notarized signatures of one trustee from the employer group and one trustee from the labor organization group.

In our opinion, the Report and Statement correctly set forth the financial and statistical data of [name of pension fund] as of December 31, 19x8, and may properly be approved and signed by the appropriate trustees.

[Closing],

YOUR SIGNATURE

LETTER TRANSMITTING PENSION PLAN AMENDMENT

YOUR LETTERHEAD

[Date]

INSIDE ADDRESS

[Salutation]:

Enclosed are three copies of the amended and restated Pension Plan in conformity with our understanding of the provisions of the Tax Equity and Fiscal Responsiblity Act of 1982, the Deficit Reduction Act of 1984, the Retirement Equity Act of 1984, and the regulations pursuant to each.

Please sign all three copies and return two to us. In order for us to complete Form 5300 with the appropriate attachments for requesting a favorable letter from the Internal Revenue Service, we will need a complete census of all employees, as well as the approximate contribution to the profit-sharing plan for 19x4. We have enclosed our annual census request for that purpose.

If you have any questions, please call.

[Closing],

YOUR SIGNATURE

TRANSMITTING LETTER OF RECOMMENDATIONS TO MANAGEMENT

The envelope that contains this transmittal letter and the accompanying report should be marked "Personal and Confidential."

YOUR LETTERHEAD

[Date]

INSIDE ADDRESS

[Salutation]:

We enclose one copy of our letter report containing observations, comments, and recommendations based on our review of the organization, personnel, and reporting practices of [name of client company].

We will be pleased to discuss this report with you at your convenience.

[Closing],

YOUR SIGNATURE

LETTER TO BANK SUPPORTING PROPOSED PLANT-EXPANSION MORTGAGE

While management letters are, by definition, directed to executives of a client company, you may occasionally have to submit information directly to a bank to clarify the company's financial projections. This letter is addressed to a bank and deals with such a situation.

YOUR LETTERHEAD

[Date]

INSIDE ADDRESS

[Salutation]:

We herewith submit the Comparative Projected Income Statement and accompanying Projected Cash Flow Statement for the period September 1, 19x6, through July 31, 19x7. These statements were prepared for the purpose of projecting whether the proposed plant expansion can generate sufficient cash to meet the related debt service requirements of an anticipated $625,000 mortgage. The statements were prepared using the assumptions and rationale contained therein.

We have reviewed the assumptions and rationale underlying these projected statements, and we believe them to be reasonable and appropriate for the purpose of this projection.

Since projections are based on assumptions about events and circumstances that have not yet taken place, they are subject to the variations in operations that may in fact occur in the future. Accordingly, we cannot give assurance that the predicted results will actually be attained.

If you have any questions, please do not hesitate to contact us.

[Closing],

YOUR SIGNATURE

TRANSMITTAL TO BANK OF FINANCIAL STATEMENTS RE MORTGAGE

YOUR LETTERHEAD

[Date]

INSIDE ADDRESS

[Salutation]:

We are enclosing the financial statements of Equipment Leasing, Inc., for the year ended June 30, 19x6.

These statements are provided to you in accordance with provisions contained in the mortgage agreement dated May 23, 19x4.

[Closing],

YOUR SIGNATURE

TRANSMITTING COPIES OF PRIOR CORRESPONDENCE

YOUR LETTERHEAD

[Date]

INSIDE ADDRESS

[Salutation]:

Thank you for your letter of [date]. I regret that you failed to receive copies of the correspondence relating to our audit for the period ended [date]. To remedy that situation, I am enclosing copies of the following letters:

2/7/x6: [description of letter]
2/11/x6: [description of letter]
2/16/x6: [description of letter]
2/18/x6: [description of letter]

Please note that copies of these letters were sent to [name of recipient] in your accounting department.

If you wish, I will have copies of all future audit correspondence marked to your attention.

[Closing],

YOUR SIGNATURE

LETTER ACCOMPANYING ACCOUNTING REPORT TO PARTNERS

YOUR LETTERHEAD

[Date]

INSIDE ADDRESS

[Salutation]:

Enclosed are the revised copies of our accounting report on the partnership of [name of partnership] for the year ended December 31, 19x7.

As you requested, we have removed from each partner's copy of the report the schedules for business and personal expenses that apply to the other partners.

[Closing],

YOUR SIGNATURE

TRANSMITTAL OF SPECIAL REPORT TO STOCKHOLDERS

YOUR LETTERHEAD

[Date]

INSIDE ADDRESS

[Salutation]:

Enclosed are four copies of your special published report to stockholders relating to the acquisition of [name of company].

We have manually signed the accountant's report in each copy.

[Closing],

YOUR SIGNATURE

PART VI

WRITING MORE EFFECTIVE LETTERS AND REPORTS

CHAPTER 17

Word Processing in the Accounting Office

- The Power of Word Processing
- Nine Specific Applications
- A Hard Look at Software
- Storage Media in Transition
- Choosing Among Printers
- The Right Vendor
- Ten Tips on Word Processing

The basic difference between typewriting and word processing is this: In typewriting, what you enter on the keyboard appears immediately on paper. You can correct errors in typewriting, to be sure, but these are after-the-fact remedies. Word processing provides the intermediate step of words on a video display screen, which gives you a chance to make the necessary corrections *before* anything is printed on paper.

THE POWER OF WORD PROCESSING

Word processing allows the typist to do many things that are impossible in traditional typewriting.

Word wrap. The first thing an experienced typist notices about word processing is the lack of any manual carriage return. At the end of a line of text, the program automatically moves the text down to the beginning of the next line. It does this by determining whether the last word will or won't fit at the end of a line. If it won't, the program begins a new line.

Delete. If you type a word, phrase, sentence, or paragraph that you want to eliminate—or if you make a major error—you can get rid of your mistake without strikeovers, line-outs, correction tape, or white-outs. All you have to do is hit the DELETE key, highlight the unwanted text, hit the ENTER key, and, presto, the mistake disappears. Moreover, the program automatically adjusts all following lines to their proper length.

Insert. Just as you can get rid of text, so you can add text. To do so, you hit the INSERT key when the cursor (a small, flashing, place-marking symbol) is where you want the new text to be. Then you type in the desired text. No matter how long or short the new text is, the program will make appropriate adjustments for every line following the insert.

Move. Words, phrases, sentences, even whole pages can be moved from one place to another in a document. No more cutting, pasting, and retyping. Just highlight the text to be moved, find the spot where it is to go, and press ENTER (or EXECUTE, or whatever key your system uses for this function).

Copy. Not only can you move text from place to place, you can also copy an unlimited sequence of characters from place to place. With repetitive text, this feature can be a tremendous timesaver. The copied text appears in its new location as well as in the place where it was originally typed.

Search and replace. Suppose you have entered the figure $2,567 a dozen times in a document. Later you discover that the figure should have been $2,634. How do you change it? In word processing, you use the search-and-replace function. By pressing the search-and-replace keys that your program uses, your computer will locate in sequence every appearance of the $2,567 entry and will change it automatically to $2,634 (or else it will ask you each time if you want to change it).

Merge print. This is one of the greatest timesavers in letter writing. The merge-print function permits you to combine stored paragraphs or stored names and addresses with existing "shell" documents to create new, custom-designed letters and other documents. You may have a basic proposal letter, for example, stored on disk as a shell document. To it you can add a name and address, along with specific, relevant paragraphs (as well as new text), to create an original proposal that is exactly on target for the prospective client.

These are only a few of the features that word processing offers. Every program has a number of formatting options that no typewriter can match. The simplest of these have to do with line length, line spacing, and margins and tabs. Many systems allow right margins to be "justified" (aligned) so as to resemble typeset printing. Especially useful in the accounting office are graphics capabilities and column formats, including decimal alignment.

NINE SPECIFIC APPLICATIONS

Today, word processing is used in virtually every kind of business. When it was first introduced, it gained almost immediate acceptance in a number of fields, among them law, banking, and insurance. Accounting, for some reason, was somewhat slower to adopt it, yet the advantages of word processing to an accounting practice are such that professional accounting journals soon began to include articles on its uses and its implementation. Here are a few of the applications:

Proposals. Many sections of a proposal are the same from letter to letter, as shown by the letters in Chapter 1. Where new text is needed, it can easily be slotted in. With minimal additional work the name and address can be added, and the result is a proposal that is precisely right for the client.

Confirmation letters. Dozens of standard requests for confirmation can be stored on disk and used when needed. In many instances, all that will have to be entered is the particular client's name and address, which can be inserted from a stored name-and-address file.

Tax preparation and transmittal letters. Form letters have always been common and useful in the tax field. The elimination of repetitive typing saves countless hours and at the same time it ensures a high degree of accuracy. Whenever you are able to use stored text—as is always possible with word processing—you can obtain perfect text, because it has already been edited and proofread. In addition to using your own stored letters, or your firm's, you may want to look into word-processing programs geared to various tax forms.

Financial statements. Robert F. Stencel in his article "Are You Overlooking the Benefits of Word Processing?" in *Computers in Accounting,* states that financial statements are the primary word processing application in most accounting firms. They may well be the primary *computer* application in accounting offices regardless of the software program chosen to accomplish it. A word-processing program may be a good choice for financial statements, although specialized accounting packages should certainly be considered.

Audit documents. Audit reports, with their formalized language, are highly simplified with the use of a word-processing system. The handling of figures may prove more satisfactory on another program, however. If you have an integrated program, such as Framework or Symphony, it can handle both figures and text efficiently.

Letters of recommendation to management. Certain types of business problems are recurring ones. In a small company, for example, the lack of segregation in processing cash receipts is a common difficulty. If you store one or more paragraphs relating to this situation, you may not have a word-for-word recommendation ready for every client, but you will probably have a paragraph that can be modified quite easily to fit the circumstances.

Management advisory services reports. Any lengthy report can, in fact, benefit from word processing. Since MAS reports must present facts clearly and accurately, they often have to go through several drafts. Revision is one of word processing's greatest strengths. Long and complex documents do not necessarily become shorter or simpler through electronic editing, but they do get done better and faster. With word processing, half a dozen laboriously typed drafts are a thing of the past.

Invoices. The figures change depending on the client, but the form of the invoice remains the same. A stored collection of invoice forms simplifies and speeds the task of billing. Likewise, a group of letters dealing with overdue accounts makes it easy to send the appropriate letter to slow-paying clients at the appropriate time without needless retyping.

General correspondence. Any narrative text lends itself to word processing. Although you may not be able to store a paragraph for every occasion, the other advantages of word processing—especially the text-editing capabilities—make the production of all kinds of correspondence more efficient. Beyond that, your letters are almost sure to look neater and more professional when errors are caught and corrected on the video display, rather than on the printed page.

This nine-item list barely scratches the surface of possible applications. It is not overstating the case to say that nearly everything produced in an accounting office can be stored on disk.

A HARD LOOK AT SOFTWARE

A computer is only as good as the software that runs on it. Unless the word-processing program you choose is the right one for your circumstances, you will not obtain all the benefits you should.

If you have a personal computer or are networking with a larger computer (a system sometimes called "shared logic"), you can choose from a wide variety of word-processing software. New programs appear almost weekly, as do new versions of established programs. Old programs fade away. A trip to a well-stocked software store, or the careful reading of one or more of the many computer magazines, will give you a general picture of what today's choices are for word-processing software.

The tough question is this: Even if you know what programs are available, how will you know which one to choose? It may seem almost as perplexing as which phonograph album or cassette to buy. "If you like a couple of the songs," said one of the authors' sons, "buy the album and pray." Is this the best you can do in choosing word-processing software? No. Many software companies, new as they are, have acquired reputations, good or bad. Moreover, there are ways to obtain information on specific programs, although until recently there was not much reliable comparative information available. In the past few years, some useful directories have begun to appear. These directories, like software itself, may prove to be ephemeral, and any directory is quickly outdated. The best place to look for recent directories is in your local library or bookstore. A directory that is more than two years out of date will be of virtually no use.

The best way to evaluate software is to try it out. This may or may not be practical, however, because even a fairly extensive office test has its limitations. In the end, you may still feel a bit uneasy. Actually, almost any well-reviewed, widely sold word-processing package has its advantages and disadvantages. Given a reasonable amount of investigation, whatever choice you make will probably work for you—and you may never know whether "Word Processor X," instead of the one you got, would have worked slightly better.

STORAGE MEDIA IN TRANSITION

The current choice in storage media is between disks or diskettes (so-called "floppies") and hard disks. The advantage of hard disks over floppies lies in the vast storage capacity and speed of the hard disk. The main disadvantage, besides the high initial cost, is that a hard disk cannot be replaced like a floppy. Once it is filled with data, you have to erase, or "purge," some copy to record more. That sounds like a serious flaw, but in reality the storage capacity of a modern hard disk is so large—20 to 30 metabytes; up to a thousand or so text pages—that erasure may not be required.

A few years ago, a hard-disk drive for a personal computer would have been out of the question. Today, it is probably the best choice. Prices have come down drastically. Storage capacity has gone up. Anyone who has incessantly switched floppy disks, particularly on a single-disk drive, will appreciate the convenience and efficiency of having all information—all blank forms, all shell letters, all standard paragraphs, all address lists—stored on a single hard disk.

Every aspect of computer technology is in transition. New methods of storage may be on the way, but, for the time being, an accountant or a small accounting firm buying a computer system for the first time should certainly consider the possibility of a hard-disk drive. A firm with an established computer system using floppies might also want to take a careful look at hard disks.

CHOOSING AMONG PRINTERS

The choice of a printer is not so puzzling as some of the other choices, because you can observe with your own eyes what a printer does. An inexpensive dot-matrix printer produces copy that is too fuzzy for most of your letters and reports. Because of its speed, it is ideal for printing rough drafts, internal correspondence, and perhaps a few of the documents that leave your office. It is also good for charts and graphs.

But for the kind of sharp, typewriter-style printing you need for proposals, engagement letters, representation letters, audit reports, promotional materials, and the like, you will want what is called a *letter-quality* printer. Letter-quality printers are slow compared to dot matrix printers—and *very* slow compared to laser printers, which, however, cost more than most small accounting firms may want to pay.

Most letter-quality printers use a daisy-wheel printing element. This element can easily be switched, which permits the use of various typefaces and type sizes. A few printers use what is called a "thimble"—it looks just like one—but the best printing (short of laser printing) comes from daisy wheels.

THE RIGHT VENDOR

An automobile dealer whose factory-trained mechanics are all thumbs is not your best bet when it comes to buying a new car. The dealer may offer a great price and toss in some free accessories. At first those clumsy fellows lurking in the garage may not matter much. The car runs fine. The manual has a chart that shows when and how the car should be serviced. So far, so good. But sooner or later you will need to make repairs, and at that point a ten-thumbed mechanic can really cause headaches.

The same applies to selecting a vendor. You have to weigh a number of factors when you decide to buy. Peat, Marwick, Mitchell & Co. puts out a useful fact sheet on selecting a vendor. It is reproduced on the following page.

SELECTING A VENDOR

Advantages and Disadvantages of Vendor Options

Vendor	*Advantages*	*Disadvantages*
Large manufacturers	They understand the importance of service and support; will stay in business and be available for support.	Prices are higher than for comparable products with lesser-known names.
Manufacturer-owned stores	They can offer ongoing support; provide packages of hardware and software, plus training.	They have little flexibility in inventory and in pricing policies.
Independent dealers	They can stock whatever brands they want; they are accessible.	If they go out of business, client support is no longer provided; some do not have resources to tailor system to clients' needs; usually charge full list price.
Other retail outlets (department, discount, computer stores)	They are convenient; offer some variety	They offer no customized equipment; some salespeople are not knowledgeable; cannot come to client's office to confer; usually charge full list price.
Original-Equipment Manufacturer (OEM) and systems houses	They provide integrated sytems, ready to run.	If they go out of business, client support is no longer provided; charge full list price.
Mail order houses	They offer almost every kind of equipment at the lowest possible prices.	They offer no support.
Consultants	They provide any or all desired services or support.	The consulting costs are extra.

TEN TIPS ON WORD PROCESSING

Now that your word-processing system is in place, productivity increases, office morale goes up—and text-editing problems arise. Although word processing has all the advantages that its warmest supporters claim, it is not without its pitfalls. Certain glitches can occur with word processing that were unlikely or impossible with your old Remington typewriter. And since the new technology is so impressive, you can easily miss them. A few tips may help.

1. Pay close attention to formatting. The very versatility of word processors sometimes leads to inconsistencies. It is so easy to make changes in line length, line spacing, margins, tabs, and so on, that you have to be on guard not to begin a long document in one format and end it in another. For instance, suppose you change the line length in a letter from 63 to 67 characters to accommodate one troublesome line. If you forget to change it back again, the rest of the letter will look subtly (or maybe not so subtly) different. More serious problems, as when one boldfaced word turns into half a boldfaced document, are easier to spot in the printed copy, but are nonetheless annoying.

2. Delete everything you intend to. This kind of problem seldom arises in typewriting, but it comes up quite often in word processing. If, for example, you delete a paragraph about "inventory control" from the body of a letter report, the deletion is quick and easy, but once the paragraph is gone, it is gone forever. There is no lined-out text to remind you of the fact that "inventory control," mentioned twice on page three and left there, was deleted from page two. This kind of problem can show up in many ways, such as when a single word is deleted, which grammatically affects the words before or after it in the same sentence. The only remedy is careful proofreading.

3. Make sure that copied text does not appear twice. Many word-processing operators have the habit of *copying* text to a new location rather than *moving* it. They do this because they are afraid of losing it in the transfer, since text disappears from the screen in the MOVE mode, while it remains in place in the COPY mode. This is probably an unnecessary safeguard, and one that can lead to trouble. If you forget to go back—and it may be pages back—to delete the text from its original location, you will present the surprised reader with the same block of text twice, once where you want it, once where you don't.

4. Be aware of possible character-string problems with search and replace. The global search-and-replace function allows you to replace a given string of letters automatically. This can be a tremendous timesaver. Let's say you want to replace the name "Estrin, Inc." with "Drew and Company." By using global search and replace, you can define "Estrin, Inc." as the character string to be replaced, and then define "Drew and Company" as the replacement. The computer does the rest. But suppose you want to replace the word *fee* with the word *charge* throughout a document. Look out! In most programs what the computer will be replacing is the character string *f-e-e* wherever it occurs. You forget that. Imagine your surprise when you see the following sentence:

> Our charge for this service is $75, which we chargel is reasonable in view of the amount of chargedback you are likely to receive.

5. Remember that replacing text can affect formatting. In the previous example, you replaced the character string "Estrin, Inc." with "Drew and Company." You were replacing 12 characters (including spaces) with 16 characters. That may not seem like much of a difference, but such a charge can occasionally wreak havoc. Suppose, for instance, you have inserted a number of required line-end codes so as to hyphenate some words or make full use of the format line length. Here is what can happen:

> We have examined the balance sheet of Drew and Company as of
De-
cember 31, 19x7, and the related statements of income and

This is by no means the only kind of odd change that can occur. Let's say that in a column format with tabs you replace "CEO" with "C.E.O." The additional three character spaces may push tabs to the right in the second column, giving you an unaligned left margin in that column. Proofreading is the only remedy for such mishaps. You cannot always rely on automatic functions to make needed adjustments.

6. Watch out for errors in merge-print salutations. Automation is marvelous, but computers are unable to think—yet. For example, if you have the computer pick up the first name of an inside address and use it after "Dear" in the salutation, you may produce some howlers. On the left of the following example is how the procedure is supposed to work. On the right is how it may work:

Dwight Eckstein	Boy Scouts of America
34 Weldon Road	1325 Walnut Hill Lane
El, Paso, TX 79940	Irving, TX 75038
Dear Dwight:	Dear Boy:

7. Be careful to check the text of a form letter. Once again, word processing is so versatile that you may be inclined to follow the lead of modern direct-mail advertisers and sprinkle the name of your addressee throughout what is basically a form letter. That may be the thing to do, but if you do it, remember not to leave the body of the letter unchanged for the next client. Otherwise, you will have a letter addressed to Ms. Helene Farr (which is correct in the salutation) and then (to Ms. Farr's amusement or annoyance, depending on her mood) begins to say things like, "We hope you understand, Mr. Ackerman . . ." and "Thank you for your attention to this matter, Mr. Ackerman."

8. Avoid overreliance on spelling-check programs. If your word processor has a spelling-check feature, you are sure to find it useful. However, you must remember that this kind of built-in dictionary can find only misspelled words. If you spell *believe* as *beleive,* it will pick up the mistake and save you embarrassment. But if you spell *hear* as *here,* it will not pick it up. It has no way to. The word *here* is a correctly spelled word, and your computer cannot know that the sentence incorrectly reads: "I hope to *here* from you at your convenience."

9. Use form letters only in appropriate situations. Your good friend Sparky O'Rourke, along with dozens of other clients, needs to be reminded about the imminence of tax time. For this purpose you have a form letter on disk that accompanies a photocopied checklist. Now, it may be all right to send the covering letter to Sparky even if it is addressed to "Dear Mr. O'Rourke." On the other hand, it may not be. If the tone of the letter is formal (since you cannot be a close friend to all your clients), Sparky may conclude that you are either lazy or insensitive. If you *do* use the form letter, you may want to add a handwritten note: "Hey, Sparky. The note is from my friendly computer. I hope you and Tess are well."

10. Don't overedit. As an accountant, you want everything to be letter-perfect. As a word-processing user, you have the capability of making everything letter-perfect. However, it is possible to go overboard and to waste time editing. If you emulate Oscar Wilde, the poet and playwright, who according to one critic "spent the morning putting in a comma and the afternoon taking it out again," you will lose one of the principal benefits of word processing: increased efficiency. Try to remember how it was before you had a word processor. Recall the amount of time you spent editing back then. If you are putting in substantially more time now, it is probably best to mend your ways. One accountant-writer suggests that you edit only the first draft of a document (just as you always did), then proofread subsequent drafts.

CHAPTER 18

A Practical Guide to Report Writing

- Toward Better Audit Reports
- Who Receives the Audit Report?
- Guidelines for Dating the Report
- The Management Advisory Services Report
- Parts of a Management Advisory Services Report
- Ten Tips for Report Writers

Written reports come in many varieties. The first image that comes to mind is a neatly bound booklet, which includes a table of contents, an introduction, exhibits, and so on—in other words, a full-scale, formal report. But that is not the only kind of report. A one-page letter can be a report, too, if its purpose is to make known the results of an investigation or observations. A report is more a matter of intent than of length, although much of this chapter will deal with full-scale reports.

Report writing involves the drafting and redrafting of an often-lengthy manuscript. The job is time-consuming and demanding, although its burden can be lessened through the use of word processing. The text-editing ability of word processors—the instant insertion, deletion, moving, and copying of text—is a tremendous advantage in preparing long, complex reports.

TOWARD BETTER AUDIT REPORTS

If precast, short-form certificates, such as those in Chapter 6, are all that you use, then your audit report writing will require very little skill in producing original text. If, on the other hand, you include recommendations to management in your report—everything, as one writer said, "from computerization of parts inventories to the needs for family housing, from stream pollution to hospitalization of the elderly,"—you are going to have to write some original and demanding material. Model paragraphs, such as those in Chapters 7 and 8, can help considerably, but they can't do the whole job.

Effective report writing is a complex, time-consuming task. If you feel frustrated or inadequate when attempting to report your audit findings in writing, you have plenty of company. The art of writing is a difficult one to teach, and studies of American education have consistently shown that it is seldom taught adequately. Some students have had almost no instruction in writing prior to their freshman year in college, and many have had none afterwards. Small wonder that accountants (and many other professionals) dislike writing and do it far less capably than they could.

What can you do if you have difficulty communicating objectives, conclusions, and recommendations as clearly and effectively as you believe you should? In the broadest yet simplest terms you train yourself to become a self-editor. You must read your own writing with a critical and detached view, putting yourself in the reader's shoes— "Do I fully understand what I've written? If not, why not?" To help answer those two basic questions, ask yourself the following, related questions:

Is the material logically organized? There are a number of ways to organize the body of a report. Look back at Chapters 7 and 8 and notice how the model paragraphs have been grouped. That method of arranging items by functions within a company is one possibility. There are many other methods that depend on the nature and length of the report. You may want to organize your report from the most important to the least important point. Or you may want to use some kind of chronological scheme. The main thing to remember is that the body of the text ought to have some kind of discernible plan.

Is proper weight given to each point? Giving the proper emphasis to a subject can be rather tricky, because it may be easier to write at length about a trivial point than it is to write about a major point. But doing so may either mislead or irritate the reader who expects to find proper emphasis, and who anticipates, for instance, that a "proposed reorganization of the internal accounting department" will receive more space in your report than a "minor slip-up in the purchasing department." No matter how hard it may be to allot space according to your grasp of the importance of the point being made, you must do it. The reader, and especially the busy reader, will automatically assign the weight to a point that your report appears to give it.

Does the report show sensitivity to actual conditions? There are two aspects to this: (1) Does the report show an awareness of the effect your recommendations may have on the client-accountant relationship? In other words, is it tactful? Clearly, the report should not cast reflections on the integrity of personnel within the client company. (2) Does the report point out situations where the recommendations, excellent as they may be, might cost too much in relation to the benefits achieved? As a discerning report writer, you must keep your audience constantly in mind.

Does the report avoid extraneous topics? A report should not include items that are properly directed to an individual within the company. Nor should it include minor points that have no significant bearing on the profitability of the business. If you have assembled a number of minor points that you feel should be mentioned, put them in, but without elaboration. Give them only their proper, limited emphasis—perhaps at the end of the report.

Is the writing persuasive? You naturally hope that the recommendations you make will be put into effect. But the reader must be convinced that your recommendations are good ones. You cannot assume that their value is obvious. After all, the client had not previously recognized the deficiencies you now point out; otherwise he would already have dealt with them. Even if the client now recognizes the deficiencies, you still have to make a convincing case for your specific remedy. How do you do it? You have to rely on your skill in communicating the validity of your ideas. There is no other way. You present solid evidence. You anticipate the reader's doubts and objections and counter them in the text. You point out

- The situation that exists
- The standards or criteria violated by the situation
- The cause or effect (or both) of the situation
- The recommendation on how to remedy the situation

WHO RECEIVES THE AUDIT REPORT?

The audit report is a confidential document. It should go to a responsible person, usually the treasurer or principal executive, in an envelope clearly marked "confidential." The envelope or box used for mailing should be strong enough to withstand careless handling, since no confidentiality exists in partially opened containers.

If the audit report is a standard opinion, without accompanying recommendations, and the recipient is a corporation, the report may be addressed to the board of directors of the client company or to the stockholders. If the report contains recommendations, it should ordinarily be addressed to a single, named person.

A report to an unincorporated client may be addressed to the partners, a general partner, or the proprietor, depending on the terms of the engagement or on what has been discussed prior to mailing.

Sometimes a client may request that copies of the report be mailed to a third party or parties. You should comply with this request only if (a) you have the request in writing and (b) you mention the client's request in your transmittal letter to the third party.

GUIDELINES FOR DATING THE REPORT

Obviously, the date of an audit report is later than the end date of the reporting period, since you need time to do the work on which the audit report is based. It is important to date an audit report correctly, because the date establishes a cut-off point, beyond which you cannot necessarily be expected to know about events in the client company.

The usual date of an audit report is the date on which the accountants' fieldwork ended. This may not be cut and dried, because of possible loose ends; but it tends to be fairly clear.

You may have to update a report on occasion, as when an event to be included in the financial statements occurs after the fieldwork has been completed but before the report is issued. Three possible ways to handle this situation are as follows:

1. Dual dating. By far the most common and generally the most satisfactory way to update dual dating looks like this:

February 11, 19x7, except for Note 6 for which the date is March 30, 19x7.

2. Redating. In redating, the entire report gets a new date. This may occasionally be appropriate, but it does pose a problem unless the time span involved is very short. In the case above, if the date of the whole report to become March 30, 19x7, the accountant would seem to be accepting responsibility for all occurrences between February 11 and March 30.

3. Unaudited disclosure. The exclusion or deletion of an event from the opinion requires the addition of a disclosure in a note to the financial statements. The note makes it clear that the event occurred after the date of the auditor's opinion, and its effects do not play a part in that opinion.

The matter of report dating can become quite complicated, and this book does not presume to deal with it in any exhaustive way. There are many useful sources of information on the topic, including *Montgomery's Auditing*, 10th Edition, and the *AICPA Audit and Accounting Manual.*

THE MANAGEMENT ADVISORY SERVICES REPORT

Although audit reports remain the stock in trade of accountants and small accounting firms, MAS reports have been gaining in importance in recent years.

Management advisory services are a natural outgrowth of what accountants do routinely in their auditing engagements. MAS reports, however, are different in format and content from auditing reports, and their recommendations are often more far-reaching, owing to the terms of the engagement.

The first step in MAS reporting is the engagement letter, or memo of understanding. A sample MAS engagement letter is included in this book on pages 18–20. Note, however, that while the model letter is brief, an MAS engagement letter can be long, involved, and specific.

Because the engagement must focus on a variety of circumstances unique to the client company, the letter detailing it has to be an original piece of writing in most cases—and it has to be very carefully done. The engagement letter should cover the following points:

- Objectives of the MAS engagement
- Extent, description, and limitations of the work
- Responsibilities of the parties
- Final deadline and schedules for the various tasks
- Arrangement for fees
- Statement concerning the reports to be issued

As the work proceeds, you should keep the client informed by supplying progress reports at frequent intervals. These can be either written or oral, depending on the agreement you have reached with the client. In these interim reports you will explain the findings to date, make preliminary recommendations, discuss problems that have arisen, and ask the client to make any specific decisions that may be needed. The interim reports will be valuable not only to the client but also to you as you assemble the information needed to prepare the final report. The feedback you receive will help you in reaching sound conclusions and in shaping viable recommendations.

In most cases you will deliver the final report in two forms: oral and written. Although the content of both reports will be similar, you should not simply read the written report aloud. The oral presentation should be relatively informal. The written report, on the other hand, while it shouldn't be stuffy, is a well-written and well-edited document. It should look neat and professional enough to impress the most critical client. As one writer-accountant notes, "Your personal prestige and reputation are on the line each time you prepare a written report."

PARTS OF A MANAGEMENT ADVISORY SERVICES REPORT

The simplest kind of report is probably the single-paragraph recommendation in a management letter. All it requires is a clear description of the problem and a brief statement on how to solve it. But when you have to write a full-scale MAS report, what are the minimum requirements? There are three:

1. Table of contents. Assuming that the report is properly organized, a table of contents provides an ideal summary for readers. It should include both main headings and subheadings so as to give a fairly complete picture of the entire contents.

2. Introduction. The purpose of the introduction is to place the circumstances of the report in perspective. It indicates the intent, nature, and scope of the engagement. A person who knows nothing about the study should be able to read the introduction and gain a reasonably accurate picture of the parameters of the report.

3. Body of report. In general, the longer the report, the more precise and probably the more extensive use you will have to make of headings, subheadings, and perhaps sub-subheadings. These function as guideposts for the reader throughout the report.

Most long reports contain more than just these three basic elements. The majority have exhibits of one kind or another, and many have an executive summary as a concise afterword. Other common additions to the bare essentials are transmittal letters, summaries of recommendations, appendices, and abstracts. Let's glance quickly at each of them:

Abstract. The abstract (the item is probably the one least often added) is a very brief narrative description—perhaps half a typewritten page—of the contents of the report. Its intent is to make it possible for the client to locate one specific report among the many in the files. An abstract appears at the beginning of a report.

Transmittal letter. An example of a transmittal letter appears on page 374.

Exhibits. Graphs, charts, financial statements—indeed, anything that graphically illustrates the statements made in the body of the report—can be exhibits. They should appear in a position as near as possible to the relevant text.

Appendices. An appendix contains material supportive of the points made in the body of the report. Although an appendix is not needed for a full understanding of the report, it does provide persuasive backup. An appendix or appendices appear in the back of the report.

Summary of recommendations. A summary of recommendations provides a convenient listing of the recommendations made in the body of the report. The list may be included as a supplement to an executive summary. Ordinarily it goes at the end.

Executive summary. An executive summary states the main points contained in the report. If it is placed at the beginning of a report, it serves as a preview. However, this placement has two disadvantages: (1) The executive summary may parallel the introduction in certain respects. (2) Its placement at the beginning may influence top management to read only the summary, not the entire report. An executive summary is perhaps best placed at the end of the report.

TEN TIPS FOR REPORT WRITERS

Carl Sandburg, the great American poet, wrote, "If God had let me live five years longer I should have been a writer." It does seem to take a lifetime—or more—to master the intricacies of the English language. It is probably true that no report has ever been written that could not have been written better. The number of how-to books published each year on the subject of writing is a clear indication of how much postschool study is devoted to finding effective ways to put words on paper. The learning task is never-ending. Here are ten tips relating especially to report writing.

1. Allow enough time. The advice to allow enough time may sound a bit like asking a pit trader to stop and smell the roses, but it is sensible advice all the same. A good report requires *time* to write. No matter how busy you are, you will have to find the time to draft and redraft your report. If the time you set aside is too short, your report will suffer. If the time is adequate, you will be able to do your best.

2. Begin with the easy part. Since a report is a long, segmented project, there is no real need to start at the beginning. If a particular segment is easy to do, why not do it first? That way, you will have something on paper, which will perhaps inspire you to keep going.

3. Find common ground. Jeremiah J. Sullivan, in *Handbook of Accounting Communications,* mentions the need to find common ground. What he means is this: In order to show the client how much work you have done, you may be tempted to present a massive amount of data (not information) as evidence of the effort you have made. Don't do it. The client will not be impressed and may even be confused into making inappropriate decisions.

4. Establish textual connections. Angela Maniak, writing in *The Internal Auditor,* points out the need for establishing textual connections. She includes an example of an audit finding in which a situation is clearly and fully defined, but where no connection is made between it and the standard being violated. She points out that even the best reader cannot read your mind. The accountant in this case knew what standard was involved, but he failed to mention it. Such connections must be established on paper, not inferentially.

5. Paraphrase long regulations. It is easy but not always wise to quote relevant policies, standards, or regulations. If the quotation is short, it poses no problem. But if it is long, the reader's mind is likely to wander. He or she probably knows the regulation in the first place. Rather than quoting it at length, try paraphrasing it. Give only a brief summary. When it becomes a part of the text in this way, not as a turgid quote, the reader will be less prone to skip it.

6. Interpret raw data. Most readers need help in making sense of what you have assembled in your working papers. They need your assistance in analyzing and interpreting the data. You don't want to patronize your readers, but nine out of ten report writers supply too little help rather than too much. Ask yourself how much a reader needs to know in order to accept your findings. The answer should suggest the optimal amount of help you should provide.

7. Explain exhibits when necessary. Exhibits may be self-explanatory, but often they aren't. Either a note at the foot of the exhibit or an explanation within the text will help clarify a chart or graph that might otherwise be passed over or misinterpreted.

8. Put your first draft aside for a while. Although this advice is as old as the abacus, its worth has been proven countless times. A few days spent *not* looking at the first draft of your report will almost always pay dividends. When you come back to it, you will see things that you would have missed in ten straight readings the first time through. Your revising and editing can be speeded up amazingly if you follow this practice. Total writing time will be substantially reduced.

9. Have the report read by an outsider. By "outsider" we mean a person who did not participate in writing the report. It does not mean your gossipy Aunt Jenny. In fact, you will benefit from having as many people as possible read a near-final draft. They will all find a few of the same problems—and each of them will probably find something different, too. It can be eye-opening.

10. Turn mistakes to your advantage. In a letter to *The Journal of Accountancy*, George E. Hunt recounts what he did when a certified report was handed out incorrect, then withdrawn and corrected. The banker-client was furious, even though the mistake was essentially his. Mr. Hunt was embarrassed, but he turned the occasion to good account with, as he said, "honesty, forbearance, and compassion." His follow-up letter to the banker, shown on the following page, is a classic example of tact and gentle instruction.

______________________________ [Date]

INSIDE ADDRESS

____

[Salutation]:

Our firm appreciated the opportunity to meet with you regarding one of our reports, and your questions regarding the accounts payable were interesting. I will use this letter to summarize our conversation.

We can see how you originally termed the accounts payable "estimated" since the original report had an error which we corrected later. As we discussed, this error resulted from an incorrect confirmation received by us originally from the client's debtor. When we discovered the correct amount, we immediately prepared new reports and asked for the original reports to be recalled and destroyed.

This useful discussion between us also gave us an opportunity to discuss accounts payable in general and the audit process concerning them. We told of our confirmation posting procedure and our checking of later payments of accounts payable. We also stated that we check the accuracy of the accounts payable to the best of our ability but that there *can* be accounts payable not known to us.

In summary, we certify reports only when we have done all of the procedures we deem necessary and have satisfied ourselves that the statements presented are substantially correct. Unfortunately, this particular report was incorrect and, as you know, was the first one like this in many years. We hope it won't happen again, but we did value the opportunity to discuss these matters with you.

[Closing],

____

SIGNATURE

____

CHAPTER 19

Handbook of Letter Format

- Date
- Inside Address
- Salutation
- Body of Letter
- Closing
- Signature
- Optional Elements
- Identification Line
- Full-Block Format
- Block Format
- Semiblock Format
- Short Letter Format

Part of the impression a letter makes depends on the way it appears on the page. The basic elements of a business letter have to be included—the date, inside address, salutation, body, closing, and signature—but there are different ways to format them. Here is a look at each of these elements and a number of optional elements.

DATE

Every letter you send out should be dated. Your secretary is responsible for supplying the date—you do not have to include it in your dictation. The letter should be dated the day it is dictated, even if it is typed later.

The position of the date depends on your letter format. The four common letter formats are illustrated on pages 411–414. Regardless of format, the date is usually positioned three or four lines below the letterhead, although in a very short letter it may look better somewhat lower.

Do not use abbreviations (*Feb.* 10, 19x9, or *2/10/x9*), and do not spell out dates or add suffixes to the numbers (February *tenth*, 19x9, or February 10*th*, 19x9). The proper form is this:

February 10, 19x9

Audit reports and the letters accompanying them present special dating problems, which are discussed on page 398.

INSIDE ADDRESS

In most letters the inside address begins two to four lines below the date, and it never starts more than twelve lines below it. See the sample letter formats on pages 411–414.

The inside address ordinarily consists of four or five lines, the first of which is the name (and sometimes the title) of the recipient:

Ms. Arlene Mapes, President

If the name plus the title causes the first line to extend more than halfway across the typed page, put the title on the second line, using no comma after the name:

Mr. J. Wellington Throckmorton
Assistant Vice-President, Finance

The next line is the company name. It is important to get the name exactly right. For example, if *Co.* is part of the official name, use it; if *Company* is the proper style, use it. Refer to the company letterhead for the official name:

Sligo Paint Products Co., Inc.

In general, use the same address style that the company uses. There are no hard-and-fast rules for addressing, but in the case of state names you may want to decide on a consistent style—either spelling out the state names in all cases or using the two-letter abbreviations.

25 South 17 Street, Suite 3-A
Polk City, IN 46500

Chapters 1 and 2 of this book show a number of acceptable models for inside addresses.

SALUTATION

The salutation is placed flush with the left margin and two lines below the last line of the inside address. Its first word is capitalized, as are the person's title and name. Use the abbreviations *Mr.*, *Mrs.*, and *Dr.*, but no other abbreviations of titles. A colon follows the salutation, even when you know the recipient well and are using a first name or nickname. (A comma is used only in social letters.)

Dear Mr. Imbriani: Dear Phil:

If you don't know whether a woman is married or not, use *Ms.* Use *Ms.* also if the woman has indicated a preference for it. In writing to a company composed entirely of men, the standard *Dear Sirs:* or *Gentlemen:* is appropriate. For a company composed of both men and women, common practice today calls for one of the following forms:

Dear Sir or Madam: Ladies and Gentlemen:

Some businesses today use a simplified letter style in which the salutation is omitted entirely. In that kind of letter a subject line takes the place of the salutation. No illustration of the simplified style is included in this book, but a subject line with salutation is shown in the full-block letter format, page 411.

In a letter addressed to no person or organization in particular, such as a letter of recommendation, use *To Whom It May Concern.*

BODY OF LETTER

Even a short letter has a beginning, a middle, and an end. For example:

Dear Mr. Irwin:

Enclosed is a confidential letter addressed to Ms. Adrian Bell. According to our records, Ms. Bell, a former associate here, joined your firm last August. Would you please see that she gets the letter?

Each of the sentences fills one of three roles:

Beginning: "Enclosed is a confidential letter addressed to Ms. Adrian Bell."

Middle: "According to our records, Ms. Bell, a former associate here, joined your firm last August."

End: "Would you please see that she gets the letter?"

Most letters are much longer, but they all have the same essential parts. The *beginning* introduces the subject of the letter, telling why the letter is being written. The *middle* elaborates on the subject to the extent necessary. The *end* explains what the letter writer wants the recipient to do.

The body of the letter should be typed in one of the standard formats shown on pages 411–414.

CLOSING

The closing of a letter, like the salutation, can have varying degrees of formality. The closing, however, differs more in ordinary business correspondence than the salutation does. Here is a ladder of formality for closings:

Very formal:	Respectfully yours,	Respectfully,
Formal:	Very truly yours,	Yours truly,
Less formal:	Sincerely yours,	Cordially yours,
Informal:	Sincerely,	Cordially,

SIGNATURE

Ordinarily, the signature will be yours or your firm's, but in representation letters the signature is the client's. The acceptable form for the signature in proposal and engagement letters is illustrated in Chapters 1 and 2.

The name of your firm may be signed manually when the letter expresses a professional opinion or advice, as in audit correspondence and reports. In such instances the name of the firm should be typed in capital letters, exactly as it appears on the letterhead, four spaces below the closing:

Very truly yours,

Janowitz, Wise & Blasingame

JANOWITZ, WISE & BLASINGAME

To allow for the manual signature, leave four or five lines of space between the closing and the typed signature in all correspondence. Your manual signature should match your typed signature, but should not include *CPA,* if that appears:

Very truly yours,

Bernard D. Coles

Bernard D. Coles, CPA
Partner

When a secretary signs the letter manually, her or his initials should appear after the signature:

James F. Ross   tld

Sometimes the secretary will sign the letter personally, as in this example:

Very truly yours,
Donald S. Lassetter

Maureen Dittmer

Secretary to Mr. Lassetter

OPTIONAL ELEMENTS

The following parts of a letter are often useful:

Reference line. References to file numbers, order numbers, and other numerical references should be set four spaces below the date. The word *reference* does not have to be used, but sufficient information should be given so that the recipient knows what the number or numbers represent.

File No. 89-726

Attention line. Even though a letter is addressed to a company, you may want to send it to the attention of a particular person. An attention line identifies the letter as being a business letter, rather than a personal letter, and another employee will open it if the named person is not there. The attention line goes after the company name:

Gaspar Enterprises
Attention: Eldon Reyes
200 Route 96
East Millport, PA 18600

Subject line. Some letter-writing manuals suggest a subject line as a good way to reference all correspondence on the same subject. The subject line appears after the salutation, not before it. The usual way to begin a subject line is with SUBJECT (followed by a colon) or RE (with or without a colon). A subject line is often typed in capitals and may or may not be underlined.

Dear Mrs. Buhl:

SUBJECT: TAX EXAMINATION OF LUX-TUX, INC. 19x8

If the subject line contains more than one line, only the last line should be underlined. One blank line space should be left above and below the subject line.

IDENTIFICATION LINE

A number of items can appear after the signature in a letter:

Initials. The initials go flush left two lines below the last line of the signature. The capitalized initials are those of the signer or dictator of the letter. The lowercase initials are those of the typist. Here are three common forms:

JH/ds   JH:ds   JHds

Enclosures. You should indicate if other documents are included with the letter. The usual way to show this is by typing *Enc.* or *Enclosures* two lines below the initials. If the enclosures are very important documents, they can be individually listed by identifying names.

Enc.   Enclosures (2)   Enc.: Certified check

Mailing notation. If the letter is sent by some means safer or faster than first-class mail, a note to that effect should go on the next line after the enclosure line.

Registered Mail   Express Mail

Carbon copy notation. Those who receive carbon copies of a letter should be listed two or more lines below the previous notation. Names can be arranged by order of importance or in alphabetical order.

cc: David Ardourel Nancy Blanchard Thomas Cheney	bcc: Arthur Dobson ["blind" carbon copy—no notation on original]

Postscript. Try to avoid postscripts. Their content should usually have been included in the body of the letter. If you do use one, however, indent it five spaces from both margins to set it off clearly.

FULL-BLOCK FORMAT

MITCHELL HAKOUN
CERTIFIED PUBLIC ACCOUNTANT
277 NEWTON-SPARTA ROAD
POST OFFICE BOX 775
SPARTA, NEW JERSEY 07871

(201) 383-7969

November 12, 19x8

Mr. Dale Covington, President
DC Wholesale Drygoods, Inc.
585 State Street
Fitchburg, New Jersey 07700

Dear Mr. Covington:

SUBJECT: FEE INCREASE FOR INCOME TAX PREPARATION

For the past several years I have been preparing your federal and state income tax returns. Although my costs have been rising each year, I have not passed these costs along in the form of higher billings.

If I am to continue preparing your returns, I will have to adjust my rates upward. For this year's work, my projected billing to you will be $450, assuming that this year's returns require comparable preparation time to last year's.

I look forward to a continuing association with you, and hope this fee will be satisfactory. If, however, you should find it necessary to seek other assistance, I will cooperate fully in transferring your account.

Please let me hear from you when you have had time to reach a decision on the preparation of your returns.

Yours truly,

Mitchell Hakoun, CPA

MH/vp

BLOCK FORMAT

MITCHELL HAKOUN
CERTIFIED PUBLIC ACCOUNTANT
277 NEWTON-SPARTA ROAD
POST OFFICE BOX 775
SPARTA, NEW JERSEY 07871

(201) 383-7969

November 12, 19x8

Mr. Dale Covington, President
DC Wholesale Drygoods, Inc.
585 State Street
Fitchburg, New Jersey 07700

Dear Mr. Covington:

For the past several years I have been preparing your federal and state income tax returns. Although my costs have been rising each year, I have not passed these costs along in the form of higher billings.

If I am to continue preparing your returns, I will have to adjust my rates upward. For this year's work, my projected billing to you will be $450, assuming that this year's returns require comparable preparation time to last year's.

I look forward to a continuing association with you, and hope this fee will be satisfactory. If, however, you should find it necessary to seek other assistance, I will cooperate fully in transferring your account.

Please let me hear from you when you have had time to reach a decision on the preparation of your returns.

Yours truly,

Mitchell Hakoun, CPA

MH/vp

SEMIBLOCK FORMAT

MITCHELL HAKOUN
CERTIFIED PUBLIC ACCOUNTANT
277 NEWTON-SPARTA ROAD
POST OFFICE BOX 775
SPARTA, NEW JERSEY 07871

(201) 383-7969

November 12, 19x8

Mr. Dale Covington, President
DC Wholesale Drygoods, Inc.
585 State Street
Fitchburg, New Jersey 07700

Dear Mr. Covington:

For the past several years I have been preparing your federal and state income tax returns. Although my costs have been rising each year, I have not passed these costs along in the form of higher billings.

If I am to continue preparing your returns, I will have to adjust my rates upward. For this year's work, my projected billing to you will be $450, assuming that this year's returns require comparable preparation time to last year's.

I look forward to a continuing association with you, and hope this fee will be satisfactory. If, however, you should find it necessary to seek other assistance, I will cooperate fully in transferring your account.

Please let me hear from you when you have had time to reach a decision on the preparation of your returns.

Yours truly,

Mitchell Hakoun, CPA

MH/vp

SHORT LETTER FORMAT

MITCHELL HAKOUN
CERTIFIED PUBLIC ACCOUNTANT
277 NEWTON-SPARTA ROAD
POST OFFICE BOX 775
SPARTA, NEW JERSEY 07871

(201) 383-7969

November 19, 19x8

Mr. Dale Covington, President
DC Wholesale Drygoods, Inc.
585 State Street
Fitchburg, New Jersey 07700

Dear Mr. Covington:

Thank you for your prompt reply to my letter of November 12. I am delighted that you will be remaining with me as a tax client.

Within the next few weeks I will be sending you my annual reminder, along with a checklist to help you assemble the necessary documents.

Yours truly,

Mitchell Hakoun, CPA

MH/vp

Bibliography

A number of books and articles have been written for accountants on the subject of letter writing and report writing. Some of them are listed here, along with a few other readings of general interest.

Abrego, Gilbert F., Jr., "Applying Word Processing in Accounting Practice," *The Journal of Accountancy,* February 1976, pp. 42-45.

AICPA Audit and Accounting Manual. New York: American Institute of Certified Public Accountants, looseleaf subscription service.

AICPA Management of an Accounting Practice Committee, *Management of an Accounting Practice Handbook.* Fort Worth, TX: Practitioners Publishing Company, 1986.

Aronson, Joseph H., "Estate Planning: An Overview of the Basic Techniques," *The Practical Accountant,* April 1985, pp. 21-38.

Ashton, Robert H., and Robert E. Hylas, "Increasing Confirmation Response Rates," *Auditing,* Summer 1981, pp. 12-21.

Ballard, Charles R., "Some Tips on Improving Your Report Writing," *The Practical Accountant,* November 1980, pp. 43-47.

Benis, Martin, "The Small Client and Representation Letters," *The Journal of Accountancy,* September 1978, pp. 78-84.

Block, Max, *Proposal and Engagement Letters. . .* (3rd ed.) New York: The CPA Journal, 1979.

Bromage, Mary C., *Writing Audit Reports.* New York: McGraw-Hill, 1979.

Connor, Richard A., Jr., and J. Larry White, "Write a Better Management Letter," *CA,* May 1976, pp. 58-60.

Corbett, William J., "Boosting the Profession with Effective PR." *The Journal of Accountancy,* February 1986, pp. 76-82.

Donohue, J. Roger, *Engagement and Alternative Letters (for Use by Small and Medium-sized Accounting Firms)* (4th ed.) New York: The CPA Journal, 1980.

Eder, Bernard B., "How to Write More Effective Collection Letters," *The Practical Accountant,* May-June 1974, pp. 23-25.

Eder, Bernard B., "Use an Engagement Letter to Clarify Your Fee Arrangement," *The Practical Accountant,* May-June 1976, pp. 51-52.

Greene, Richard Jay, and Mark D. Grant, "How to Use Word Processing Equipment in Your Accounting Work," *The Practical Accountant,* May 1983, pp. 98-105.

Harris, Hubert L., Jr., "Personal Financial Planning: The Competition," *The Journal of Accountancy,* July 1985, pp. 64–76.

Harrison, Victor, "How to Design a More Effective Engagement Letter," *The Practical Accountant,* August 1980, pp. 63–67.

Hubbard, Thomas D., and Jerry B. Bullington, "Positive and Negative Confirmation Requests—A Test." *The Journal of Accountancy,* March 1972, pp. 48–56.

Hunt, George E., "Errors in Reports: What to Do?" *The Journal of Accountancy,* May 1976, pp. 97–98.

"Management Representation Letters—Adapting Them to the Circumstances," *The Journal of Accountancy,* March 1979, pp. 87–90.

Maniak, Angela, "Clear Writing: RX for Foggy Audit Reports," *The Internal Auditor,* August 1981, pp. 44–50.

Montgomery's Auditing (10th ed.) Jerry D. Sullivan et al., eds. New York: The Ronald Press/Wiley, 1985.

O'Neill, Elizabeth A., "Word Processing Simplifies the Preparation of Financial/Accounting Reports and Statistical Tabulations," *The National Public Accountant,* July 1980, pp. 21–23.

Pierce, Milt, and Scott Leventhal, "Don't Let Collection Letters Spoil Your Public Relations," *The CPA Journal,* August 1982, pp. 75–76.

Pilié, Louis H., *ARAF Management Letters Guide.* Atlanta: Associated Regional Accounting Firms, 1975.

Scionti, Paul M., "Some Tips on Writing Better Management Letters," *The Practical Accountant,* September 1980, pp. 52–54.

Slaymaker, John H., ed., "Samples of Tax Engagement Correspondence," *Taxation for Accountants,* March 1974, p. 191.

Stencel, Robert F., "Are You Overlooking the Benefits of Word Processing?" *Computers in Accounting,* September–October 1984, pp. 64–72.

Stover, Beryl C. Argall, "Firm Brochures and Client Newsletters—Two Vital Marketing Tools," *The Practical Accountant,* July 1981, pp. 30–36.

Sullivan, Jeremiah J., *Handbook of Accounting Communications.* Reading, MA: Addison-Wesley Publishing Co., Inc., 1983.

"Telephone vs. Letter," *The Practicing CPA,* October 1981, p. 8.

Van Duyne, J., *Director's and Officer's Complete Letter Book* (2nd ed.) Englewood Cliffs, NJ: Prentice-Hall, Inc., 1982.

Vasarhelyi, Miklos A., et al., "The Usage of Computers in Auditing Teaching and Research, *Auditing: A Journal of Practice & Theory,* Spring 1984, pp. 98–103.

"Writing Business Letters," *The CPA Journal,* January 1981, pp. 78–79.

Index

A

Abatement of tax penalties, 272, 273
Abstract of MAS report, 400
Acceptance data sheet, new client, 21
Acceptance line (*see* Approval line)
Accepting speaking engagement, 352
Accounting report to partners, transmittal, 378
Accounts payable:
  confirmation of, 89
  minimizing discrepancies in, 82
  request for list of, 90
Accounts receivable:
  confirmation of, 65
  controlling delinquent, 186
  improving collection of, 204
  positive and negative confirmations, 65–71
Adequacy of insurance coverage, 187
Adjusting entries, transmittal, 363
Advances, confirmation of, 73
Adverse opinion, audit report, 128
Adverse opinion, personal financial statements, 133
All-purpose tax transmittal, 239
Annual report to stockholders, transmittal, 368, 369
Annual report, working papers, transmittal, 370
Annual vacation policy, need for, 173
Apology for late reply to tax notices, 278
Appendices in MAS report, 400
Applicant, inviting for interview, 322, 325
Application for tax ID number, 253
Approval line in engagement letter, 4, 23
Assets and liabilities, recommendations, 187–188
Attention line in letter format, 409
Attorney, agreement on fee collection, 317
Attorney, letter to client's, concerning confirmation, 99
Audit:
  adverse opinion, personal financial statements, 133
  confirmations, 63–104
  compilation reports, 144–152
  disclaimer of opinion, lack of independence, 132
  disclaimer of opinion, personal financial statements, 133
  draft, transmittal, 365
  engagement, letters for, 38–47
  kinds of reports, 118–120
  memorandum of information for, 48
  nature of, 40
  nonprofit organization, 14
  observing inventory for another accounting firm, 104
Audit (*cont.*)
  personal financial statements, engagement letter, 46
  proposal, 12
  review reports, 135–143
  special reports, 153–157
  tax, postponement of, 284
  word processing in, 386–387
Audit report:
  adverse opinion, 128
  disclaimer of opinion:
    inadequate records, 131
    limited examination, 131
    prior year's unaudited statements, 124
    unobserved inventory, 130
  personal financial statements, standard report, 132
  qualified opinion:
    departure from GAAP, 124
    inadequate disclosure, 126
    inconsistent application of GAAP, 125
    limitation on scope of audit, 126
    review of prior year's statements, 124
    uncertainty about "going concern," 128
    uncertainty about lawsuit, 127
  unqualified opinion:
    accepting other auditor's report, 122
    reversing prior year's qualified opinion, 123
    standard report, 121
    two years' financial statements, 122
  word processing in, 386–387
  writing techniques, 394–398 (*see* Report writing)
Audited financial statements, transmittal, 366
Authorization for payroll deductions, 173
Authorization for release of tax records, 229
Automation, need for, 170

B

Backup, software, need for, 186
Balance sheets, monthly preparation of, 175
Bank confirmation inquiry, 86–87
Bank cutoff statements, request for, 85
Barter credits, 168
Benefit pension plan (*see* Employee-benefit pension plan)
Bibliography, 415–416
Bids, competitive, need for, 181
Billing policies, 297, 299 (*see* Fee; Invoice)
Birth of child, congratulations on, 335
Block letter format, 412
Body of letter, 407
Body of MAS report, 400

Bond issue confirmation, 96
"Boxed" format for tax transmittal, 243
Brochure, public relations 339
Budgeting and forecasting, recommendations, 174-175
Business:
congratulations on opening new, 354
planning session, engagement for, 205
termination of, 236
Business advisory letter (*see* Recommendation letter)

C

Cancellation of invoices, 177
Capital stock registrar, confirmation of, 95
Cash:
in custodian or trust accounts, confirmation of, 88
investing idle, 188
management of, 167, 176-177
position, maximizing, 202
receipts and disbursements, 176-177
value of life insurance, confirmation of, 97
Cash basis statements:
compilation reports, 146-147
review reports, 141
special audit report, 153
Certificate letter for inventory, 107
Change in engagement circumstances, 58
Changes in tax law, informing client, 232
Checklist for estate administration and probate, 217
Checklist for real estate holdings, 213
Checks, manual signatures on, 177
Check-writing materials, security of, 177
Client:
acceptance data sheet, 21
memorandum of information for audit, 48
representation letter: (*see also* Representation)
alternate, 115
concise, 113
general, 108
modification, 111
Client's personal goals, estate planning, 211
Closing in letter format, 408
Collecting:
accounts receivable, 204
overdue fee, letter to attorney, 317
past-due accounts, 185
Collection agency, confirmation of accounts receivable, 100
Collections and sales, recommendations, 184-185
Combined federal and state tax, transmittals, 243, 246
Company policy on personal computers, 185
Comparative financial statements, compilation reports, 149-152
Comparative financial statements, review reports, 135-139
Competitive bids, need for, 181
Compilation engagement, 36
Compilation reports, 144-152
Complaint concerning fee, 308
Compliance with contractual provisions, separate report 155-156
Compliance with regulatory requirements, separate report, 156
Computer operating procedures, need for manual on, 186
Computer security, 186
Computers and data processing, recommendations, 185-186
Computers, personal, need for policy on, 185
Conference, introductory proposal based on, 7
Conference, pre-engagement, 38
Confirmation:
accompanying monthly billing, 67
accounts payable, 89
accounts receivable, 65-71, 101
advances, 73
amount being held in special fund, 72
attorney, letter to client's, 99
auditor's direct request for information, 101
bank cutoff statements, 85
bank inquiry, 86-87
bond issue, 96
capital stock authorized and issued, 95
cash in custodian or trust accounts, 88
collection agency, accounts receivable, 100
contracts, 98
deposit premium, 82
grants, 98
included with statement, 67, 70, 71
indebtedness, 91
instructions for, 64
insurance policies held by others, 79
inventory:
in public warehouse, 80
observed by out-of-town auditor, 103
on consignment, 81
request to warehouse, 102
kinds of, 63, 83
legal considerations, 99
life insurance, cash value, 97
long-term debt, 93, 94
marketable securities held by others, 77
mortgage indebtedness, 93, 94
negative approach, 70-71
not a request for payment, 67
notes payable, request for schedule of, 92
notes payable to vendors, 75
notes receivable, 74
payables and consignment items, 90
petty cash, 73
positive approach, 65-69
printed letter of, 69
securities in custodian or trust accounts, 88
securities, marketable, held by others, 77
standard bank inquiry, 86-87
sticker or stamp method, 71
stock authorized and issued, 95
word processing in, 386
Congratulations to client:
appointment to office, 355
community achievement, 357
joining organization, 356
new position, 359

Congratulations to client (*cont.*)
opening new business, 354
promotion, 358
retirement, 360
Congratulations to employee:
birth of child, 335
marriage, 334
outstanding work, 333
salary increase, 332
Consignment inventory, confirmation of, 81
Consignment items, request for list of, 90
Continuation of family business, estate planning, 215
Contracts, confirmation of, 98
Control over cash receipts, 176
Copy function in word processing, 385, 391
Corporate refund (Form 1139) transmittal, 263
Corporation:
estimated tax payments, federal, 260
estimated tax payments, state, 262
tax, federal, transmital, 256, 357, 259
tax, state, transmittal, 261
Correction of taxpayer's account, 269
Correspondence, prior, transmittal, 377
Correspondence, word processing, 387
Cost accounting system, installing, 184
Cost control, 174
Credit for tax payment made, 268
Credit memoranda, approval of, 185
Current rates to measure operations, 175
Custodian account, securities and cash in, confirmation of, 88
Cutoff statements, bank, request for, 85

D

Data processing and computers, recommendations, 185–186
Data sheet for new client, 21
Date in letter format, 406
Dating audit reports, 398
Debt, long-term, confirmation of, 93, 94
Debt, mortgage, confirmation of, 93, 94
Declaration of estimated tax, filing, 226
Declining speaking engagement, 353
Deductible expenses, details for tax return, 231
Deficiency, recommendation that tax client accept, 290
Definition of technical term in client representation letter, 117
Delinquent receivables, controlling, 185
Delete function in word processing, 385, 391
Departure from GAAP:
compilation reports, 145–146
review reports, 139–141
standard report, 124
Deposit premium confirmation, 82
Depreciation policies, standardizing, 188
Disbursements and cash receipts, recommendations, 176–177
Disclaimer in engagement letter, 23, 36, 40
Disclaimer, model paragraph, 36
Disclaimer of opinion:
inadequate records, 131
Disclaimer of opinion (*cont.*)
lack of independence, 132
limited examination, 131
personal financial statements, 133
prior year's unaudited statements, 124
unobserved inventory, 130
Discrepancies in accounts payable, minimizing, 182
Disks in word processing, 388
Document control, 177
Dot-matrix printer for word processing, 389
Draft audit, transmittal, 365

E

Editing in word processing, 393
Employee:
congratulations, 333–335
get-well note, 336
offering position to, 326, 327
review, need for, 169
stock ownership plan, 167
Employee-benefit pension plan:
amendment, transmittal, 373
engagement for, 52
Form 5500-C, transmittal, 264
general information form, 56
proposal for, 16
qualification of, 233
report, transmittal, 373
specification sheet, 54
transmittal of notice about, 371
Employment, response to inquiry about, 321
Engagement:
annual or biannual letter, 34
audit, letters concerning, 38–47
business planning session, 205
change in circumstances from original, 58
compilation, 36
disclaimer in, 23, 36, 40
employee-benefit pension plan, 52
estate planning, 209
expert witness, 50
feasibility study for office building, 195
file copy of letter, 34
financial accounting system, 191
fund raising for small business client, 193
general letter, small business client, 24
general letter, special circumstances, 27
IRS representation, 30, 32
items to cover in letter, 23
kinds of, 22
leading to an opinion, 38
limitations on, 36
longtime client, 34, 42
management advisory services, 18, 399
memorandum of information for audit, 48
out-of-town auditor to observe inventory, 103
personal financial statements, audit of, 46
projected financial statements, proposed venture, 197
review, 34
special, 50

Error in report, using to advantage, 402–403
Errors made by prior tax accountant, correcting, 275
Estate planning:
  administration and probate checklist, 217
  client's personal goals, 211
  continuation of family business, 215
  definition, 190
  engagement, 209
  kinds of letters, 189
  real estate holdings checklist, 213
Estimated tax, filing declaration of, 226
Estimated tax payments, transmittal, 250
Examination, IRS, representing client, 32
Executive summary of MAS report, 400
Exemption forms (W-4), keeping, 173
Exhibits in MAS report, 400, 402
Expanded introduction, recommendation letter, 164
Expenses, travel, summary of, 172
Expert witness, special engagement, 50

F

Facilities and organization, recommendations, 169–171
Family business, continuation of, estate planning, 215
Feasibility study for office building, 195
Fee: (*see also* Invoice)
  amounts charged, 297, 299
  collection arrangement with attorney, 317
  complaint concerning, 308
  confirming oral agreement, 307
  escape provision in engagement letter, 58
  in engagement letter, 23, 30, 58
  in proposal, 12
  kinds of letters, 295
  overdue reminders, 309–316
  payment plan for, 314
  promissory note, 315
  request for increase, 304, 305
  tied to performance, 313
  urgent request for payment, 316
Fiduciary income tax transmittal, 251, 252
File copy of engagement letter, 34
Filing tax forms, reminder, 224
Filing tax return late, 267
Financial accounting system, engagement to set up, 191
Financial planning, personal, 206, 208
Financial services, definition, 190
Financial services, kinds of letters, 189
Financial statements:
  audited, transmittal, 366
  comparative, compilation reports, 149–152
  comparative, review reports, 135–139
  nonpublic entity, compilation report, 144
  nonpublic entity, review report, 139
  personal:
    adverse opinion, 133
    audit of, 46
    disclaimer of opinion, 133
    standard audit report, 132
  projected, for proposed venture, 197
  re mortgage, transmittal, 376
Financial statements (*cont.*)
  unaudited, transmittal, 367
  word processing in, 386
Fiscal closing, transmittal, 364
Fixed assets ledger, 187
Forecasting and budgeting, recommendations, 174–175
Form:
  1040, acceptance as filed, tax audit, 289
  1040, transmittal, 240–248
  1040-ES, transmittal, 250
  1139, transmittal, 263
  5500-C, transmittal, 264
Form letters in word processing, 385–387, 392–393
Format, letter, 404–414 (*see* Letter format)
Formatting in word processing, 385, 391–392
Full-block letter format, 411
Fund raising for small business, 193

G

General:
  client representation letter, 108
  engagement letter, 24, 27
  preliminary proposal, 5
Get-well note to employee, 336
"Going concern," uncertainty about, audit report, 128
Grants, confirmation of, 98
Growth, planning for, 170

H

Handbook of letter format, 404–414
Happy face/sad face tax transmittal, 248
Hard disks, advantages of, 388
Humorous letter to state tax department, 281

I

ID number, application for tax, 253
Identification line in letter format, 410
Inadequate disclosure, qualified opinion, 126
Inadequate records, disclaimer of opinion, 131
Income tax basis statements:
  compilation report, 147–149
  review report, 142
  special audit report, 153
Inconsistent application of GAAP, qualified opinion, 125
Increase in salary, informing employee, 332
Indebtedness, request for statement of, 91
Independence, lack of, disclaimer of opinion, 132
Inquiry about employment, response to, 321
Insert function in word processing, 385
Inside address in letter format, 406
Insurance:
  adequacy of coverage, 187
  confirmation of cash value, 97
  policies, confirmation of, 79
Internal accountant, request for tax data from, 230
Internal Revenue Service:
  agent's request for more data, 283
  asking how to proceed with problem, 277

Internal Revenue Service (*cont.*)
examination, representing client, 30, 32
postponement of tax audit, 284
resolving problem with, 270
Interview, inviting applicant for, 322, 325
Interview, second with good applicant, 325
Introduction in MAS report, 400
Introductory paragraph, recommendation letter, 163
Introductory proposal, 7
Inventory:
certificate letter, 107
confirmation of, 80, 81, 102–104, 107
consignment confirmation, 81
control, eliminating weaknesses in, 183
observed by out-of-town auditor, 103
observing for another accounting firm, 104
request to warehouse, 102
software program, replacing inadequate, 186
Inventory and warehousing, recommendations 182–184
Investing idle cash, 188
Invoice: (*see also* Fee)
cancellation of, 177
explanation of, 303
higher bill than expected, 306
kinds of letters, 295
list of services, 302
unpaid, request for payment, 311, 312
word processing in, 387
Irregularities, meaning of term, 117
IRS (*see* Internal Revenue Service)

J

Job applicant:
inviting for interview, 322, 325
no position open, 323, 324
offer declined, reason why, 328
rejection of, 329
Job descriptions, need for, 169
Jury duty, postponement of, 330

L

Lack of independence, disclaimer of opinion, 132
Late filing of tax return, 267
Lawsuit, uncertainty about, qualified opinion, 127
Lawsuits, information concerning, 99
Lawyer (*see* Attorney)
Ledger, fixed assets, 187
Letter format:
block, 412
body of letter, 407
closing, 408
date, 406
elements of, 404
full-block, 411
handbook of, 404–414
identification line, 410
inside address, 406
optional elements, 409
Letter format (*cont.*)
salutation, 407
sample letters, 411–414
semiblock, 413
short, 414
signature, 408–409
Letter-quality printer for word processing, 389
Letter to editor, public relations, 347
Liabilities and assets, recommendations, 187–188
Life insurance, confirmation of cash value, 97
Limitation on scope of audit, qualified opinion, 126
Limitations on engagement, 36
Limited examination, disclaimer of opinion, 131
Long-range planning, need for, 174
Long-term debt, confirmation of, 93
Longtime client, audit engagement, 42

M

Management advisory services:
engagement, 18, 399
proposal, 6, 15, 18
report writing, 398–400
word processing in, 387
Management information systems, proposal, 15
Management letter (*see* Recommendation letter)
Management planning, 168, 174–175
Manual of computer operating procedures, need for, 186
Manual signatures on checks, 177
Marketable securities, confirmation of, 77
Marriage, employee's, congratulations, 334
MAS (*see* Management advisory services)
Media coverage, public relations, 346
Memorandum of information for audit, 48
Merchandise in public warehouse, confirmation of, 80
Merge print in word processing, 385, 392
MIS (*see* Management information systems)
Mortgage:
agreement, financial statements re, transmittal, 376
application, projected financial statements to support, transmittal, 375
indebtedness, confirmation of, 93, 94
Move function in word processing, 385

N

Negative assurances, special report, 155–156
Negative confirmation, 70, 71
New business, congratulations on opening, 354
New client acceptance data sheet, 21
New client, welcoming, 350
Newsletter, public relations, 341
Nonprofit organization, audit of, 14
Nonpublic entity, financial statements of, compilation report, 144
Nonpublic entity, financial statements of, review report, 139
Notes payable, request for schedule of, 92
Notes payable to vendors, confirmation of, 75
Notes receivable, confirmation of, 74

O

Observing inventory for another accounting firm, 104
Obsolescence, criteria for determining, 183
Offering position with firm, 326, 327
Office building, feasibility study, 195
Office operations, kinds of letters, 295, 319, 337, 361
Omission of substantially all disclosures, compilation report, 144-145
Operating procedures for computer, 186
Opinion, engagement leading to, 38
Oral fee agreement, confirming, 307
Organization:
  chart, updating, 169
  nonprofit, audit of, 14
  of reports, 396, 399-400
  special fund, amount being held in, 72
Organization and facilities, recommendations, 169-171
Out-of-town auditor as observer of inventory, 103
Overdue fee:
  collection arrangement with attorney, 318
  reminder about, 309, 316
  thank-you for paying, 318

P

Paragraphs in recommendation letters, 163-188
Partners, accounting report to, transmittal, 378
Partnership tax return, filing final, 234
Partnership tax return, transmittal, 254, 255
Past-due accounts, collecting, 185
Payables (*see* Accounts payable; Notes payable)
Payment plan for overdue fee, 314
Payments and purchasing, recommendations, 181-182
Payroll and personnel, recommendations, 172-173
Payroll deductions, authorization for, 173
Payroll tax returns, items needed for, 225
Penalties, abatement of tax, 272, 273
Pension fund amendment, transmittal, 373
Pension fund report, transmittal, 372
Pension plan (*see* Employee-benefit pension plan)
Perpetual inventory, need for accurate, 183
Personal computers, need for policy on, 185
Personal financial planning, 206, 208
Personal financial statements:
  adverse opinion, 133
  audit of, 46
  disclaimer of opinion, 133
  standard report, 132
Personnel and payroll, recommendations, 172-173
Personnel records, need for formal, 172
Petty cash, confirmation of, 73
Planning, long-range, need for, 174
Planning session, business, engagement for, 205
Policies, insurance, confirmation of, 79
Policy on personal computers, need for, 185
Positive approach to confirmation, 65-69
Postponement of jury duty, 330
Postponement of tax audit, 284
Pre-engagement conference, 38
Preliminary proposal, general, 5
Prenumbering documents, 177
Press release, public relations, 344
Price offers, special, reviewing, 184
Pricing of products, interim report, 199
Printed annual report, transmittal, 369
Printed confirmation letter, 69
Printer for word processing, 389
Prior correspondence, transmittal, 377
Prior tax accountant, correcting errors made by, 275
Prior tax accountant, letter to, 228
Probate, checklist for, 217
Problem resolution, IRS, 277
Procedures manual, need for written, 176
Processing cash receipts, separation of duties in, 176
Profile (*see* Résumé)
Profit participation, special audit, 155
Projected financial statements, proposed venture, 197
Projected financial statements, to support mortgage applications transmittal, 375
Promissory note, 315
Promotion, congratulations to client on, 358
Proposal:
  as engagement letter, 4
  audit, 12
  audit of nonprofit organization, 14
  features of, 4
  financial accounting system, set up, 191
  general preliminary, 5
  introductory, based on conference, 7
  kinds of, 3
  management advisory services, 18
  responsiveness to client's requests, 14
  résumé included with, 11
  two basic kinds of, 4
  word processing in, 386
Proposed venture, projected financial statements, 197
Public relations:
  advice to staff, 343
  brochure explaining capabilities, 339
  definition, 338
  kinds of letters, 337
  letter to editor, 347
  media coverage, 346
  newsletter, 341
  press release, 344
  reprinting article, 342
  sending article to client, 349
  speaking engagement, 345, 352, 353
  thank-you note for recommending client, 351
  welcome to new client, 350
Public warehouse, confirmation of inventory in, 80
Purchasing agent, making use of, 181
Purchasing and payments, recommendations, 181-182

Q

Qualification of retirement plan, 233
Qualified opinion:
  departure from GAAP, 124
  inadequate disclosure, 126
  inconsistent application of GAAP, 125
  limitation on scope of audit, 126
  uncertainty about "going concern," 128
  uncertainty about lawsuit, 127

R

Real estate holdings, checklist, 213
Receivables (*see* Accounts receivable)
Receiving report forms, 182
Recommendation letter:
  brief, 167
  contents of, 163
  covering note for, 201
  general, 165
  kinds of, 161-162, 179-180
  transmittal, 373
  word processing in, 387
Recommendation of client by outsider, thank-you note, 351
Reconciling vendor statements, 182
Record storage, 171
Reference line in letter format, 409
Refund, corporate (Form 1139), transmittal, 263
Refund due on taxes, requesting, 235, 242
Registration number, eliminating state taxpayer's, 280
Rejection of job applicant, 329
Report, interim, on pricing of products, 199
Report writing:
  audience awareness, 396-397
  audit reports, 396-398
  dating audit reports, 398
  kinds of reports, 394-395
  logical organization, 396, 399-400
  MAS reports, 398-400
  objectives of MAS engagement, 399
  parts of MAS report, 399-400
  persuasiveness in, 397
  proper emphasis in, 396-397
  recipient of audit report, 397-398
  tips for improvement, 401-402
  turning error to advantage, 402-403
Representation:
  alternate client letter, 115
  concise client letter, 113
  general client letter, 108
  inventory certificate letter, 107
  kinds of letters, 105
  modification of general client letter, 111
  technical term in, 117
Reprinting published article, public relations, 342
Reserve meeting, request for excuse from, 331
Résumé included with proposal, 11
Résumé, job applicant's retained, 324
Retirement, best wishes to client on, 360
Retirement plan (*see* Employee-benefit pension plan)
Review:
  employees' need for, 169
  engagement, 34
  of prior year's financial statements, 124
  reports, 135-143
Royalties, special audit report, 154

S

Salary increase, notifying employee, 332
Sales and collections, recommendations, 184-185
Sales forcasting, 184
Salutation in letter format, 407
Search and replace function in word processing, 385, 391-392
Securities in custodian or trust account, confirmation of, 88
Securities, marketable, confirmation of, 77
Security for check-writing materials, 177
Security of computer system, 186
Semiblock letter format, 413
Separation of duties in processing cash receipts, 176
Short letter format, 414
Sick pay, control over, 173
Signature in letter format, 408-409
Signatures on checks, manual, 177
Small business client, engagement, 24
Software:
  backup, need for, 186
  choosing programs, 387-388
  inventory program, replacing inadequate, 186
Speaking engagement, public relations, 345, 352, 353
Special:
  audit reports, 153-157
  engagement, 50
  fund, confirmation of amount in, 72
  price offers, reviewing, 185
  report to stockholders, transmittal, 379
  services, engagement, 26, 30
  services, proposal, 6
Specification sheet for employee-benefit pension plan, 54
Spelling check in word processing, 393
Staff involvement in public relations, 343
Stamp method of confirmation, 71
Standard:
  audit report, personal financial statements, 132
  audit report, unqualified opinion, 121
  bank confirmation inquiry, 86-87
State:
  corporation estimated tax payments, transmittal, 262
  corporation tax return, transmittal, 261
  taxpayer registration number, eliminating, 280
Status of taxpayer's account, 270, 279-281
Sticker method of confirmation, 71
Stock authorized and issued, confirmation of, 95
Stockholders' annual report, transmittal, 368, 369
Stockholders' special report, transmittal, 379
Storage of records, 171
Style for résumé, 11
Subject line in letter format, 409
Summary of MAS report, 400
Supporting vouchers, need for, 177

T

Table of contents in MAS report, 400
Tax audit:
  acceptance of Form 1040 as filed, 289
  asking client for information, 285
  kinds of letters, 265
  postponement of, 284
  recommendation that client accept deficiency, 290

Tax audit (*cont.*)
recommendation that client sign waiver, 291
summarizing results of, 287
Tax return:
abatement of penalties, 272–273
advising client to compile data, 223
apology for late reply to notices, 278
asking IRS how to proceed with problem, 277
authorization to release tax records, 229
correcting errors made by prior accountant, 275
correcting taxpayer's account, 269
credit for payment already made, 268
details on deductible expenses, 231
eliminating state taxpayer registration number, 280
filing declaration of estimated tax, 226
final partnership return, 234
informing client of changes in tax law, 232
items needed for payroll, 225
kinds of letters, 221, 265
late filing, reason for, 267
letter to prior tax accountant, 228
preparation not included in audit, 44
proposal, 6, 15
qualification of retirement plan, 233
reminder on filing, 224
request for data from client's internal accountant, 230
resolving problem with IRS, 271
request for refund due, 235
status of taxpayer's account, 270, 279–281
termination of business, 236
word processing in, 386
Tax services (*see* Tax return)
Tax transmittal:
all-purpose letter, 239
application for tax ID number, 253
"boxed" format, 243
combined federal and state, 243, 246
corporation estimated payments, 260
corporation return, 256, 257, 259
estimated tax payments, 250
fiduciary income, 251, 252
Form 1040, general, 240
Form 1040, refund due, 242
Form 1040, tax owed, 241
Form 1040-ES, 250
Form 1139, 263
Form 5500-C, 264
happy face/sad face, 248
kinds of, 237
partnership return, 254, 255
state corporation estimated payments, 262
state corporation return, 261
word processing in, 386
Technical term, explanation of, 117
Termination of business, 236
Thank-you note for payment of overdue bill, 318
Thank-you note for recommending client, 351
Transfer agent, confirmation letter to, 95
Transmittal:
accounting report to partners, 378
adjusting entries, 363
annual report to stockholders, 368, 369
audited financial statements, 366
definition, 362
Transmittal (*cont.*)
draft audit for comments, 365
employee-benefit plan notice, 371
financial statements re mortgage, 376
fiscal closing, 364
kinds of letters, 361 (*see* also Tax transmittal)
pension fund amendment, 373
pension fund report, 372
prior correspondence, 377
projected financial statements, to support mortgage application, 375
special report to stockholders, 379
unaudited financial statements, 367
working papers for annual report, 370
Transmittal letter, general (*see* Transmittal)
Transmittal letter, tax (*see* Tax transmittal)
Travel expenses, summary of, 172
Trust account, securities and cash in, confirmation of, 88
Two-part engagement, 27

U

Unaudited financial statements, transmittal, 367
Unobserved inventory, disclaimer of opinion, audit report, 130
Unpaid invoices, request for payment, 311–312
Unqualified opinion:
accepting other auditors' report, 122
reversing prior year's qualified opinion, 123
standard audit report, 121
two years' financial statements, 122

V

Vacation pay, control over, 173
Vendor for word processing, 389–390
Vendor statements, reconciling, 182
Vendors, notes payable to, confirmation of, 75
Vouchers, need for supporting, 177

W

W-4 Forms, keeping, 173
Waiver, recommendation that client sign, 291
Warehouse, inventory request to, 102
Warehouse, public, confirmation of inventory in, 80
Warehousing and inventory, recommendations, 182–184
Welcome to new client, 350
Word processing:
applications, 386–387
definition, 384
editing in, 393
features of, 385–386
form letters in, 385–387, 392–393
printer for, 389
software for, 388–389
spelling check in, 393
tips on using, 391
vendor for 389–390
Word wrap, in word processing, 385
Working capital, sufficiency of, 169
Working papers for annual report, transmittal, 370
Written job descriptions, need for, 169
Written procedures manual, need for, 176